BUSINESS COMMUNICATION

BUSINESS COMMUNICATION

Madhukant Jha

genNEXT Publication

Business Communication

Rs. 890

ISBN: 978-81-908675-5-9

Published in 2009 in India by
Gennext Publication
23 Main Ansari Road, Darya Ganj,
New Delhi-110002
E-Mail:GenNextpublication@hotmail.com
Phone: 23282060

Printed at : Young Art Press, Delhi - 92

Contents

Preface

Business requires skilful communication, and presumptions and misunderstandings about language and behaviour can be barriers to success. This book illustrates the importance of communication in real life business communications. Effectual communication skills are indispensable in the new millennium. Today's fast-moving, competitive business world calls for employees with splendid communication skills. So to meet this need, business schools try to raise students with both skills; verbal as well as written. Courses in communication stress techniques through writing assignments, oral presentations and term papers.

While the business world regret the absence of effective writing and speaking skills, the fast pace of the working environment leaves very less time for learning these skills. In order to successfully facilitate communication skills for students, this volume illuminate clear guidelines, well-structured outlines, and well placed examples.

This book answers basic questions on grammar and offers research tools, research resources, and information sources. Overviews found in the chapters allow anyone to learn to communicate more effectively. The well-written materials ensure that students are able to understand these topics clearly. It boasts of important communicative skills such as presentations, telephone etiquette, e-mailing, memos and public speaking.

Author is confident that this book will be a handy tool for the students learning business communication. Sincere feedback, suggestions and comments are always welcome.

1

Communication Strategy

Effective business communication is more than the ability of an individual to create a clear memo, a useful executive summary, a good report, or a persuasive presentation. It is a set of individual skills, team or group decisions, and company-supported policies, philosophies, and actions that promote the linkage of individuals and groups within an organization. Such linkages ensure that the key strategic and operational information is shared appropriately and effectively. Managers and companies that do not develop and encourage the use of such processes give up potential competitive advantages and may underutilize company strengths.

It is clear that profound changes are occurring in such a way that businesses are both doing business and communicating. Changes are occurring in what is being communicated within and outside of organizations, why it is being communicated, and who is doing the communication. Having closely held information within groups (departments) and not sharing that information was once commonly viewed as appropriate and in the best interest of a company.

Now, companies seek to eliminate those barriers because of necessity. Managers need to build teams, share information, and appropriately delegate authority to facilitate the completion of projects. A supply-chain view of a corporation, its suppliers, and customers is now accepted and widely implemented as part of an integrated resource management approach. Managers who keep information private and closely guarded are obstacles to teamwork and to reaching common, companywide goals. Managers who do not accept input from others within and outside of their groups risk failing to identify and solidify critical connections that will make the company fast and innovative.

More than ever, businesses need to promote communication skills to facilitate quick and precise decision making that keeps them competitive.

To promote communication skills, it is necessary to focus on companywide perspectives (policies and support), implementation by teams and groups, and the skills of individual contributors. Our goal is to help facilitate that competitive advantage.

One of the problems facing most businesses is how to keep up with internal and external change. This includes changes in business communication strategies and requirements.

DRIVING CHANGES IN BUSINESS COMMUNICATION

The need for improved business communication strategies is being driven by the fast demands of business, globalization, and the technology revolution, as well as leadership challenges that require improved business communication strategies and skills at company, team or group, and individual levels.

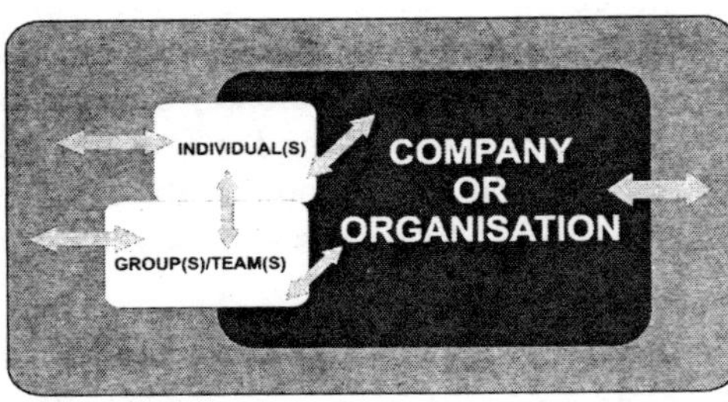

Figure: Common communication patterns within and outside of a company.

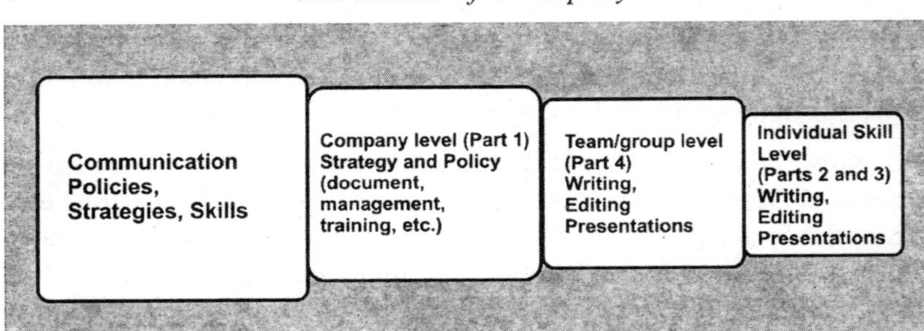

Figure: Effective business communication depends on a series of interrelated policies, strategies, and skills at the company, team, and individual levels.

As shown in Figures above, changes in strategy need to be viewed from three perspectives: companywide, group or team, and individual contributors. Options available are both constrained and enhanced by decisions made at each of those levels. For example, if a company decides to implement a document life-cycle management strategy or a document management system, to offer training to employees in communication skills, to use project management systems, to teach effective writing and editing skills, or to make persuasive presentations, the entire capacity of a company will be enhanced.

New communication strategies have become necessary as a result of the rise of several movements:

- The quality movement pioneered by Deming
- The implementation of integrated supply chains
- The advent of integrated resource management
- These initiatives forced a new and improved kind of communication and leadership, as evidenced in the following:
  - — ISO 9000 standards
  - — The growing use of standards and benchmarks throughout industry and in other areas

Technology has placed new demands on us to order and make sense of data-making effective communication a top priority. This means that information (data) must be collected and assembled into database that can be queried so that computerized systems for tracking and analyzing all aspects of a company become a reality, not a pie-in-the-sky idea. Management groups must work with information systems that link data, facilitate analysis, generate query-based reports, and expedite decision processes if they are to sustain a competitive advantage.

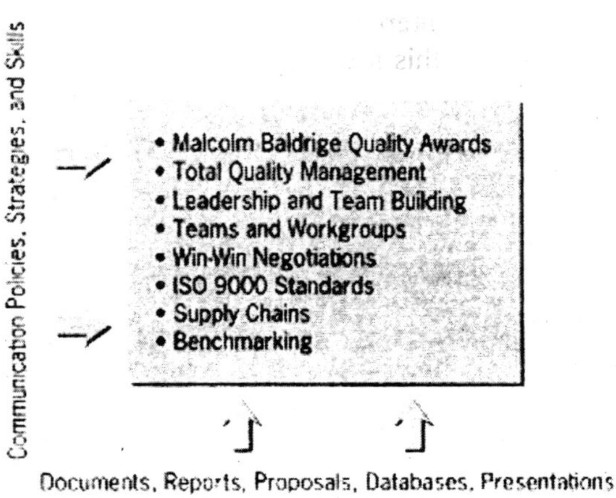

Figure: Communication Strategies and Skills are Central to Multiple Business Initiatives and Requirements.

BENCHMARKING AND TEAMWORK

In Thomas Kayser's Mining Group Gold, in Michael Hammer and James Champy's Reengineering the Corporation, and in Robert Camp's insights on benchmarking, the authors make it clear that successful managers and companies effectively share goals, strategies, and other pertinent information.

William Russell indicates that integrated resource management requires that everyone in an organization understand the terminology of other functions-and the impact of those functions on his or her own area. In addition Russell notes that individuals need to understand how the decisions in their own areas will affect other areas. These are all communication issues. Peter Drucker, arguably the "founder" of modern-day management, in his work on manufacturing makes parallel points.

Russell and the American Production and Inventory Control Society (APICS) note that surveys of the most successful companies show that:

"improving communications between management and workers" is the number one activity those companies are pursuing.

Companies need to know how to share information successfully by using multiple tools (one-on-one meetings, phone calls, e-mail, memos, reports, group meetings, and presentations), which are often dependent on the skills of individual contributors.

In addition, to win a Baldrige award or comply with ISO 9000 requirements, effective internal and external communication processes are needed. Support for this idea can be seen in the work of pioneering thinker.

Robert Camp, who examines benchmarking leadership and management processes, the leadership focus of the Baldrige requirements, and the manner in which supply-chain management is implemented in companies such as Xerox, Westinghouse, Texas Instruments, the Ritz-Carlton Hotels, and others.

The era of the information age and the demand of the New Economy require extraordinary leadership and negotiation skills-in other words, excellent communication skills. As Stephen Covey writes in Principle Centered Leadership, and as the work of Fisher, Ury, and Patton, Getting to Yes suggests, successful negotiations implicitly acknowledge the need for managers and other leaders to communicate well.

COMPANYWIDE, TEAM, AND INDIVIDUAL PERSPECTIVES

The success of individuals, teams, and companies is becoming increasingly dependent on effective business communication because of the growing complexity of business transactions, products, and services. It is quite common for one company to provide services and products to other companies that are located at some distance. Equally true, more companies need to manage internal information across multiple business locations, locations that are often global. Each of these tasks requires effective communication processes that will decrease transaction and data-sharing time and costs. Because specific barriers-and solutions-to business communication can exist at multiple levels in an organization, answers to the following three broad questions will help to identify communication concerns, potential strengths, and weaknesses or barriers:

- Why should a company use a companywide approach to improve business communication, and specifically, what can a company do?
- How can a workgroup or team improve business communication on specific projects?
- How can individual contributors improve business documents and presentations, as well as related processes and personal skill sets?

For example, if a manager can spend less time in creating a proposal that is more clear and more useful, and a senior executive can evaluate it without requesting further data or clarifications, companies should be able to make decisions more rapidly and with greater accuracy. The issue then becomes, what can a company do to make certain that managerial time is not wasted producing and/or using ineffective documents and presentations?

DECIDING COMMUNICATION STRATEGY

COMPANY-LEVEL DECISIONS

Communication issues cut across all levels of a business, and key decisions need to be made at different levels. For example, at a company level, decisions must include the following:

- Should our company design and implement databases to support projects that need to be coordinated across various workgroups?

- Would it be cost-effective to develop and use standard formats for internal reports and/or proposals?
- At what point and in which documents or presentations do we support or require the use of colour?
- Can we gain efficiencies by standardizing our word processing and presentation software? Should we use Lotus Notes to share information, or should we use Microsoft Word? Should we adopt and support a presentation package (for example, PowerPoint) on a companywide basis, or should we support department-by-department use of whichever presentation package a current manager prefers?
- What are the costs and benefits of providing staff training to improve writing skills or document development processes? What do we train them to do? To what degree of proficiency do we train users?
- Should we install and support voice recognition software for managers who earn $100,000+ a year and type by the hunt-and-peck method?
- What are the costs and benefits of installing an intranet (internal computer network) to share data, documentation, and other information? Which software packages allow documents to be shared (or imported and exported to other packages) with ease and security?
- Should we adopt a document management system (for example, Xerox's DocuShare) so that we can share documents within our company and with outside customers, vendors, and/or consultants?

TEAM-LEVEL DECISIONS

At the team or workgroup level, decisions at the level of a specific project can be resolved, often dependent upon the company-level supports that are or are not available. Pertinent decisions include the following:

- Do we use project management concepts (timelines, Gantt charts, PERT charts) for a specific project? Do we use manual or software-based solutions?
- Do we send out a report, or do we make a formal project presentation and provide a report? Do we distribute the report or presentation electronically or as hard copy? What are the advantages, the disadvantages, and the barriers?

- If we do a presentation in person, do we use overheads or a computer-controlled presentation? Can we benefit from real-time access to databases, spreadsheets, and what-if calculations?
- Which team member would be the best presenter, or do we use a team of presenters?
- Which team member will edit the final report or proposal, or do we hire a professional editor?

INDIVIDUAL DECISIONS

There are also decisions that an individual contributor needs to make, taking into consideration the restrictions of specific work environments and the guidance of managers. Decisions at this level include the following issues:

- Do I use a writing and editing process in order to be more effective and efficient?
- Would it be valuable to use tables to display key information in a report, or is it okay or better to leave it as several paragraphs of text?
- Should I ask a colleague to proofread the materials?
- Do I need to improve my basic grammar skills, or is the 40 to 50 percent accuracy rate of my word processor sufficient?
- Do I need to use a computer-projected presentation, or would overheads or handouts be best, or would just talking with no visual aids be best?

IMPLEMENTING COMMUNICATIONS STRATEGY

As you can see, these issues are not discrete; they overlap among individuals and groups within a company. That's one reason that business communication issues need to be raised and answered: There are broad issues with very positive or negative effects on individual careers, the outcome of specific projects, and the overall efficiency and profitability of a company.

Evaluating an individual's ability to write, edit, and present information is critical but not sufficient. To improve business communication, specific requirements, strengths, and barriers must be identified and handled at all levels. The current literature on business communication seldom addresses these issues, and it fails to identify processes that can be used to resolve them. Further, the connection of these issues to leadership and management is not addressed. As a result, individuals and teams are often unable to identify strengths, weaknesses, or barriers, and they cannot get the resources they need to improve business communication and increase efficiency and effectiveness.

DEVELOPING INTRAORGANIZATIONAL EFFECTIVE BUSINESS COMMUNICATION

It is important to complete the following steps at a company level:

- Identify internal and external requirements for communication (documents and presentations).
- Identify resources/strengths.
- Identify barriers (process, personal skills, interpersonal, hardware, software, standards, etc.).
- Develop and implement processes that will eliminate or decrease the barriers.
- Determine the type of support (for example, hardware/software/networks) that can be useful.
- Establish/adopt templates/standards for documents and presentations.
- Determine what training support is needed to increase effectiveness and meet requirements.

COMPANY-LEVEL BUSINESS COMMUNICATION TRENDS

A number of key trends have been emerging in business communication. E-mail is now a staple in the business world, and companies need to address and continually reassess the extent to which to they use the Internet (World Wide Web) for advertising, marketing, research, and document sharing. Beyond the Internet, whether to use intranets is also a key business communication decision. Sophisticated document management systems that use both the Internet and intranets are allowing companies to move closer to, if not paperless offices, offices that can create and share electronic versions of documents easily and securely.

E-MAIL

Many company-level policy decisions (including software, networks/hardware, and training/support) impact the extent to which e-mail is successfully used. In later chapters, we offer suggestions on how to create more functional, useful e-mail messages-literally billions of e-mail messages are sent on a daily basis- and we also review commonly accepted ways to improve e-mail. At a company level, a policy discouraging the sending of trivial e-mail could save hundreds of hours of time for every employee every year-and eliminate the need to read items that have no value to one's functions.

Using Intranets and the Internet

Both powerful tools, the Internet and intranets pose some crucial challenges when it comes to formulating an overall communication strategy.

Evaluate:

- Security, including encryption of documents via public and private keys and degrees of access
- Cost
  - — The time required to produce a document
  - — The distribution barriers and advantages
- Speed
- Colour and complexity (for example the use of Visio and Acrobat software solutions)

DOCUMENT MANAGEMENT SYSTEMS

The key to successful use of the Internet and intranets is the use of document management systems ideas.

Putting Paper-Intensive Tasks On-Line

Companies experience greater efficiencies by putting databases, inventory control (JIT (Just in Time), etc.), advertising, marketing, customer service, benefits information, personnel manuals, newsletters, and management announcements/bulletins on an intranet. The sky's the limit. Employees who can use electronic document management systems become better informed and are able to make faster, more qualified decisions.

Developing Effective Business Communication within Teams

Intranets and the Internet offer parallel advantages for facilitating communication to groups and teams.

To optimize communication advantages, teams need to do the following:

- Identify requirements.
- Identify resources/strengths/barriers (for example, the presence/absence of processes, personal skills, interpersonal, hardware, software, and standards).
- Establish/adopt templates/standards.
- Establish/adopt/implement processes (especially a writing and editing process, document sharing, and project management).

DEVELOPING INDIVIDUAL BUSINESS COMMUNICATION SKILLS

For an individual contributor, some choices are constrained by company-level and team or project decisions. However, a decision to improve specific skills can be made by individuals and can be done without extensive support, especially when justified as part of a personal career advancement effort. To optimize communication, individuals need to do the following:

- Identify requirements and define products that meet those requirements.
- Determine resources, strengths, and barriers (hardware, software, processes, personal skills, knowledge, etc.).
- Implement processes.
- Improve personal skills.

INTEGRATED SUPPLY CHAINS AND RESOURCE MANAGEMENT

Over the last several years, the idea of supply-chain linkages in manufacturing environments has gained momentum as the need for more effective sharing of information throughout a company, and with outside vendors and customers, has increased. If a company cannot efficiently share information, it is unlikely that supply-chain linkages can be identified or continuously improved, which can lead to a noncompetitive situation. Companies need to create processes that enable their employees to appropriately and successfully share information within and across organizational units. Companies that do not develop and encourage the use of such processes give up potential competitive advantages and underutilize the strengths of their employees.

An important communication question is: What barriers exist in current processes that inhibit sharing of information? From a management communication perspective, are there opportunities to share and leverage information that can improve processes and products? Are there opportunities to increase communication efficiency and eliminate barriers? Pertinent questions include the following:

- What information can Market Research share with Hardware Design that will help develop the best product?
- What can Customer Service share with Software Design that will improve ease of operation for customers or help hardware designers in creating a more dependable machine?
- How can Manufacturing and Hardware Design work together to create an easier-to-build machine?
- Can Logistics and Distribution and Customer Service decrease the quantity of low-use spare parts held in multiple locations by Customer Service?
- Do field technicians have information (for example, part reliability) that is not shared with Hardware Design for lack of an appropriate communications mechanism?
- What information does the Corporate Strategy group need-and need to share?

SUPPLY-CHAIN LINKAGES IN NON-MANUFACTURING ENVIRONMENTS

Supply-chain-linkage problems are also inherent in service organizations. Nonprofit and government organizations have customers, boards of directors, and customers or clients, and the problems associated with effective communication in a business environment also exist in those organizations.

MANAGEMENT STYLES AND COMMUNICATION STRATEGIES

We advocate using win-win approaches to management, problem solving, and communication because they increase the efficiency of individuals, teams, areas, and companies. If these approaches are linked to appropriate incentive and reward systems (for example, performance pay, merit pay, or profit sharing), they can lead to performance improvements at all levels of an organization.

EFFECTING CHANGE

If your company, area, or team (or yourself as an individual) does not use win-win approaches, how can you implement a change in your communication styles? From a strategic perspective, improved communication enhances the performance of the whole company, from sharing knowledge and innovative ideas to being able to make faster and better decisions. Deciding to improve overall communication requires support at a company, team or group, and individual contributor level. Win-win approaches can promote successful communication, and change a win-lose to a win-win or interest-based approach. It is important to stress how the win-win approach can benefit individuals, teams, and the entire company.

SUMMARY

Communication used to promote a product, service, or organization; relay information within the business; or deal with legal and similar issues. It is also a means of relying between a supply chain, for example the consumer and manufacturer. At its most basic level, the purpose of communication in the workplace is to provide employees with the information they need to do their jobs. Business Communication encompasses a variety of topics, including Marketing, Branding, Customer relations, Consumer behaviour, Advertising, Public relations, Corporate communication, Community engagement, Research & Measurement, Reputation management, Interpersonal communication, Employee engagement, Online communication, and Event management. It is closely related to the fields of professional communication and technical communication.

Business is conducted through various channels of communication, including the Internet, Print (Publications), Radio, Television, Ambient media, Outdoor, and Word of mouth. Business Communication can also refer to internal communication. A communications director will typically manage internal communication and craft messages sent to employees. It is vital that internal communications are managed properly because a poorly crafted or managed message could foster distrust or hostility from employees.

Note: Wipro is renowned for its communication strategy. . In 2007, Wipro was listed among top companies in Europe and the world in a "Top Companies for Leaders" study carried on by Human Resources Company "Hewitt Associates" in partnership with "Fortune magazine". For detailed information, For a very good study of Communication Strategy, see Wipro company site: http:/www.wipro.com

2

Management of Documentation in Electronic Era

Over the last several years, a new focus on business communication has emerged: that of computerized document management. Document management is a concern at all levels and for all the organizations. This is due in part to the increased use of computer programs to generate and manage documents, as well as the need for increased linkages among business groups and functions. Businesses are also communicating in new ways; whereas previously a group of people would meet to talk about an issue, they now often address issues by conference calls, videoconferencing, and/or e-mail in an effort to decrease meetings, eliminate barriers created by distance, and increase efficiency.

The increasing use of e-mail, databases, spreadsheets, and other forms of communication leads to the creation and retention of more documents. And this increased production, retention, and use of documents creates a need to evaluate work processes, workflow, and documents from the perspective of a document cycle: the origination, filing, use/retrieval, security, retention, and the destruction of documents.

In this section, we will highlight some of the key ideas that are moving to the forefront; however, to gain a fuller understanding of these rapidly evolving issues and potential solutions, we strongly recommend a quick search of the Internet. You will discover tens of thousands of sites, documents, consulting firms, and software providers that focus on document management.

We will briefly review some of the approaches being taken by major corporate players in document management systems: Xerox (DocuShare), IBM (Documentum Enterprise Document Management Systems, EDMS), Microsoft (Microsoft Exchange, BackOffice, and Document Management

Extensions), Lotus (Lotus Notes and Domino), and Adobe (Acrobat, Acrobat Reader), among others.

Table below shows software solutions and web site locations of companies with major document management efforts.

Changes in Document Management

As recently as 10 years ago, the use of hard-copy documents was the preferred way of conducting business. That preference is now giving way to the use of electronic documents that are linked in complex electronic systems. Today, the use of e-mail is likely to be deemed a more effective way to share information. Several years ago, a report would be written, and sharing that report would mean copying or printing it and then mailing or otherwise physically delivering it. Today, reports are efficiently shared over intranets and the Internet, and the primary focus is not only to get the report printed and distributed, but also on who should be given what levels of electronic access (such as the right to modify content) to these documents. This is a serious issue related to the security of the document.

TABLE: Web Site Addresses For Document Management Software Solutions

Company	Software Solution	Web Site(s)
Xerox	DocuShare	xerox.com/products/docushare
IBM	EDMS	edms.solutions.ibm.com
Microsoft	Exchange, BackOffice, Extensions	microsoft.com and 80–20.com
Adobe	Acrobat, PDF fusion	adobe.com and docctrl.com/fusion
Lotus	Lotus Notes, Domino	lotus.com/products
Axiom	Cabinet NG	cabinetng.com
Aviator	Aviator for Lotus Notes	aviatorsoftware.com

DOCUMENT LIFE CYCLES

Software solutions are driving changes in how companies view the management of documents and document life cycles. Document life cycle stages include the following:

- Origination
- Filing/use/retrieval
- Security
- Retention/destruction

Origination

When evaluating strategies for the creation of documents, a companywide perspective should include:

- Project requirements
- Sufficiency and compatibility of software programs and data
- Training that users will need to perform required functions
- Technical (computer) support needed
- Total cost of ownership issues

Any one of these issues can be an extremely expensive barrier to eliminate after a software decision has been made.

Project Requirements

The capabilities of document management systems are extensive, and in-depth evaluation is required to determine which system to implement. Topdown management of this decision would be counterproductive. Input is needed from multiple layers of management (including project managers) and also from your technological staff. The people who hold critical knowledge about the requirements for document management and the barriers that need to be overcome are not high-level managers, but rather, those doing day-to-day document-handling tasks, be they database managers, assistants, or employees in contact with external clients and vendors. A document management system's value extends beyond the immediate internal needs of a company; additional value comes from your improved ability to exchange data with sources external to the company (vendors, bidders, customers, etc.).

Sufficiency and Compatibility

Many heavily promoted document management systems and tools, such as Xerox's DocuShare, IBM's EDMS, and Adobe's Acrobat, are designed to support multiple software packages and operating platforms. An evaluation of a document management system or tool should include its ability to handle your current software and documents, files from your legacy applications, scanned documents, and data from external sources (again, vendors, bidders, customers). Another valuable by-product of document management systems is the ability to implement document templates that will produce consistency and eliminate the need to reinvent reports or other document formats/templates for every project. Reports will be easier to write and you'll be able to connect them to other reports in your database.

TRAINING

Training employees to use document management systems is costly; but not training them is often more costlier.

Technical (Computer) Support

One of the major requirements for effective document management is excellent technical (computer hardware, software, and networking) support.

You can find a wealth of information on document management support through vendors' web sites, such as Xerox and IBM.

Filing/Use/Retrieval

The filing, use, and/or retrieval of documents are critical issues. For those of us who use every available flat surface to accumulate paperwork, using file drawers is overwhelming, and storing electronic (nonvisible) documents can be catastrophic. Equally true, anyone who has worked on a multiyear project or who is part of a major corporation that is continually growing or down-sizing knows that well-organized document classification, sorting, and retrieval systems are essential.

Linking and Locating Documents

When a company has multiple projects running concurrently, or thousands of pages of documentation (and revisions and updates) on one project, being able to locate a document quickly is critical. Being able to cross-reference documents (be it by project, employee, raw material, or another basis) is also a must.

Creating Documents on Demand

Document management systems can improve the production and distribution of customized "documents on demand." Producing documents on demand eliminates the need to print and store multiple (in some cases thousands) of copies of manuals and other documentation, which can greatly reduce waste (especially in terms of revisions and updates). To remain competitive, companies need to develop document classification, filing, and retrieval strategies that not only handle existing requirements, but also have the flexibility to grow as requirements change and expand. Adobe Acrobat, a viable solution for sharing documents, is growing in acceptance.

SECURITY

Generating electronic documents has created new security problems. For example, in a recent case, an employee of a major East Coast-based corporation, fearing upcoming layoffs, e-mailed years of her confidential research work to her sister at another corporation based on the West

Coast. It is quite possible for an employee to either copy, alter, relocate, or destroy years of work in a matter of seconds if the proper backup and access rights to files have not been established or maintained. Document management systems allow different levels of access (i.e., none, read-only, write) to be assigned to different users, which can help mitigate such problems.

Retention and/or Destruction

The retention and destruction of documents have gained visibility in recent years, in part due to high-profile lawsuits (tobacco, asbestos, silicon breast implants, etc.) where millions of pages of documentation have been subpoenaed. As a result, more companies are establishing policies regarding if and when specific documents should be retained or destroyed. (And no, you can't wait to make that decision until after you've received a subpoena; destroying documents at that point will probably be a felony in the United States.) Equally important, some documents-for example, inventions, patents, and corporate policies-need careful evaluation before they are destroyed.

SUMMARY

Using a document management system and establishing a coordinated document life cycle policy can increase productivity and decrease liability related issues. Companies need to establish clear and consistent document management systems that involve individuals at all levels of the organization in order to ensure their effective implementation and maintenance.

Note: The Toyota Way incorporates the Toyota Production System. For further knowledge on Document Management in Electronic Age, reader can visit Toyota's site www.toyota.co.jp

3

Writing and Editing Process

It would be rare to find an executive who doesn't count business writing as one of the most important and significant parts of his or her job description. Most executives and managers spend a significant portion of the workday generating e-mail, memos, and letters. They also frequently write reports, proposals, and requests for proposals. Yet many executives have very little formal training in how to write beyond the freshman composition courses required in college. The business writer has two main concerns:

- How can I write more effectively and efficiently?
- How can I get the results, the response, which I want to get?

Using a writing and editing process will (1) help you make better decisions about your writing and (2) help you to identify and avoid common writing problems. A writing and editing process is useful and cost-effective; it saves time and improves results by helping both the writers and the readers of a document. As a writer, you will learn to organize documents so that their logic and structure are visually clear to your readers, thus helping your readers to quickly grasp your key points. If you have the right content, you'll get the results you want.

USING WRITING AND EDITING PROCESSES

If you are like most managers and executives, you're spending too much time writing reports, proposals, memos, e-mail, and letters. In this section, we demonstrate our "writing and editing process," which can help you decide whether writing is the most appropriate way to get your message across and, if so, how to write more efficiently and effectively.

Using a specific writing and editing process will help you systematically organize your goals, evaluate your logic, build stronger arguments, and avoid common errors.

The four primary steps to the writing and editing process are prewriting, drafting, editing, and postwriting.

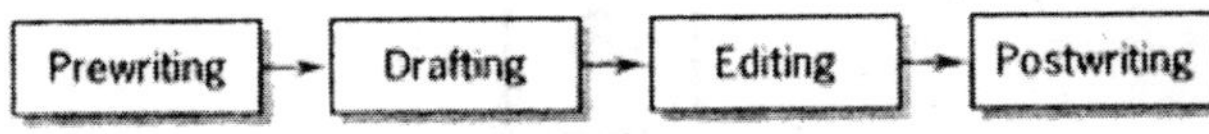

Figure: A four-step writing and editing process.

However, you will find that your writing will be easier and more effective if you use our six-step writing and editing process.

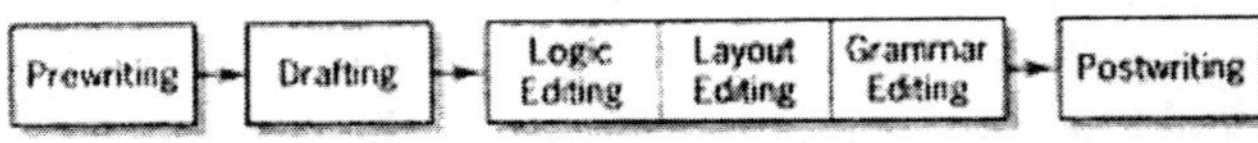

Figure: The six-step writing and editing process.

This six-step process uses three sequential editing steps to save editing time and generate more effective documents.

MAKE THE PROCESS A HABIT

Think of the writing and editing process as a set of good habits, not as a laborious task. When you use a writing and editing process, you're replacing inefficient, unconscious writing habits with a systematic process that will improve your message's effectiveness.

Most of us share at least one inefficient writing habit. We try to perform several editing tasks simultaneously. For example, we try to check a 50-page document for errors in verb tenses while simultaneously deciding where to insert figures or tables to reduce text and worrying about including contents needed by a senior manager. Then, about 35 pages into the report, we notice a major error, become distracted, and go back to the beginning to try and correct it. We then find another problem, and pretty soon, we forget what we have and have not checked. All this rechecking and reediting become very time-consuming, which is why a systematic process can save your time and effort.

CLARIFY YOUR GOALS

Many business writers revise and revise and revise their documents because they don't know what they really want to accomplish. They don't have clearly defined goals. By using our writing and editing process, you will be able to do the following:

- Define your message.
- Identify and meet the requirements of those using your materials.

- Work more efficiently by improving the organization of your work processes and materials.
- Evaluate your logic, build stronger and clearer arguments, and avoid common errors.

In this chapter, we define and explain our process steps. In subsequent chapters, we demonstrate how to apply these steps to a variety of documents. We will guide you through our writing and editing process with a series of figures that illustrate the process and show you where you are in the process. A shadowed box indicates the current step being described.

PREWRITING

Prewriting, the first step in the writing and editing process, is a decision-making step that helps you:

- Decide if your document is appropriate to write.
- Determine what to include.
- Avoid common initial writing errors.
- Avoid writer's block.

Many people writing in business settings get off on the wrong foot because they start to write without knowing where they want to end up. Having only a general idea of what you want to say means you're not quite ready to begin writing. As a result, you'll probably have to revise what you've written because you haven't evaluated the following items:

- Where are you trying to go? What's your objective, purpose, and goal?
- Who will be reading the material? Who is your audience?
- What do your readers already know?
- What do your readers need to know to evaluate your points?
- What action do you want readers to take?

The prewriting process includes answering these related questions.

AVOIDING WRITER'S BLOCK

At the start of writing seminars and classes, we always ask, "How many of you get writer's block when you are writing memos or business letters or reports?" Typically, over 40 percent indicate that writer's block is a problem.

However, when you make decisions about your goals and content at the prewriting stage, you effectively eliminate any doubts about what you need to write. Your task becomes one of systematically organizing and writing down your key points, drafting your material, editing it, and then evaluating it.

Remember, too, that deciding not to write or deciding not to include some information in a written document or public presentation can be a viable alternative. Although we provide instruction on how to write, we advocate writing only when you've decided that it is necessary. In summary, remember the following key points about prewriting:

Prewriting Questions: Using the following questions during your prewriting process can help you make key decisions about the direction the document takes.

"What do I want to accomplish?"

- What are my primary objectives?
- What do I want my readers to do or not do, and by when?
- How important is my reader's action or inaction?
- How much effort and cost are justified-in reading or in writing?

"Who is going to read the document?"

- Who are my intended readers?
- Who are other potential readers-now and in the future?

"What content, ideas, or data are needed in the document?"

- What do my readers already know?
- What do my readers want to know?
- What specific content, ideas, and/or data do I include or exclude?
- What format (memo, letter, report, phone) do I use to distribute the information?

"How can I best organize my points into a coherent argument?"

- What organizational plan (e.g., problem-solution) will link my ideas/data?
- Should I use several organizational plans (e.g., time sequences, geographic locations, problem/ solutions) to organize ideas within and across sections?

- Can I improve my transitions and improve the strength of my argument?

"Do my layout and design make this document clear?"

- Are my design elements (heads, subheads, bullets, margins, bolding, fonts, graphics, etc.) making my logic and structure both logically and visually clear?
- Am I using design elements consistently, thus reducing the need for revisions-especially for group projects?
- Am I using figures, tables, charts, and graphics to advance my arguments and reduce text?
- Prewriting is a decision-making step.
- Prewriting leads to success because it makes you think before you start writing.
- Thinking before writing and knowing your goal eliminates rewriting and wastage of effort.
- Prewriting helps you to determine the type of document you need to create (persuasive or informative, long or short, etc.) to fulfill your goals and your readers' needs.

Why Write: Why do we write at all? Most often it's because the written records:

- Encourage precise thought and control of language.
- Can reduce misunderstandings and ensure uniform instructions.
- Can overcome problems of distance and time.
- Facilitate retention of information.
- Allow readers to read and reread their own schedules.
- Allow controlled, consistent, and rapid distribution.
- Fix responsibility (e.g., for authorship or actions).
- Provide a record and can be checked for accuracy.

However, poorly written documents can undermine your goals. Keep the following in mind:

- Ineffective, unclear, or ill-conceived documents create confusion.
- Documents are costly to create and to read. (How much do you earn an hour? How much do your readers earn an hour? How restricted or strategically valuable is their time?)

- The amount of time it takes to create a document can lead to critical delays and impersonal, oneway communication.

In Business Reports: Oral and Written, Ruch and Crawford (1988) indicate memos, letters, and reports are useful for documenting a process or creating a legal record. This suggests that you:

- Don't write if you don't want to create legal records.
- Write (or elicit) a letter/memo to help create legal records.

To create more effective documents, know your audience. Know what they need. Know what you want done or what you want to say or accomplish, and state it clearly. Most important, if you can't write coherently, get a second opinion on your document. A poorly written document can become a permanent record of your error and a source of problems that are more complex than the ones you are trying to solve.

Drafting

Creating a draft version of a document-a version that you intend to modify to improve your organization, logic, structure, persuasiveness, and/or grammar-is a common practice, especially with important reports, proposals, and business letters.

Drafting is a straightforward step if you have completed the prewriting process.

What points should you consider when you start to draft a document? First, review the four basic questions associated with the prewriting step:

- What do you want the document to accomplish?
- Who is going to read the document?
- How can you effectively organize or link your points into a coherent argument?
- What layout and design standards will make it a successful (professional) document?

After you've answered these questions, your drafting process steps are as follows:

- Complete any needed research or data gathering.
- Expand your notes and identify your key points.
- Double-check your notes for other key points.
- Choose an organizational plan or plans to link your ideas, such as moving from problem to solution or writing chronologically.

Improve the impact of your writing:

Use your readers' viewpoints and address their concerns.

State your key point, action, or requirement in your first paragraph.

KEY DIFFERENCES BETWEEN EDITING AND DRAFTING

When you're drafting, your goal is to get your ideas down, not to have the document letter-perfect. You shouldn't stop every five words to validate the logic of your argument, to modify a head or subhead, to review your phrasing, or to correct your spelling. Those are editing steps, not drafting steps. If something seems problematic while you are drafting your material, just highlight it, type a couple of stars beside it, leave an underscored blank (______) after it, circle it, or underline it, but don't stop and try to fix it. If you stop, you will interrupt the flow of your basic ideas and linkages. If you draft and edit simultaneously, you will tend to get into endless loops and revisions.

Don't stop to create or insert figures, tables, or graphics during drafting. That, too, is part of the editing process. Just note where you'll need to add a figure or table. Your goal is to keep ideas flowing and to focus on your purpose. Fix and tighten the linkages among your ideas when you edit. Don't stop to edit your grammar and spelling. That is not a drafting step. In fact, fixing your grammar is your third editing step.

During your first editing step, when you edit for logic (your conceptual or content points), you will probably eliminate material from your draft, so getting the letter perfect while you are drafting wastes time and breaks your thought patterns, which can lead to multiple loops and revisions. It is important that you allocate time to edit your work.

How rare is it to find people who don't need to edit their work? Very. We have met only two or three people who can perhaps bypass this step, and we don't include ourselves among them!

Treat all of your documents as drafts, even electronic messages. Set your e-mail messages aside for a few minutes before clicking the Send button. When you come back and look at them, you will often have a new perspective, and you might see glaring errors as well as ways to make the message more effective. Best of all, you might save yourself and your department or company some embarrassment.

If you use a word processing program, such as Microsoft Word, that has automatic spell checking and grammar checking, consider turning off those features. Many people find it hard to ignore those red and green squiggly lines, but seeing what they've misspelled or misphrased can break their concentration. Some writers find it more helpful to complete grammar and spell check after having drafted the material.

EDITING

Editing is the key to creating a good document. Many writing processes use steps that are parallel to your prewriting, drafting, editing, and postwriting steps. However, we break the editing step into three sequential substeps, which helps you work more efficiently. Our three-step editing process allows you to improve your draft document systematically without wasting time and effort.

Step 1: Editing the Logic and Structure

Editing logic and structure to enhance the flow of information is the first editing substep. Unfortunately, it is also the most frequently ignored. When business writers assume that all they have to do is start writing without choosing an organizational plan, they end up with documents that ramble.

One way to provide structure and logical organizational patterns, especially with longer documents, is to use the popular "Army approach" to teaching, speaking, and writing:

1. Tell your readers what you're going to tell them.
2. Tell it to them.
3. Tell them what you've told them.

Here's a parallel approach in writing:

1. Use an introduction-either a sentence, a full introduction, a table of contents, or an executive summary.
2. Make your points concisely, and use heads, subheads, and graphics to emphasize them.
3. Summarize and conclude.

You can also improve the logic, structure and organization of your documents by asking yourself the following key questions:

- Can your reader immediately identify you, your position, and your company?
- Is the action you want the reader to take clear in your first or last-paragraph?
- Is the action you are going to take clear in your first or last paragraph?

- Are your recommendations clear, supported, and in your first or last paragraph?
- Are your organizational plan and content easy to understand?
- Would a different organizational plan make your content easier to understand?
- Can readers skim the documents (does it have good heads, subheads, transitions, etc.)?
- Are your assumptions justified and supported?
- Is the content factual, correct, and persuasive?

Step 2: Editing Layout and Design

Good layout and design make the logic of your message visually clear.

One important, yet often overlooked, task is to determine where you need to add graphics, figures, and tables to make your message easier to follow or to strengthen your argument. Include a transition that helps the reader is seeing how to use it, and create a transition that moves your reader to your next point.

Don't just plunk a graphic, figure, or table into your text and assume that it is self-explanatory or that it automatically leads to your next idea. A figure or a table on a page of text material is a magnet for a reader's eye. It is one of the first things a person will scan. If it is well done, it will help drive home your key point on that page or in that section. Make sure you label it clearly and refer to it in the text of the document.

How do you choose your layout and design elements? Most of us just highlight, bold, and/or add italics at will. There are better ways. You need to take your reader's perspective and evaluate how you would react if you received this document.

We have provided above some questions to ask yourself as you evaluate your document for organization, layout, design, and style sheets. Use a style sheet. Style sheets allow you to establish and use consistent formats for paragraphs, heads, subheads, fonts, italic, bold, and so forth. If you establish your layout and design criteria before you start, you'll save yourself and your team extensive time and revision. Word processing packages with style sheets are now quite common (unfortunately, however, some are poorly designed). Take the time to learn how to use a style sheet effectively, especially if your company prefers a particular style.

Step 3: Editing for Grammar

The third editing substep is editing your grammar. This process is the only editing step that many writers complete. It includes such things as identifying and fixing commas and other punctuation problems, poor phrasing, subject-verb agreement problems, wrong pronouns, and article errors. But editing for grammar only does not address the equally important components of your document's logic and structure, layout and design.

Often, writers correct grammar errors at the wrong time-before they're finished with the editing process. This wastes time, and you run the risk of forgetting to edit for grammar after making last-minute fixes to the logic or content. Check for grammar errors by reading aloud. To help identify grammar errors in a document, treat it as you would one of your favorite children's books. If you can read your document aloud without pausing or stumbling, it's probably well written. If you stumble over a sentence that you yourself wrote, what will your readers do?

Be cautious when using grammar checkers. It is helpful is to run a grammar checker, but don't expect perfection. Every generation of grammar checkers is greatly improved, but many grammar checkers are only about 40 percent accurate. They identify both false positives and false negatives; you have to know enough grammar to recognize when they are wrong. If you are like most of us, you have not taken a grammar test since ninth grade, so consider completing the self-diagnostic test for grammar. It can help you identify and correct your personal error patterns.

Organization, Layout, and Design:Look at your finished document in terms of layout and design:

- If I received this document, would I read it or toss it aside for later?
- Would I be more likely to read the document if key points and organization were easier to see visually?
- Can I make the linkages among the ideas visually clearer by changing heads and subheads or using figures or tables?
- Is the document visually pleasing? Is it in an appropriate business format? Did I use clear laser typeface(s) or font(s)? Does it fit together as whole (font, margins, heads, etc.)?
- Would adding colour emphasize my key points better or be a distraction?
- Does my document look like others my company creates?

Postwriting

Many writing and editing processes end with the editing step. However, editing is not the end of the process. When you're done, set your memo or report aside for a few hours and then check it again for problematic errors before you send it out. And before you send it, check with your manager or supervisor to be sure anything you've promised can be delivered. If you don't regularly complete these two simple steps, we guarantee you will eventually regret it, especially if you cannot provide the service or product. In the postwriting process, change your perspective from writer to reader. Among the postwriting questions you should ask yourself are the following:

- Have I met the reader's requirements or does she need more information?
- Am I writing statements that I'll later regret?
- Did I proofread my document? Should a colleague proof it? Is it worth proofreading twice?
- Did I spell check and grammar check?
- Have I arranged for reproduction, distribution, and storage?
- Do I need clearance to send or distribute the document?
- If I was angry when I wrote it, have I let it sit overnight?

SUMMARY

The sequential, multiple-step writing and editing process is effective because it helps writers segment what appears to be an overwhelmingly complex task into a series of manageable steps. Using a writing and editing process can help you accomplish the following:

- Build documents that are complete, supported, persuasive, and effective.
- Save yourself and your reader's time and money.
- Spend your weekends with your family, playing golf or bringing balance to your life.

Note: For Business writing and editing process in working atmosphere, Virgin is a very good example. Virgin group is the best example in "Business Writing and Editing". For more information visit www.virgin.com

4

Logic and Structure of Documents

In the writing and editing process, we noted that creating an effective, well-organized, written document requires the writer to address three broad topics in a sequence:

- Logic and structure
- Layout and design
- Grammar

The most easily recognized errors in documents are often those associated with grammar, including spelling errors and inconsistencies in phrasing. These errors are becoming more easily identified, if not corrected, by the use of word processing programs that include spelling- and grammar checking programs, which, although not optimal, can serve as a helpful way to double-check your own proofreading and editing.

But, obviously, no software program can adequately tell you how to better organize your logic and structure, or your design layout. In fact, structure problems are often exacerbated by errors in layout and design. For example, if the logic and structure of a document is faulty, the visual cues, the layout and design of the document, cannot be effective and may, in fact, misdirect the readers' attention. Together, these two categories of problems are important causes of unpersuasive documents.

In this chapter, we address issues related to improving the logic and structure of your documents.

- Think first.
- Create an organizational plan
- Build strong arguments.
- Use figures and tables.

THINK FIRST

Before you start writing, you need to think seriously. It is extremely important to spend a couple of minutes just thinking about your purpose and your readers. We suggest some questions you may wish to ask yourself in the prewriting phase of the writing and editing process in previous chapter. The same basic principles apply to both writing and presenting orally.

To improve the logic and structure of a document, consider the following:

- Identify who will be reading your document.
- Decide what you want your audience to do after reading your material.
- Identify what they want to know, their needs or requirements, what they already know, and what they don't know.
- Decide if your goal is to persuade or to give an informative overview of ideas.
- Identify the key points that you need to address.
- Determine how to order or sequence those points most effectively.
- Choose an organizational plan (for example, give the problem and a proposed solution, the costs and the benefits, and an implementation plan).
- Use sufficient material to support your points.
- Help your reader to see at a glance how your ideas fit together.

If you spend some time for thinking about these issues before you begin writing, you will find it easier to organize your ideas and structure your document.

CREATE AN ORGANIZATIONAL PLAN

Good organization in effective communication cannot be overstated. Good organization helps your readers understand your message in a better way and improves your credibility. Novice writers sometimes use an organizational plan we have dubbed "the random generation of nonconnected ideas." This is definitely not an effective way to present information or to enhance its retention. Rather, effective writers use commonly identified and standard organizational patterns. Effective summaries of organizational plans have been developed by Penrose,

Rasberry, and Myers in Advanced Business Communication ; in Sterkel's Effective Business and Professional Letters; and others. Penrose, Rasberry, and Myers stress that you can enhance the retention of information by using an appropriate organizational pattern, such as:

- Chronology
- Causal
- Structure/function
- Order of importance
- Problem-solution
- Spatial/geography
- Topical

These plans are basically self-explanatory. For example, chronology implies that you link ideas by order of time-for example, what is to be done in the first, second, third, and fourth fiscal quarters. These plans are extremely useful because they provide options that can help you establish a framework for emphasizing different types of information and relationships. A common mistake is to believe that you can use only one organizational plan or one logical structure in a document. Often, more than one can work, and your task is to anticipate which plan will work most effectively with your readers. In many instances, it is helpful to use several organizational plans in a document to show different interrelationships among ideas. For example, an overall organizational plan for a memo might be to discuss a problem and a solution to that problem. The solution to that problem, however, might need its own organizational plan-for example, a plan emphasizing the quarterly implementation (chronology) of the proposed solution and/or the costs and benefits associated with specific aspects of the solution.

DIRECT AND INDIRECT ORGANIZATIONAL PLANS

Karen Sterkel, among others, suggests that it is helpful to establish a direct or indirect psychological plan. For example, you can construct effective routine memos, letters, and reports by using a direct plan, a plan that presents a concise main idea in the first sentence or paragraph to focus the reader. Next, you present your main ideas, add supporting details, and add a close. In contrast, an indirect plan can be effectively used for bad news or unfavorable memos, letters, or reports. In an indirect plan, Sterkel suggests placing your main idea in middle of your material. First, you develop and present your supporting ideas to act as a buffer.

You state your reasons for a decision, offer a compromise, and close. Sterkel suggests that the indirect plan is effective for persuasive documents because you get the readers' attention, give details, minimize obstacles, anticipate action, and close.

BUILDING STRONG ARGUMENTS

In addition to the use of organizational plans, we suggest building stronger arguments in your documents and presentations by eliminating two common logic and structure problems:

- Unsupported statements
- The so-what problem

Unsupported Statements

We often see inexperienced managers who fall into the trap of making unsupported statements: They state their ideas as facts; they fail to support their points with data; they use invalid data; and/or they fail to use appropriate statistical analyses of data. As a result, readers are left floundering on their own to develop the missing data or analyses. Often, writers fail to supply the data to prove their point or to properly analyze it because they were not thinking clearly or had not properly evaluated the logic of their arguments.

Remember, facts must be supported by verifiable information. Citing highly credible sources in your document strengthens your image and avoids any suggestion of plagiarism.

The So-What Problem

Larry Matteson, a retired vice president at Eastman Kodak, while teaching at the Simon Graduate School of Business at the University of Rochester, often emphasized the "so-what" problem to MBA candidates. As writers and as managers, we often fail to make connections among our ideas for our readers. We assume they know where we are going. We assume they know how to get there. We even assume they agree we should go there!

All these assumptions are faulty, and they prevent us from building organized arguments that help our readers to see not only our end points, but also the processes and data that helped us get there. In addition, we fail to tell them the reasons we should get there-the so-what! Avoid the so-what problem. Make your statements, give your assumptions and supporting data, and eliminate extraneous information. Close the loop and make certain that your reader understands your point, your conclusion, the value you are trying to point out. Make certain your readers get to the end of your memos, reports, or proposals without lingering, "So what?"

USING FIGURES AND TABLES

One of the most effective ways to help your readers grasp and follow the logic and structure of your materials is to help them invisualising your ideas. Graphics, tables, figures, and graphs help accomplish this in at least three ways. First, properly designed graphics explain complex information in ways that highlight the relationships among ideas, thus providing insights into those relationships. Rather than writing two or three paragraphs of text to p ›vide a conceptual overview of the material, it is often possible to show complex relationships visually.

Second, graphics, tables, and figures force a writer to analyze and better understand, from a reader's perspective, the ideas that are being presented. Tables and figures do not lend themselves to rambling. Third, graphs, figures, and tables simplify and emphasize key points. Figures, tables, charts, and graphs catch a reader's eye and help to isolate your key points. By focusing a reader's attention in this way and by visually displaying the connections between your ideas, your argument becomes easier to follow.

DESIGNING EFFECTIVE TABLES AND FIGURES

Creating an effective table or figure involves an analysis process, a design process, and consistency.

Analysis

First, you need to decide what you want to accomplish. This is the audience analysis task that comes with the prewriting questions and the audience analysis for presentations.

Design

Second, you need to decide how to emphasize your key point or simplify the complexity of the information. For example, Figure given below shows how you can simplify a complex set of information by eliminating implicit information (the zeros that function as placeholders, in this example). Further, you can add highlighting (by changing colour or fonts or by adding italics or bolding) so that readers see at a glance the key points in a complex figure. In addition, use an effective label or title, one that calls attention to the point you want to emphasize. The title of a figure, graph, or table can serve the same function as a subject line in a memo or an e-mail: It focuses the reader.

Before

	Location						
Part	SF1	SF2	Sea	Dal	Atl	Bos	Tor
1AB1	0	0	10	20	15	0	0
1AB2	0	0	10	20	15	0	0
2BC1	25	0	0	0	0	25	25
2BC2	25	0	0	0	0	25	25
2BC3	5	0	0	0	0	5	5
3CD1	0	50	0	0	0	0	0
3CD2	0	50	0	0	0	50	0
3CD3	0	50	0	0	0	50	0
3CD4	0	50	0	0	0	50	0

After

Inventory Stock and Shortages by Warehouse Location/City

Shaded cells indicate critical shortages on 10/31/2002

	Warehouse Location/City→						
Part ↓	SF1	SF2	Sea	Dal	Atl	Bos	Tor
1AB1			10	20	15		
1AB2			10	20	15		
2BC1	25					25	25
2BC2	25					25	25
2BC3	5					5	5
3CD1		50					
3CD2		50				50	
3CD3		50				50	
3CD4		50				50	

Figure: Improve tables and figures by eliminating implicit nformation, adding highlighting, and using effective labels and titles to focus readers.

Consistency

Consistency among multiple graphs, tables, and figures is another key factor in a document and in the presentations that are linked to the written documents. Help your readers by focusing on your information; don't force them to spend time in trying to decode variations in your visual cues and emphases. For example, if you use a 5 percent gray background to highlight a key cell in a table or spreadsheet, don't switch to bold and eliminate the 5 percent gray background in the next figure, table, or spreadsheet in the same document. If the basic table or figure works for the written portion of your material, don't totally redesign it for your oral presentation. Yes, it might help to add colour, but don't switch the rows and the columns without an extremely good reason.

Effective Charts, Figures, and Tables

To be effective, figures and tables don't have to be outsourced to a graphic designer. Frequently, you can use a template from your presentation package to import figures and tables to your written document. Alternatively, you might choose to design a figure or table in your word processor and then import it into your presentation package. Microsoft's Word, Excel, and PowerPoint packages all offer user-friendly ways to design charts, tables, and figures that can easily be imported and exported into the other programs for documents and presentations.

When using figures and tables, do more than just stick them into a document; add transitions to help a reader understand:

- Why the figure or table is there?
- How to use it?
- What it emphasizes?
- Where to focus attention?

Transitions help the reader move to the next point in your message. Tables and figures should not be added just to create white space, to break up the text, or to decorate a page. Tables, figures, and graphs should advance and clarify the logic of your argument.

SUMMARY

The ways in which you enhance the logic and structure of materials is, in most instances, basic common sense. Unfortunately, we frequently don't take the time to build logic and structure into a document or to verify that they work in the draft material that we have created. Evaluate the logic and structure of all documents, verifying that you have used an appropriate organizational plan, that you have used graphs, figures, and tables to advance your arguments, and that you've knitted your argument together with transitions. Given below is a checklist to help you improve logic and structure. It is easy to improve the logic and structure of a document when you adopt the mind-set of your readers. Improve the logic and structure of your documents by thinking the process through before you start, by implementing organizational plans, by building stronger arguments, and by using figures and tables appropriately. Using these steps can help you create a logical, well-structured document that will advances an argument successfully.

Note: For knowing more about " Developing the Logic and Structure of Documentation" reader can study documentation process of Microsoft company by visiting their site: www.members.microsoft.com

5

Document Layout and Design

To the novice writer, the appearance or layout of a document may not seem all that important. As long as the document is neat and has no glaring typographical errors, the writer may assume it is acceptable. However, the layout and design of a document are really crucial for two main reasons:

- Good layout and design of your document can help in clarifying your logic and structure, which become visible at a glance, allowing the reader to better understand your organization and follow your points.
- Good layout and design concepts also improve crucial esthetic elements of a document. Our seminar and workshop participants almost unanimously indicate that they pay more attention to documents that look professional. Such documents are much better received and are more likely to get the results you need.

At what point do you start to work on the layout and design of your documents? The shaded areas in Figure below show the steps in which layout and designs are considerations. Because these concerns are central to the complete writing and editing process, you need to start thinking about them early on.

Figure: Layout and design concepts are used during most writing and editing steps.

As we discuss earlier, it is important to establish minimum standards for common layout and design features, especially for team projects. Individuals also need to establish standards for the various types of documents (memos, e-mail, business or form letters, proposals, reports, etc.) that they commonly create. In the following paragraphs, we discuss which layout and design points you can establish, and often need to revisit, during different writing and editing steps.

LAYOUT AND DESIGN DURING THE PREWRITING STEP

The prewriting step is the first place where you're concerned with layout and design, because your goal is to save your reader's time and to make it easy for him or her to understand your key points. You should be designing the layout of a document to highlight your key points and provide a visual overview of your organization. Evaluating potential layout and design features at this point in the process will also help you recognize when the conceptual organization of your document needs improvement.

TEMPLATES AND STYLE SHEETS

Checklist for Improving the Layout and Design of Documents.

- Use appropriate levels of heads and subheads to show relationships among ideas.
- Use displayed lists or bulleted lists to highlight key points and clusters of related points.
- Include integrated tables, figures, charts, and graphs that simplify information and ideas.
- Vary margins and indentations to show relationships among ideas.
- Use sufficient font(s) or typeface(s) and vary the size to add emphasis without adding visual clutter.
- Use bolding, italics, and underlining to add visual emphasis.
- Use borders, boxes, and shading to show relationships.
- Use colour to highlight key points.
- Use headers or footers to identify document, author/contacts, dates, and pages.
- Use white space to reduce concentrated text.

An effective way to bring consistency to documents and to save design efforts is to use templates and style sheets. Major companies, such as Xerox, have developed publications manuals designed to help establish corporate visual standards, provide uniform ways to emphasize key points, and save time. Other companies, including Procter & Gamble, traditionally have trained new managers on the "corporate look" for specific types of documents.

The advantages of style sheets or document templates are twofold:

- Employees don't have to reinvent the wheel or waste time designing every memo, report, and proposal. This saves extensive amounts of time and money.
- Managers and others who share documents across functional areas or with outside companies become familiar with a generic template and know exactly where to locate key points or sections without searching. This, too, saves extensive amounts of time and money.

USING STYLE SHEETS FROM WORD PROCESSING AND PRESENTATION PROGRAMS

Most small companies don't have the resources to develop extensive standards; however, the style sheets included with first-tier word processing and presentations programs provide very useful options. Such style sheets facilitate the consistent use of styles (for fonts, margins, heads, subheads, and other features such as shading, borders, and colour). Software style sheets allow you to design a consistent look within and among documents- designs that might be as simple and effective as using bullets to show action items and due dates in a two-paragraph memo or as complex as forJohnng a series of proposals to a government agency. Style sheets also allow you to coordinate documents with presentation visuals and materials.

Style Manuals

Another important tool in layout and design is the use of styled manuals. Widely used styled manuals include the following:

- The Chicago Manual of Style
- Prentice-Hall's Words into Print
- The APA Publication Manual (American Psychological Association)
- The New York Times Manual of Style and Usage
- The Gregg Reference Manual

These style manuals offer insights into design features and usage information (grammar, reference). For example, when do you hyphenate specific words? How do you use specific honorary titles with international clients? How do you cite a book or a journal article in a report? How do you handle references in footnotes and reference lists? How do you create clear tables and figures? How do you emphasize key points of information?

Consider choosing a single, well-accepted style manual as a universal reference for your company or team. Such a manual will provide a standard source of information that will decrease work interruptions, improve document consistency across the company, facilitate creating a unified document from the work of multiple authors, and help decrease the need for constant reediting.

The design that you develop or choose in your prewriting step should visually emphasize your organizational plan (for example, problem-solution, cause effect, implementation across fiscal quarters) and effectively demonstrate your points.

LAYOUT AND DESIGN DURING THE DRAFTING AND EDITING STEPS

After establishing layout and design points during your prewriting step, your next writing and editing step is to draft and then edit your materials. When you are editing for content, ask yourself: "Does my logic support my points?" At the same time, try to figure out if your layout and design choices make the information clear. For example, if you have five key points, do those points stand out at first glance, catch the reader's eye, and help to provide cues for what you're trying to accomplish?

Layout and Design during the Postwriting Step

After you've edited your document, check your layout and design for one more time during your postwriting step. Use a reader's perspective to make certain that your logic and organization are visually clear. Make certain that your key points are easy to see and follow. If they're not, consider using a different organizational pattern, rephrasing the material, or using different layout and design cues. Of equal importance, remember what didn't work- save yourself editing time on your next document.

Specific Layout and Design Concepts

You don't have to become a graphic artist to improve your documents, but understanding basic layout and design concepts can help you plan, edit, and create more successful documents:

Heads and Subheads

Heads and subheads are the visually emphasized words at the start of sections, paragraphs, and topics that are often referred to as L1, L2, L3, L4, and so on. An L1 head is the main or most visually prominent concept in a document. L2, L3, L4, and succeeding subheads are of decreasing (often hierarchical) conceptual importance and visual strength.

Margins and Indents

These need little explanation. Remember that there are, however, left, right, top, and bottom margins, and that indenting material on both the left and right sides may be very effective. Wide margins also allow readers to add notes.

Displayed Lists

Displayed lists are created by simply pulling the left and right margins around a piece of information. Changing the font, for example, to italic, can add more visual emphasis.

Bullets

Bullets are symbols that are used to show where a piece of information starts or to set off a list.

Font(s) and Typeface(s)

The two most commonly used are some variant of Times New Roman and Helvetica or Arial. Times New Roman is probably the safest choice. Anything too unusual can distract the reader from the message-this includes using all capital letters, all italics, or all boldface.

Integrated Graphics

Graphics are used to simplify information and decrease complex text. They include, among others,

- Tables
- Figures
- Charts

These design cues are important because they allow you to bring consistency and repeating patterns to your work. In addition, they allow you to create white space-open places on a page that can help focus your reader's attention. When you use visual cues, remember to apply them to your headers and footers. Effective headers and footers, especially footers that contain identifying information such as authorship, document title, origination date, computer file name/location, and page numbers, can make a report extremely easy to use and locate in the future.

Applying good layout and design concepts makes it easy for your readers to find what they need and what you want to share.

APPLYING LAYOUT AND DESIGN CONCEPTS IN SAMPLE DOCUMENTS

We have found that simply discussing these concepts is insufficient. Even though people see them every day, many writers find it helpful to see actual before-and-after examples showing how to use these concepts and tools effectively.

Using Bullet Points, White Space, and Inset Margins

When you create a document like the memo, your readers will be scratching their heads trying to figure out what you want them to know or do. The revised memo should have them nodding in agreement with your points. When you compare the verbose memo to the revised memo, you will notice that both documents have the same audience and goal, and they contain essentially the same information.

However, the verbose memo is not only too long, it also lacks the simple visual cues (e.g., bullet points, inset margins, and white space) that focus your attention on key points in the revised memo. It lacks a useful subject line, and, compared to the revised memo, most people would find the original hard to skim. In fact, most people would need to read it several times to understand the main point.

CLEAR SECTIONS, SUBJECT LINES, TABLES, AND HEADS

Effective, visually and logically consistent memos can also be created by systematically editing your material, adding useful section divisions, heads, figures, charts, or tables. Most readers would find the complex, original memo to be ineffective because it has extensive text and no visual cues to show its organization. In contrast, the improved memo has a good subject line and is well organized, partially because the integrated table forces the writer to think clearly by providing a structure that organizes ideas and data.

The table and the head ("Interpretation of the Data") effectively focus the reader's attention. To gain the information you need from the original memo, you need to read the entire memo-probably twice. To get the information you need from the improved memo you can simply skim the table. Which memo would you rather receive, and on which memo would you want senior management to find your name?

LAYOUT AND DESIGN CONCEPTS WITH OTHER DOCUMENTS

The same concepts apply to e-mail messages, letters, resumes, reports, and proposals. For example, consider the e-mail messages. They demonstrate that applying these concepts to e-mail adds value, although in many instances, creating a good e-mail message is more difficult than creating a good memo because of the inherent limitations of many e-mail editing packages. Many e-mail packages do not support underlining, bold, or switching of fonts, let alone useful embedding of figures, tables, or graphics. Because of these shortcomings, the writer must write with more clarity and use other visual cues to organize the materials. One effective solution is to use short, well-structured ideas that are broken into short paragraphs with indented margins and lists.

USING LAYOUT AND DESIGN IDEAS WITH RESUMES

When you want to move up in your organization or to find a new job, remember to use layout and design ideas and tools with your resume. The resumes using layout and design cues can improve the visual organization of a document by reducing hard-to-read blocks of text. Resumes are often given only a minute or two of a manager's time, so they need to make an immediate, positive impact. They are seldom read for pleasure-especially when the manager takes them home to read in the evenings or on weekends!

SUMMARY

Common layout and design tools can help you in improving documents to get the results you need. Using tables and figures can be especially effective in simplifying information and advancing arguments. As you move through the writing and editing process, it is crucial for you to consider the look of your documents as a way to visually reinforce your written word.

Note: For detailed information and understanding more on layout and design tools, reader may visit this site www. informationr.net/ir

6

Successfully Using E-mail

E-mail is playing an increasingly important role in business communication, with tens of millions of pieces of mail being transmitted daily. In 1998, the Electronic Messaging Association estimated that by the year 2000, users will send approximately 6 trillion electronic messages.

Forrester Research, in a 1996 report titled "People and Technology Strategies," estimated that 60 million Americans were exchanging e-mail and that the use of email would grow tenfold over the next five years.

Elsewhere, Kate Delhagen of Forrester Research noted (in 1998) that e-mail has exploded over the last five years and that within 10 years, over 80 percent of the U.S. population will have an e-mail address.

E-mail is also becoming a problematic form of business communication because of barriers that exist at both the company and individual user levels:

- A lack of common standards and expectations (etiquette) among users
- A need for universally supported software/forJohnng features
- Security questions (internal, external, encryption)
- Increasing concerns about the document life cycle of e-mail

In addition to the material in this chapter, useful and regularly updated information is available about these and other e-mail topics at various web sites, some of which are cited in Table given below. Regularly updated information will be of extremely valuable because of the rapidly evolving nature of this field.

Table: E-mail Sources

E-mail, Internet Issue	*Web Site*	*Web Site*	*Web Site*
E-mail growth	emailehlp.com/email-ed.html	emailhelp.com/forrester.html	emailhelp.com/ema.html
E-mail etiquette/issues	albion.com/netiquette/book/index.html	iwillfollow.com/emailetiquette.html	everythingemail.net
E-mail glossary/emoticons	newbie.net/jumpstations/SmileyFAQ.html	windweaver.com/emoticon.htm	everythingemail.net/glossary.html
E-mail style and layout	albion.com/netiquette/book/index.html	webfoot.com/advice/email.top.html	
Business etiquette International etiquette	bspage.com/Inetiq/netiq.html	newbie.net	
Ethics	fau.edu/rinaldi/net/index.html	newbie.net	

LACK OF COMMON STANDARDS AND EXPECTATIONS

There are not commonly accepted standards for e-mail that are parallel, for example, to those for business letters. Writers who have style questions about business letters and documents can quickly check the commonly available references, such as The Prentice-Hall Style Manual, The Chicago Manual of Style, 14th, or The Gregg Reference Manual. However, guidelines for e-mail are less common and less widely circulated.

This is changing, but the problem of accepted standards remains to be solved. Perhaps the best-known and most widely accepted source for standards is Netiquette by Virginia Shea, which is available both in hard copy and on-line.

MAXIMIZING E-MAIL COMMUNICATION

Be sure your e-mail messages carry the impact to get the recipients' attention and achieve your intended goal. Table below details some frequently encountered problems of e-mail and links them to the writing and editing process. Whether it's making your subject line too vague or forgetting to spell check, you can maximize communication and avoid pitfalls by keeping the writing and editing process in mind when you create e-mail.

Here is a brief overview of common e-mail problems and some recommendations to help solve them.

SUBJECT LINES

Missing or uninformative subject lines are problem for e-mail senders and readers. Subject lines for e-mail, as for memos, are intended to focus both the sender and the reader: The sender can check the subject line to see if the goal of a memo was met, and the reader can decide when, or whether, to open the incoming message.

Recommendation: Use subject lines that are concise and informative and that highlight the goal of the message or a needed action.

Table: E-mail problems Linked to a Writing and Editing Process

Individual User E-mail Issues	Prewriting	Drafting	Editing Logic	Editing Layout	Editing Grammar	Postwriting
Missing/poor subject line						x
Weak structure/ organization	x		x			
Too much information	x	x	x			x
No attachments	x		x			
Unusable attachments	x					x
Sloppy work		x	x	x		
No spell check					x	x
All caps	x				x	x
No caps	x				x	x
Visual cues				x		x
No visual cues				x		x
Getting too fancy				x		x
Emotives				x		x
Oops, I sent it!						x
Paper trail	x		x			x
Copying the world	x		x			x
Forwarding to the world	x		x			x

WEAK STRUCTURE OR ORGANIZATION

Early users of e-mail simply dashed off notes and forgot about them, causing bad habits to develop among generations of e-mail users. Those bad habits are proliferating as e-mail becomes the preferred method of correspondence. Some companies, such as Microsoft, pride themselves on their extensive use of e-mail for internal correspondence. Unfortunately, many people don't take the time and care with e-mail messages that they might with a hardcopy memo or business letter. This leads to ineffective messages that require more follow-up for clarification and response.

Recommendation: Spend the same amount of time in the writing and editing process drafting and editing e-mail as you would memos and letters.

TOO MUCH INFORMATION

One of the most frustrating problems facing e-mail users is how to impart a lot of information. When you have a long (multiple paragraphs or pages) message, it can be helpful to use attachments to reduce the size of the e-mail to make the information less intimidating and more user-friendly. However, especially for cross-company and cross-platform (UNIX versus Mac versus Windows) document exchanges, it is often difficult to know if the receiver will be able to open the attachments that you want to include. For example, if you want to summarize a page of text by using a table or graphic, will the receiver's e-mail or other software open it?

Recommendation: Before you send e-mail attachments, verify that the receiver has the ability to open and use them. It is often preferable to avoid software-specific file formats (such as Microsoft's.doc files) and to instead use formats that can be interpreted by multiple software packages (such as.rtf).

SLOPPY WORK

Sloppy work is an increasing problem as more people begin to use e-mail. Common failures include the following:

- Not knowing the goal of an e-mail
- Treating an e-mail more as a conversation than as a concise memo
- Failing to develop logical transitions among ideas
- Not using a spell checker
- Using poor typing habits

Using ALL CAPS or no capitalization can eliminate cues that readers unconsciously use to recognize the visual patterns (outlines) of words. These types of errors are often made by users who lack basic keyboarding/typing skills and by users who try to hide their lack of grammar skills (albeit, unsuccessfully).

The problem of sloppy work is briefly addressed in "A Beginner's Guide to Effective Email, revision 2.0" by Kaitlin Duck Sherwood. Sherwood indicates that e-mail is often viewed as being more conversational than traditional paper-based media and that, as a result, e-mail tends to be sloppier than communication on paper. Recommendation: Reread your e-mail message before you send it. Avoid being sloppy. Sloppy errors can create significant liabilities. As a case in point, embarrassing e-mail often gets forwarded to others without the sender's permission. Use the editing and postwriting substeps from decrease sloppy errors. You risk embarrassment if you send out an e-mail before editing or proofreading it.

VISUAL CUES

A multitude of visual cues can help in making your e-mail messages easier to read. Unfortunately, senders frequently don't know if the receiver's software will support (interpret) the codes that are used to represent those visual cues in the document. Many times, the visual cues (bolding, margin changes, italics, colour, etc.) end up as embedded gibberish in the receiver's document. This is because many e-mail programs support only a basic ASCII code set instead of extended or special-character sets. In her "Beginner's Guide to Effective Email," Sherwood offers a useful overview of some of the barriers to effective forJohnng of text materials.

Recommendation: If you are sending e-mail to specific individuals on a regular basis, send a test message to verify whether the receiver's software can interpret your embedded forJohnng. If your e-mail message is a one-off document, play it safe and use simple, straight text or ASCII characters; don't try to get fancy. Instead, focus on writing materials that are well organized, go straight to the point, use good transitions, and use numbered or lettered points and line spacing as visual cues.

CREATING A FANCY DOCUMENT

For many e-mail users, the fundamental goal is quick, concise communication. Spending too much time creating a fancy document is wasted effort, especially when the e-mail is just to let a colleague know that you going to a 30-minute meeting.

Recommendation: Match your effort to the importance of your message. Use visual cues, but first know what you need to say, say it clearly, and then stop.

EMOTICONS

Emoticans are cute, but cute doesn't necessarily fit in a business message. In addition, unless you and the receiver use a "smiley" web site or newbies.net) to understand their meaning, those little cues can have mixed messages. For example, you might be tempted to use the emoticon: X with a new client who asks you to guarantee nondisclosure. Unfortunately, X can mean "my lips are sealed," or it can mean "a big wet kiss."

Recommendation: Avoid using emoticons and smileys except for casual messages to colleagues you know extremely well or to friends. Emoticons seldom add value to business correspondence, and they can be counterproductive.

WRONG EMAIL ADDRESS

There are hundreds of horror stories involving e-mail messages that never should have been created or sent. In many recent cases of litigation-for example, those related to tobacco, silicon breast implants, automobiles, and software-individuals have created paper trails that have greatly helped litigants.

FORWARDING E-MAIL AND COPYING THE WORLD

Two chief caveats: Do not copy the world or forward e-mail to everyone. It is all too easy to send trivial e-mail to dozens of people by using distribution lists rather than targeting appropriate individuals. The reverse is also true: It is easy for those receiving e-mail to forward it, intentionally or unintentionally, to a multitude of others-perhaps including individuals whom the original sender deliberately excluded.

Recommendation: Complete your postwriting step before you let your finger hit the Return key or click the mouse. Decide whether you might better send the material by conventional mail or discuss it in a phone call. Decide who should receive the material and establish a document cycle for the message (for example, read and delete, do not distribute, etc.).

NONSTANDARD FORJOHNNG FEATURES

One of the problems facing both individual users and companies is the lack of universally supported software features. For the purposes of this discussion, we are defining software features as those that provide various text-emphasis techniques, such as margins or indents, bolding, italics, underlining, colour, inserted figures or graphics, attachments, and so forth. ForJohnng features become a problem when, for example, a person sends an e-mail to a receiver at another company or at another branch of the same company. Depending on the software package being used (and in some cases the service provider), the sender doesn't know whether the e-mail will be readable by the receiver. It may be filled with gibberish. The response may read *?#$%?*&???-or there may be no response at all!

Recommendation: At a company level, make certain you adopt a commonly used and widely supported e-mail package that allows for the forJohnng of text. At the individual level, verify that the e-mail capabilities of key contacts are compatible with yours.

SECURITY CONCERNS

One of the problems that is being faced by many business users is the question of security, especially with content-sensitive materials being sent out over the Internet. At the company level, data security (internal and external) and encryption are vital to be considered.

Recommendation: Companies need to establish protocols dealing not only with the use of encryption software, but also with the integrity and protection of the e-mail/server system from external and internal threats. Companies need to address the practical problems that can result from a failure to screen for viruses, and they need to protect against hackers and unauthorized access to systems, software, and documents. Valuable ideas on security and data encryption are available at the Electronic Messaging Association web site, at www.newbies.net, and at the following sites for Pretty Good Privacy (PGP):

http://www.web.mit.edu/network/pgp.html

http://www.nai.com/products/security/security.asp

http://www.thegate.gamers.org/~tony/pgp.html

DOCUMENT LIFE CYCLE OF E-MAIL

The explosion in the use of e-mail has led to the creation of massive numbers of documents that do not have a defined life cycle. They are often not destroyed by the sender or the receiver and, in fact, are stored permanently due to the archiving practices of computer support groups.

Recommendation: As part of their document management policies, companies need to establish document life-cycle procedures to ensure that critical documents (such as patent information) are retained and other documents having potentially negative legal implications are appropriately handled. In addition, companies need to establish access restrictions for users to ensure that only authorized users can view or alter documents.

SUMMARY

E-mail is fast becoming a mandatory means of communicating in the business world. In the very near future, the vast majority of families in the United States are expected to have e-mail addresses. The use of e-mail to communicate effectively, to reduce meetings, and to save time and money on both local and international levels cannot be ignored. Spend time learning how to improve your e-mail messages and how to use this means of communication more effectively. In the long run, you'll save time and money-and produce the results you want.

Note: E-mailiing plays an important role in communication of a company, as can be seen in the case of Google. In 2007 and 2008, Fortune Magazine placed Google at the top of its list of the hundred best places to work. Google's corporate philosophy embodies such casual principles as "you can make money without doing evil," "you can be serious without a suit," and "work ought to be challenging and the challenge ought to be fun." Reader can visit their site: http://www.google.org/about.html

7

Memos

Managers and executives write so many memos in the course of the day that they seldom stop to think about the characteristics of a good memo. Their goal, quite often, is to get the memo written and check that task off their to-do list. This can create problems, especially when the writers have not made a habit of using a writing and editing process. Writing good memos can be a fairly simple task when the writing and editing process is consistently used.

In this chapter, we examine some of the factors that increase the chances your memo will be read and acted upon, and we offer tips for improving the content and design of your memos. Many of the concepts that we discuss throughout Part 2 (logic, structure, organization, layout and design, and grammar) apply to multiple types of documents, because the requirements and goals are often overlapping. You can easily recognize and use those overlaps to save time by applying similar "solutions" to seemingly different products.

QUALITIES OF A GOOD MEMO

What factors increase the likelihood that a manager or executive will read and act upon what you've written? We asked the people who do it every day. During writing workshops, we frequently ask executives to review copies of actual corporate memos, e-mail messages, letters, and reports to determine what characteristics influence whether they will read a document. Their preferences are:

- Short documents
- Documents from their bosses
- Documents clearly linked to a context or requirement
- Memos with good subject lines and/or first paragraphs (or with reports, introductions, or executive summaries)

- Well-organized materials
- Documents that are concisely phrased, well written, easy to read, and have appropriate tone
- Documents with heads, subheads, bullets, and figures-documents they can skim
- Documents that have a nice font and aren't jammed onto a page
- Very short documents!

Additionally, managers and executives indicate that they generally ignore memos, letters, and reports that are:

- Long
- Hard to skim
- Hard to understand, difficult to read, or poorly written
- Unprofessional in appearance

This implies that you should create memos and e-mail that:

- Are short
- Have clear objectives and subject lines
- Are well organized
- Have visual cues to the organization
- Use sufficient supporting data
- Are clear and concise

CREATING GOOD MEMOS

It's easy to improve memos by applying the following quick-and-easy suggestions:

- Have the right content: Define your objective and analyze your audience to be sure you meet the needs of your readers and your own purpose in writing the memo.
- Avoid excessive details: Make it easy on your readers to do their work by including only what is needed-don't write novels!
- Write a memo that readers can skim: Use good organizational cues and visual design so your readers don't have to read every word you write.

DISTINCTION BETWEEN MEMOS AND E-MAIL

Traditionally, there has been a very simple dichotomy between memos and business letters. Memos have been internal documents and business letters have been external documents. That distinction of internal and external documents has become blurred as we all begin to use email-for internal and external communication-more frequently.

This is good, but can also be problematic. It's good if it leads to quicker and less complicated communication. It can be problematic when people fail to realize their e-mailed memos are not internal documents that are automatically confidential or protected or limited in circulation. When memos are sent as e-mails to people outside to the company (i.e., external documents), they functionally become business letters, and consequently they must be held to a higher standard during all phases of their creation, editing, distribution, and life cycle. Once you send out a business letter or an e-mail, that message is no longer under your control. As a result, you need to pay more attention to your prewriting, editing, and postwriting processes. In addition, the following suggestions from Charles Brusaw, et al., in The Business Writer's Handbook can be very helpful. According to Brusaw, when writing memos, you should do the following:

- Use meaningful subject lines that convey the essence of the memo.
- Use a check-off line for __ action, __ information, or __ response.
- Write clear, focused, and forthright memos. (Don't tell a story.)
- Put your recommendations and key points up front.
- Use useful, concise, supporting detail.
- Use informative, visually sequenced heads and subheads.
- Use lists and bullets.
- Use a personal tone.

The late Malcolm Forbes also made a number of excellent suggestions on how to write good memos and letters:

- Know what you want; state it in one sentence?
- Plunge right in; give the purpose of the letter in the first paragraph.
- Write so it's enjoyable; use a reader's viewpoint; be natural; be positive.

- Give it your best; make it visually appealing; make it short; emphasize your points.
- State what you're going to do; state what you want to be done. Sum it up and get out.

SAMPLE MEMOS

Many people love to use templates to design their documents. Most word processors now offer style sheet options that include pull-down boxes with pre-designed heads and subheads. These are very useful, and they can be even more useful when you use those heads and subheads to emphasize your organization, your logic, and the structure of your messages. To help you visualize how to improve memos (and e-mail), we provide sample memos that show common problems and effective solutions. Review these samples to help you identify how you and your team can strengthen documents.

Calling the bookstore, or using the Internet (amazon.com or barnesandnoble.com), for example, would be a quicker and easier solution than drafting, revising, and following up with another memo.

SUMMARY

Memos are becoming more widely used with the advent of e-mail. Memos, which traditionally were internal documents, are being transformed into external documents that replace more traditional business letters. Because, it is important to use both document management systems and writing and editing processes to ensure that the content is appropriate and will not lead to legal liability. Further, the use of a writing and editing process can ensure that memos incorporate appropriate organizational plans and visual cues that make them easier to create and to read.

Note: For detailed study reader can visit www.nokia.com

8

Business Letters

Business letters are important link to individuals and groups outside to your company. While written communication within a company is generally done through e-mail and memos, business letters are generally thought of as a more formal means of communicating with those outside to the company.

In this chapter, we discuss the use of writing and editing processes to avoid common errors in writing business letters. We will help you improve your writing and editing processes, and thus the quality of your products, by examining five factors that help determine the success of business letters:

- Content
- Organization
- Tone and phrasing
- Correctly spelled names and titles
- Style-layout and design

CONTENT OF BUSINESS LETTERS

Most writers assume that they automatically put the appropriate content in their letters. In reality, that is often a bad assumption, which is why the writing and editing process contains a prewriting step, which includes analyzing your readers, and a postwriting step, in which you confirm that your content coincides with your goals.

VALUABLE LETTER-WRITING RESOURCES

For those of you with limited experience in writing everyday business letters, a number of excellent resources are available. Sabin, The Gregg

Reference Manual covers correspondence and usage issues in extensive detail, as does DeVries in The Prentice-Hall Style Manual. Both books contain hundreds of pages of sample documents and illustrations showing how to handle the minute details involved in creating technically correct correspondence. The first step (prewriting) will help you determine who will be reading your material, what they know, what they want to know, what you want them to do or not do, and how to give them the information they need. The last step (postwriting) will help ensure that you have met your objectives and avoided fatal errors.

One of the more effective additions to a business letter is an action statement: an indication of what you are going to do next or what you expect the reader to do. An action statement can be effective as a first sentence or a closing sentence.

ORGANIZATION

Making sure your business letter is organized, yet many overlook this crucial step, and the resulting letter resembles a rambling stroll though the countryside. If your ideas fit into a problem-solution format, then organize your letter in that mode. If you can talk effectively about your ideas in relation to time (e.g., fiscal quarters) or geographic or market areas, and that perspective will help your reader better understand the implications, then organize your letter (or a section of it) accordingly. When you use organizational plans to help your readers see the pertinence of your ideas and to make your ideas more familiar, you will decrease their work and increase the likelihood that they will be able to assimilate your points.

Apply the ideas of Malcolm Forbes:

- Know where you are going.
- Make your main point in the first sentence or paragraph.
- Use clear, concise, straightforward statements.
- Sum up.
- Get out.

Forbes's advice is excellent. You need to put your reason for writing in your first sentence or paragraph. It is sometimes recommended that you put good news in your first sentence, and if you have bad news, to buffer it by using a neutral first sentence or paragraph. For example, "We have greatly enjoyed being able to supply your company with high-quality parts for the last five years. But we can no longer supply parts to your company, as your account is 90 days past due." This technique can be problematic, however, because many people skip the buffer and go directly to the bad news.

Use the buffer cautiously.

TONE AND PHRASING

Tone is another one of those commonsense points that is often overlooked. In seminars, one of the best exercises we do is to pass out a sample letter and ask for a show of hands: Would you read this, set it aside for later, or toss it? Tone errors are the second most common reason that managers and executives give for setting aside a document to read later. Tone errors often reflect poor editing for grammar and failing to complete the postwriting step. Tone errors often result from anger. If you write a letter when you are angry, don't mail it immediately. Put it into a desk drawer, let it sit overnight, and then review it in the morning. It's easier and more effective to take the time to review it than to have to apologize or to suffer the consequences of your poor judgment.

NEGATIVE PHRASING

Some letter writers will take a negative approach:

We understand your customers have been canceling contracts due to your inability to meet milling tolerances of ±0.001 microns. Building on a positive statement is usually much more effective:

Our new CNC machines are helping our customers meet strict milling tolerances of ±0.001 microns and increase market share.

Often, the wrong tone is a result of one or two words that convey the wrong impression. Other times, tone errors are more problematic because they reflect a writer's basic personality, which is hard to hide in your writing.

Because it is difficult to take on the reader's perspective and to recognize the "wrong" tone in a letter that you have written, we strongly recommend using a postwriting step that includes letting your letter sit overnight and then rereading it or, better yet, asking a colleague to read it before you send it out.

OTHER PHRASING CONCERNS

Some phrasing errors occur as a result of being immersed in a company's culture. These include the excessive use of jargon and acronyms, genderspecific phrasing, trite phrases, and using the passive voice.

Jargon and Acronyms

How do you know you're using too much jargon and too many acronyms? One clue is writing that appears codelike: "... the SLC group at EK is very concerned about JIT delivery and ROE for the L&D function of the CNC..." When the spell checker for your word processor highlights every third word, it's time to start editing.

Gender-Specific Language

Not only is gender-specific language typically inaccurate, it is often inappropriate and can even cause legal problems. For example, do you mean security men or security officers? Managers, men who... or individuals who... ? Senior vice presidents, women who... or senior vice presidents, executives who... ? If a specific group is composed of only one gender, it is appropriate to note it; however, it is probably not appropriate, at least in the United States, to suggest that gender precludes employment in certain positions.

Trite Phrases

Trite phrases such as "Have a nice day" do not belong in business letters.

Sentence Construction

Phrasing problems can also be related to the active versus passive voice in sentence construction. In general, use concise, active voice. It is shorter and eliminates a perception of overly formal writing, and increases the effectiveness of your writing. Carol Gelderman in her chapter, "Business Letters," provides an excellent illustration of the difference between active-versus-passive construction and verb tenses-two concepts that are frequently confused. As Gelderman illustrates, it is easy to write both active and passive constructions in all verb tenses:

When you use active voice, the subject "does" the action of the verb:

- Smith writes the best letter. (active, present tense)
- Smith wrote the best letter. (active, past tense)
- Smith will write the best letter. (active, future tense)

When you use passive voice, the subject is "acted upon" by something else:

- The best letter is written by Smith. (passive, present tense)
- The best letter was written by Smith. (passive, past tense)
- The best letter will be written by Smith. (passive, future tense)

Using the active voice in your business letters will significantly shorten them and often make them more effective. The passive voice is only effective in case if you want to maintain a formal tone.

Correct Spelling

Do people work for Proctor and Gamble or Procter & Gamble? Is your potential client Kathy Smith, Cathy Smithe, Kathryn Smith, or Ms. Kaye Smith? One of the quickest ways to lose the confidence of someone with whom you hope to do business is to misspell that company's or individual's name. It shows you don't care enough to hunt through files, check a web site, or make a phone call. Remember, it's always worth taking the time to confirm the spelling of proper names.

A fatal error that ranks close to misspelling a person's name or a company name is giving someone the wrong title-be it too high or too low. There is often more than one way to use titles correctly. For guidelines, we suggest using The New York Times Manual of Style and the Chicago Manual of Style, as well as visiting web sites. For example, we recently needed to know how to use certain honorary titles in Japan.

Avoiding Fatal Errors

Fatal errors like misspelling someone's name or using the wrong title can be avoided by making a quick phone call, checking other correspondence, or logging on to a web site and checking your information. If you're lucky, you might make direct contact with the person you need to deal with- perhaps eliminating the need for your letter or making it a follow-up or confirmation letter instead.

Style-Layout and Design

Creating effective business letters requires more effort-and more writing and editing skill-than creating effective memos. We say this because writers often use visual cues in memos to help them overcome poor writing and organizational skills and to make their logic and organization easy to see and follow. In contrast, some people feel that they should not use visual cues in business letters. They think that managers and executives aren't used to seeing such cues and that they are negatively perceived.

EIGHT COVER LETTER MISTAKES

Michelle Magee, formerly Assistant Director of Placement at the University of Rochester's Simon School of Business, in her seminars on cover letters, often discussed eight deadly errors that need to be avoided:

- Typographical errors
- Gross grammatical errors
- Misspelled company or employer names
- Content that lacks substance
- Content that doesn't sell
- Templated or form letter content
- Wrong company name (often due to form letters)
- Sloppy, crumpled, coffee-stained letters with handmade corrections

Michelle Magee is now the Program Coordinator for the Office of Cooperative Education and Career Services at Rochester Institute of Technology. However, when we ask managers and executives in our seminars whether they prefer to receive business letters with or without visual cues (subheads, displayed or bulleted lists, indented margins, subject lines, etc.) to make the key points easier to read, the vast majority-90 percent in a typical seminar-say they prefer receiving business letters that contain visual cues. Why? Easy. It takes too much time to scan a traditional letter to decide what you need to do with it. They don't have any more free time to read business letters than they do to read memos and e-mail, so anything you can do to facilitate their work is a plus.

Unless you are dealing with a very conservative reader (figure this out during your prewriting step), use visual cues (subheads, displayed or bulleted lists, indented margins, subject lines, etc.) to make your letters easier to read.

SUMMARY

In a business letter, it is important to verify that you have included the right content, used an appropriate organizational pattern, avoided errors in tone and phrasing, spelled names and titles correctly, and used style layout and design features that will make your letters easy to read.

Note: For further knowledge on "Business Letters" reader can visit www.infosysblogs.com

9

Reports and Executive Summaries

If you're new to report writing, the task may seem formidable. However, most of us have had experience of writing academic reports, and you may be relieved to learn that business and academic reports share many of the same processes, such as prewriting, editing, and postwriting. Further, these characteristics can be linked to the writing and editing steps, as shown in Figures given below.

In this chapter, we discuss how a writing and editing process can help you in improving your reports and save time. We also review how to avoid specific

report-writing problems and pitfalls, how to integrate tables and figures to advance your arguments, and how to maximize the use of executive summaries.

What Makes a Good Report?

Before we begin to discuss process, it will be helpful to review the characteristics of good business reports.

- Clear structure
- Ease of use
- Visual cues
- Well written and edited
- Short format

USING WRITING AND EDITING PROCESS WITH REPORTS

Using the writing and editing process can help you and your team to create effective reports and understand where the process steps come into play when you are addressing specific report characteristics.

STEP 1: PREWRITING

Prewriting helps you to clarify your thinking before you start writing. Your drafting and editing will be easier and more effective because prewriting helps you:

- To identify your readers or users
- To determine the goals and requirements to be met
- To identify the sequential subtasks to be completed
- To establish individual responsibilities and identify potential conflicts (e.g., work, family, social)

Company's Report Standards

In some companies, report-specific or company-specific style requirements vary from department to department. In other companies, company-specific styles and standards may be poorly defined. When they do exist, they may consist of nothing more than vague instructions and generic templates: "Use two columns on a page and use a table here. That's our style," or "Here, make your report look like this one. The boss liked that report." We recommend developing consistent, clear styles and standards for reports.

1. Good reports have clear structures. A useful general report structure includes:
   - Executive summary. A stand-alone document that helps your readers in understanding information and making decisions.
   - Introduction. A paragraph or two on what's coming, where, and its importance
   - Conclusion/recommendation. Up front, so your readers aren't left guessing
   - Body with clear supporting information (shorter is better)
   - Coherently organized. Use organizational patterns (problem/ solution, fiscal periods, time sequences, etc.) that reinforce your objective and meet readers' needs.
   - Supporting data. Include the necessary data in your text or append it (preferred).
   - Figures/tables/graphics. Use visuals that advance your argument, make key points easy to understand, and have labels and visual cues that make points clear at a glance.
   - Documented sources. Include citations to help readers judge and validate information.

- Summary. One or two paragraphs to close the report and reinforce conclusions.
- Collected references/footnotes. To help readers locate key information sources.
- Appendixes. With secondary information in stand-alone, well-introduced sections.

2. Good reports are easy to use. After reading an executive summary, a reader should know your goal/objectives, conclusion, results or recommendations, and the report's structure (organization). The body of the report is as short as practical. Extra information is appended.

3. Good reports use visual cues. Your visual cues reinforce the logic and structure of the report. Your layout/design make your logic/structure visually clear. To help guide your reader and allow the reader to skim the report quickly, use
   - Consistent fonts
   - Concise, meaningful heads and subheads
   - Page headers or footers (author, title, date, page numbers, and computer file name)

4. Good reports are well written and edited. If your readers can't easily understand what you have written, your recommendations will have low credibility. When you edit, first edit for logic/ organization, then layout, and last for grammar. Remember that good reports have
   - Executive summaries that help readers make decisions
   - Clear organization (problem/solution, sequence of events, concern/recommendation/next steps)
   - Figures/tables that advance/support your argument and link to your presentation
   - Sufficient information/supporting data so your readers can make unbiased decisions

5. Good reports are short. Save yourself, your staff, and your readers time by editing your content so that it meets your reader's needs. If you don't know what your readers need, ask them!
   - Establish timeline(s) and decide how to track progress on the project
   - Establish document layout and design standards for all your group's reports
   - Decide how reports are okayed for distribution

Gantt and/or PERT Charts

To facilitate prewriting tasks, we have found that it is helpful to use simple Gantt or PERT charts to show the relationships among tasks, people, resources, costs, and timelines, as well as to sequence the substeps of a specific project.

Another tool that can help increase the effectiveness of your prewriting step is to create simple visual sketches or networks of ideas. This will help you visualize and analyze the relationships among your ideas and to best sequence them. Some people quickly sketch a flowchart with a few identifying words; others create simple or very complex outlines.

Simply list your key points and subordinate ideas using bulleted points. Or, if you want to stress the conceptual relationships among ideas, sketch a relational map (networking, mapping) that uses labeled links among your ideas to show key points and relationships.

There are several advantages to creating these visual sketches during your prewriting step:

Prewriting technique-visual representations (using labeled relationships to analyze and link concepts).

- They help you to see and analyze the interrelationships among your potential topics.
- They help you to take a user's perspective and make certain that your assumptions and "private" knowledge are shared.
- They help you to analyze your assumptions and content, just as your users and critics will be doing.
- They create a set of reference points so that you don't forget key points in your report or during your presentation(s).

In addition to sketches of concepts in a document, outlines and bulleted lists can also be effective ways to visualize the actual relationships among ideas.

STEP 2: RESEARCH AND DRAFTING

After completing your prewriting step, focus on two key ideas when you begin to draft your report:

Identify your research process and the information or data you need.

Start writing, shaping your materials to fit your goals, your users, and their requirements.

Research Processes and Techniques

We do not cover research processes or techniques here because of the complexity of the topics. If you haven't been trained in research design, measurement, and statistical analysis, add someone to your team who is knowledgeable in these areas, or hire a consultant. It is critical that you understand the assumptions you are making during your research design, measurement, and analysis tasks. If you don't have good data, and if you don't analyze it correctly, you are likely to write a report that is rejected or, worse, leads to bad decisions.

Drafting Processes and Techniques

After completing any preliminary research and organizing your material, you need to start drafting (writing) your material. Start writing by reviewing the goals and requirements that you identified in your prewriting step. Start writing on any of your topics or subtopics. Don't force yourself to start at the beginning and write linearly. Start with the topic you know best-one that will flow quickly and easily. Then, build other pieces of your report, using the structure of your outline, flowchart, or visual (relational) map. Remember, when you are drafting, your goal is to get your ideas down. Worry later about having perfect phrasing and grammar. Don't stop to punctuate your citations or footnotes. Note that you need a figure or a table, but don't stop to create them with painstaking precision. Those are editing tasks, not part of your drafting step. Get your ideas down. Fix them later.

STEPS 3: EDITING

As we explained in an earlier chapter, the editing process can be simple or time-consuming depending upon how well you have completed your prewriting and drafting steps.

As you start editing a complex report:

- Refer to the flowchart, outline, or relational map that you sketched during your prewriting step. That diagram will remind you how to sequence your ideas and build the relationships among them.
- Notice where you stumble or have to reread your own report. Make a note at those places to remind yourself to edit that specific material later for grammar or logic.
- Locate places where you can simplify your material by using charts, tables, figures, or diagrams to better show the

relationships among complex points. Reducing several paragraphs or pages of text to a useful table, figure, or chart will make your readers very happy.

As you will recall from the previous chapter, we recommend editing for logic, organization/layout, and then grammar. You'll be wasting your time later if you don't edit your materials logically and sequentially.

STEP 4: POSTWRITING

The postwriting steps are fundamentally the same for all documents. For reports, make certain that you validate the adequacy of any figures and tables, the accuracy of your citations and references, and the adequacy of your executive summary. Remember that most people do not want to write reports. Even fewer want to read them. Executive summaries that allow the report user to make decisions and locate critical sections quickly will greatly increase the effectiveness of your reports.

STRUCTURING REPORTS TO GET READ

There are several key ideas that will help you in improving the reports you write and ensure that they are read. These include avoiding problems and pitfalls, integrating tables and figures, and developing your argument.

PROBLEMS AND PITFALLS

Notice that the pitfalls and problems identified here can be addressed through the writing and editing process. Common pitfalls and problems in all writing, especially in reports. Another cluster of writing pitfalls are ethical and legal problems. Charles Brusaw, in The Business Writer's Handbook, and Joel Bowman and Bernadine Branchaw in Business Report Writing, and others cite common legal and ethical problems.

Throughout your writing and editing process, you should anticipate and eliminate the potential legal or ethical problems. From individual, company, and workgroup perspectives, you need to make a decision during your prewriting process about how to handle legal and ethical concerns.

INTEGRATING TABLES AND FIGURES

One key tool that can help you in creating more useful reports is the integration of figures, tables, and diagrams. Your goal is to reduce the text and make your critical points easier to see and interpret. This requires more than just sticking a graphic into your document. You need to create useful figures, tables, and diagrams-ones that clarify a point, reduce text, and/or advance your argument. You also need to refer to your table or figure in the text, explaining its relevance to the material and providing transitions that link it to the main ideas. When a document uses figures and tables effectively, the concepts in the document are easier to see and interpret.

DEVELOPING ARGUMENT

Another key aspect of writing a good report is to know when you have optimized the organization of your information. Your report needs to present information in a persuasive but not in biased manner. Biased reports make the readers feel as though they have not gotten both sides of an argument, which prevents making a reasoned decision.

The actual development of persuasive materials and of logical arguments requires extensive discussion, and a number of excellent books provide such information.

Litigation and Reports: Costly Errors can Result Without a Document Management System and Document Life-Cycle Process

Litigation is frequently based on the use of internal company reports. Because reports are frequently key aspects of litigation, we strongly recommend that you evaluate the need for a specific report before you decide to request or write it. We also recommend that you consider what you plan to do if you get information that you don't really want (for example, the fact that your latest product causes cancer).

Legal issues (potential litigation) should be of key concern to managers who request or create business reports-and to those who evaluate whether specific documents are retained or destroyed.

Based on litigation in the 1980s and 1990s (automobile safety, asbestos, and tobacco), reports are subject to subpoena in the United States and various other countries, and they might not be protected by attorney-client privilege or by sending them to another country.

Before you create or request a business report, keep in mind that when you get something you don't want, destroying it can be a criminal act for which you can bear personal responsibility and liability. Before you request a report that has a high probability of containing bad news, decide how you will address the problem-simply denying or destroying the report is not a legal option!

USING EXECUTIVE SUMMARIES AND KEEPING REPORTS SHORT

Most business reports are strengthened when they include an executive summary. Executive summaries save you and your readers time and money by focusing your readers' attention and making your arguments more persuasive in the long run.

CONSTITUENTS OF A USEFUL EXECUTIVE SUMMARY

There are as many definitions of executive summaries as there are problems to be solved. We find that the ideas of Charles Brusaw, et al., on executive summaries in The Business Writer's Handbook are a good starting point. Brusaw suggests that your executive summary should:

- Consolidate the primary points
- Contain adequate detail to show significance
- Be used to make decisions
- Contain little technical terminology
- Be concise, but use transitions
- Contain no new information (information not in full report)
- Include figures/tables from full report, but does not reference full report's figures/tables
- Contain definitions of all symbols/abbreviations/acronyms
- Inform the reader as to the report's:
  - Purpose
  - Conclusions
  - Scope
  - Methods
  - Recommendations
  - Findings/Results

The content in an executive summary should be developed to meet the requirements of the people reading the report, so they can best understand the issues and make effective decisions.

SUMMARY

Writing reports is a complex undertaking, which can be simplified when you use the writing and editing process to guide your work. It will help you save time and effort, and it will help you create more effective reports. Write short, concise, well-organized reports that use straightforward organizational patterns. Include a stand-alone executive summary that your readers can use to make decisions. Such reports are well received, useful, and cost-effective to create.

Note: Learning process in an establishment is an important factor in working of any establishment. Take the example of Virgin group. A research study has shown that the UK public vote Virgin as their most admired brand. It is one of the world's most recognized and respected brands. Reader can visit company's site for more indepth knowledge.www.virgin.com

10

Requests for Proposals

Proposals and requests for proposals (RFPs) vary widely in scope, ranging from informal conversations to memos to complex documents. This variations makes it important to understand the relationship between porposals and RFPs.

THE RELATIONSHIP BETWEEN PROPOSALS AND RFPs

A good proposals is a mirror image of the requirements establishment in a RFP. Because of that, the person or team developing the RFP needs to specify carefully what is being requested in the RFP. Skilled bidders supply only what you have requested. A disorganized or poorly specified set of requirements leads to disorganized proposals or multiple proposals with different organizations, which is an evaluation nightmare.

A FOCUS ON PROPOSALS

In this chapter, we discuss ideas that pertain to both proposals and RFPs, focusing primarily on four topics from the perspective of writing a proposal:

- Formal versus informal documents
- The bidding process
- Writing proposals and RFPs
- Evaluating proposals

We'll link our ideas to the writing and editing steps explained in previous chapter so that you can see how to expand the process to include both proposals and RFPs, in addition to creating more useful documents.

FORMAL VERSUS INFORMAL PROPOSALS

Proposals can vary widely in terms of their complexity and formality-and thus in terms of the cost of creating and evaluating them. In order to create a win-win situation, it is important that the two groups involved in the process (those issuing the proposal and the respondents or bidders) keep each other's perspectives, needs, requirements, and costs in mind.

SIMPLE OR COMPLEX DOCUMENTS

Part of creating a win-win situation is determining whether to request-or create-complex proposals. Requiring bidders to create complex proposals costing tens or hundreds of thousands of dollars can lead to a lose-lose situation in which excellent potential bidders do not bid. On the other hand, requesting overly simplistic proposals can also lead to a lose-lose situation, wherein both groups spend too much time clarifying information. A lose-lose situation can also result when you don't request sufficient information, when you receive inadequate proposals, and when you have to rebid the project.

Table below illustrates that the range and degree of formality is partially a function of whether proposals are solicited or unsolicited and/ or internal or external to a company or group.

Common RFP/Proposal Scenarios

In some scenarios (for example, in the defense industry), RFPs and proposals are extremely complex and are evaluated in great detail. And seemingly minor points of noncompliance can lead to the rejection of proposals that have taken months to develop. In other business settings, proposals and the resulting "contracts" are simply memos within and among businesses or groups in a company.

One of the simplest, yet potentially problematic, scenarios occurs when proposals are requested and developed during informal conversations with little or no documentation. Such undocumented agreements and informal contracts can lead to honest misunderstandings, fraud, litigation, and project failures. If an agreement is important, get it in writing, and iron out problems before a crisis occurs.

Table: The Degree of Formality of Solicited/ Unsolicited, Internal External Proposals

	Solicited	*Unsolicited*
Internal	Frequently formal, sometimes informal	Both informal and formal
External	Mostly formal	Both informal and formal

A good proposal is actually a mirror image of what is included within an RFP, a request for quote (RFQ), or a request for bid (RFB). If RFPs are poorly written, you will waste your time in evaluating, rebidding, and negotiating the contract. Putting together a good team, one with the appropriate technical expertise and writing skills, to write critical RFPs and proposals can often save significant time and money. Unsolicited proposals are to hard be sold, they have to be very persuasive to work.

TO BID OR NOT TO BID?

As we have implied, the RFP/proposal process is fundamentally about two groups negotiating. One group issues a request for proposals or an invitation for bids. A second group must decide whether to bid, and, if bidding, how to bid. To an actual bidder, a proposal is-bottom line-an attempt to sell ideas, services, or products successfully.

CAVEATS FOR POTENTIAL BIDDERS

As a potential bidder, before you commit your time and resources to developing a proposal, you need to decide if the effort required is justified-and whether you have the ability to deliver, if your proposal were to be accepted. If you decide to bid, your second decision is what to include in your proposal.

Bidders need to avoid two problematic situations:

- Making a bid for a project that has already been locked up by someone else.
- Having your expertise solicited and used by companies that are merely identifying potential solutions or developing an understanding of costs and problems without actually intending to award contracts. This often occurs when groups are trying to justify the existence of departments or head count.

Successfully identifying these situations is usually a matter of prior experience.

WRITING PROPOSALS AND RFPs

Writing proposals and RFPs should be done in a thoughtful manner, because the language and the specifications set (or not set) within an RFP or an RFB are the first part of a contract with the successful bidder. The second part of that contract is the proposal. The final requirements are specified in precise wording in the letter of authorization and the letter of acceptance (or the revised proposal), which is the third part of the contract/negotiation process.

WRITE AND EDIT WITH CARE

Part of writing and editing carefully is to determine the critical items in a project and to specify the requirements for those items precisely. For example, if one and only one specific part is acceptable, specify that part. If, on the other hand, you will accept alternative parts, indicate that fact in your RFP. If you face a $100,000 loss if the project is not completed on time, discuss a penalty clause in the RFP and insert the clause in the letter of acceptance.

Table below lists critical items that are commonly found in both RFPs and proposals.

WHAT SHOULD YOU REQUEST IN YOUR RFP?

As is true of most business documents, there is no single correct answer on what to include in an RFP or a proposal-which frustrates managers looking for cookie-cutter solutions. What you request depends on your project requirements, company policies, the relationship between the bidder and awarder, and legal issues.

Suggestions for the content of an RFP:

- General instructions to bidders
- Draft or proposed contract and schedule
- Statement of the requirements (work)
- Appendixes

Suggestions for the content of a proposal:

- Technical strategies
  - — Your understanding of the problem(s)
  - — How you will solve the problem(s)
  - — Why your solution will work
  - — The nature of your product or solution
  - — Your schedule and completion date.

Management strategies:

- How can you carry out the solution?
  - — Personnel
  - — Experience
  - — Insight
  - — Facilities
  - — Internal organization
  - — Quality control mechanisms

— Historical success
— Outside resources

Cost strategies:

- Why the customer can afford it?
- Why the proposal is reasonable/competitive?
- Your direct and indirect benefits
- Your budget/costs arranged by
  - — RFP/IFB requirements
  - — Category (personnel/supplies/equipment/facilities)
  - — Benefit
  - — Time period or project phase

IMPROVING THE LOGIC AND ORGANIZATION OF PROPOSALS AND RFPs

Using the writing and editing process can help you create high-quality RFPs and proposals. Your prewriting step will help you determine what to include and how to organize it. Your editing steps will help ensure that your organizational plan matches your goals. Your postwriting step will help you make certain that you have evaluated the risks and potential gains, as well as whether you have followed any applicable company policies.

Tips for Writing Successful Proposals

Provide What Is Needed in Your Proposal

There are variations or overlaps among different companies' definitions of what makes an adequate proposal. Ask for specific guidelines before you start writing.

Know the Company Letting the Bid

It is important to know various details about the company letting the bid, which might not be specified in the RFP. For example, does the company use a specific supplier for a subcomponent? If so, you might be more successful if you specify that subcomponent and preferred supplier. If there is a compelling reason to use a different subcomponent or supplier, justify it.

When You Win the Bid

Remember, if your proposal is accepted, you will need to live with the proposal and resulting contract. Be certain that you can complete the project according to the specified requirements. Litigation is the fact of life.

Executive Summaries

Providing an executive summary of your proposal can expedite the evaluation process by focusing attention on key requirements, how you plan to meet them, and on selling points that make your company a preferred bidder.

BUILDING ELECTRONIC TEMPLATES

To be able to produce proposals in an efficient and timely manner, we suggest building word processing files and templates that contain commonly requested information, such as company financials, company history, key resumes, compliance statements with federal/state/local laws, projects completed, and references. These boilerplates are then easily modified to fit the specific requirements of a project. This approach will save you extensive time and eliminate redundant work efforts.

EVALUATING PROPOSALS

When evaluating proposals, it is important to follow a systematic process. To enable you to systematically evaluate the various proposals, you need to specify-in your RFP-how bidders should structure (organize) their proposals. Give bidders a specific sequence (organizational plan) for submitting information. When you do so, it will be easier for you to compare multiple proposals, or the content of a specific proposal, quickly and easily. When you are evaluating a proposal, watch for subtle deviations from your RFP-in both what is stated and what is omitted.

USEFUL CRITERIA FOR EVALUATING PROPOSALS

We have found two sets of evaluation criteria that are complementary and extremely useful: those of Penrose, Rasberry, and Myers, in their book Advanced Business Communication and those of Stewart and Stewart in Proposal Writing. It is important to use both sets of criteria because the technical, cost, and management categorization of Penrose provides important insights on how to conceptualize projects, whereas Stewart and Stewart provide critical questions that clarify more specifically what to evaluate.

Penrose stresses three key categories of information that need to be specified in RFPs and used to evaluate proposals:

- Technical strategies: Why and how the proposed solution will work?
- Management strategies: How the bidder can carry out the solution(s) (their personnel, experience, insight, facilities, internal organization, and quality control mechanisms)?
- Cost strategies: Why the bid and proposed solution are cost-effective; why proposal is reasonable/competitive?

Similar to the Penrose categories are those used by Stewart and Stewart: (1) performance suitability (parallel to technical strategies), (2) cost factors (parallel to cost strategies), and (3) other factors (parallel to management strategies).

According to Stewart and Stewart, the key questions that you need to consider relative to each area are as follows:

1. Performance suitability (technical strategies)
    - Do the bidders completely understand what needs to be done?
    - Will the proposed solutions work?
    - Will their management strategies work?
        — Do they have good internal lines of communication?
        — Do they have good relationships with subcontractors?
        — Are the work schedules logical and timely?
    - Are the qualifications, experience, education, past performance, and quality of key personnel proven?
2. Cost factors (cost strategies)
    - Are the cost estimates credible?
    - Have all needed cost factors been included?
    - Are the costs the most probable ones?
    - Historically, are the company's estimates accurate?
3. Other factors (management strategies)
    - Financial condition of the company
    - Importance of the project to the company
    - Stability of labor and management
    - Extent of minority and small-business participation
    - Geographic location and distribution of subcontractors and their stability

After you have used these criteria to evaluate the proposals you receive, ask for clarification, in writing, from bidders who show inconsistencies or discrepancies. The such written clarifications will prevent misunderstandings and problems.

SUMMARY

There are no cookie-cutter answers that will provide a single correct way to write an RFP or a proposal. Writing and evaluating proposals and RFPs can be complex projects. If you aren't certain of what your manager or company wants or requires in a proposal or an RFP, take the safe, sane road. Ask.

Note: For detailed study on proposal and requests for proposals reader can visit www.ige.gov.uk/ige

11

Presentations

Is your ability to speak confidently and persuasively to a group an important part of your function as a manager or an executive? Countless surveys of employers and executives over the past two decades have consistently placed oral communication skills among the top five most desired characteristics for a manager. It is no longer possible to advance in a company or graduate program without solid communication ability. Because today's work and academic environments emphasize teams, meetings, and extensive information sharing, oral and written skills are essential. In this part, you'll learn the key process steps and tasks involved in preparing and delivering business presentations:

- Defining your purpose
- Analyzing your audience
- Gathering supporting materials
- Organizing your ideas
- Planning your visual support
- Practicing your delivery
- Preparing for the question-and-answer session
- Evaluating your presentation

In addition, we also discuss how to handle speech anxiety. While this may not be part of the preparation and delivery process for every speaker or every situation, it is a very common concern, so we address it in detail. In previous chapter, we described writing and editing process that can help you to write more efficiently and effectively. We advocated using such a process to improve your writing and save you and your company time and money. We advocate that you use a similar, multistep process when preparing your business presentations.

Recognizing the parallels between the writing, editing and presentation processes can be very helpful when you need to create a document and then present it. Mentally linking the two processes should help you recognize and break ineffective habits and establish new ways of preparing more integrated presentations and documents.

Effective presentations will help you:

- Convey information more efficiently and effectively
- Motivate work teams and groups to make faster and better decisions
- Demonstrate proficiency in subject matter to supervisors and clients
- Increase your professional profile and value to the company
- Provide confidence in all areas of communication

By strengthening your skills and improving your understanding of the presentation process, you will be a more efficient and effective speaker in interpersonal, group, and business settings.

DEFINING YOUR PURPOSE

Imagine the following scenario: When you arrive at work, your manager mentions that you need to be in Chicago on the 15th for an important meeting. You note the meeting on your calendar and go on to other business. On the morning of the 15th, you get in your car and drive to the airport, hoping to find a flight to Chicago. You find one. When you arrive in Chicago, you go to the rental car counter, hoping a car will be available. You find one. When you get in the car, you drive aimlessly around the city, looking for your meeting. You see your manager walking into a hotel and you find the meeting.

Sound pretty implausible? It is, but many executives use a similar approach when they "plan" a presentation or a report. They make a note of it, and when the time comes, they plunge right in without planning ahead, without a good idea of where they are going, what they need to accomplish, or how they are going to accomplish it. From a process perspective, they are ignoring a key preparation step of the presentation process. The first step is to define your purpose.

In order to get to where you want to go, it helps to plan your itinerary, make appropriate reservations, and get directions. Moreover, if you're going to a meeting in Chicago, wouldn't it be nice to know the purpose of the meeting, why you were invited, and your role? Similarly, when you need to write a document or make a presentation, it's best to consider where you want to go rather than just plunging right in.

Because you can't rely on luck, therefore in this chapter we discuss the following three key ideas related to planning business communication:

- Defining your general purpose
- Defining your specific purpose
- Defining your desired results

DEFINING YOUR GENERAL PURPOSE

People in business communicate to fulfill a basic need-typically to inform or persuade. It is important to know what you're trying to accomplish:

- Does your audience want to be informed, persuaded, or both? Do they want objective information? Do they want to know all the pros and the cons?
- Do they prefer a subjective evaluation of a problem? When you know your audience's expectations and requirements, you can better define your purpose and organize your ideas.

When you're presenting or writing to inform (for example, conveying the results of a market research study), your goal should be to provide information in the most objective way possible. The presenter (or writer) should present facts and use verifiable data.

In a persuasive presentation, on the other hand, your goal is to support a particular viewpoint for your audience. Your goal is to present those facts and ideas that build support for your appeal.

For example, in a persuasive proposal designed to increase your sales force, you might include sales figures, as well as workload and sales call information that support your recommendation.

Your general purpose will be your initial guide as you plan your presentation. Knowing whether you'll be informing or persuading your audience will help you decide if your purpose is primarily to teach (to impart knowledge and facts) or to guide (to interpret the facts and present alternatives). Next, we will show how your general purpose may also guide your selection of patterns of organization for your writing and speaking.

DETERMINING YOUR SPECIFIC PURPOSE

After you've determined whether your writing or presentation is to be informative or persuasive, you need to better define your purpose by writing a specific, straightforward statement of purpose. This statement of purpose, or basic thesis sentence, will focus your efforts as you zero in on what you are trying to do in your presentation or document.

In a document, this sentence should help your readers understand what you are trying to accomplish. In a presentation, it should perform the same function, and it should also stand out: If we asked your audience to hit a buzzer when they heard the thesis, all the buzzers should ring at the same time.

Some people use very blunt statements: "The purpose of this memo is..." or "The purpose of my speech is..." Less obvious examples might be phrased as follows:

- "I intend to demonstrate why our no-load mutual fund is the best place for your investment dollars."
- "Our market research shows that the population of our target country is getting younger, and in this presentation we will explore ways to attract this younger audience to our product."
- "This afternoon we will describe three key ways in which the new software can streamline our billing processes."

DEFINING YOUR DESIRED RESULTS

You will find it helpful to define the results you expect to see. This will make you to further clarify and focus your message. Typically, you do not state your operational definition to your audience. You use it to help plan your message and evaluate the response, or lack of response, that you receive. Here are some examples of how you might phrase the desired results of your presentation:

- "After this presentation, 50 percent of the audience will invest in our mutual fund."
- "After this presentation, a majority of managers will vote in favour of the proposal to add staff to the marketing division."
- "This report will clarify the goals of the assessment team, and as a result, every member will be able to participate fully in the next planning session."

SUMMARY

For a successful presentation or document, you cannot rely on luck. You need to define your general purpose, your specific purpose, and the results you want to achieve. Business executives may encounter situations that call for special-occasion speeches. These include introductions, tributes, award presentations and acceptances, and eulogies.

Note: For detailed information and understanding more on learning process, reader can visit www.baesystems.com

12

Knowing Your Audience

Successful public speakers automatically gear their material to their audiences. And just because you aren't performing at the Hollywood Bowl or delivering a keynote address to thousands of admirers doesn't mean you can skip this step. In fact, for the people in business who frequently communicate with small groups of 5 to 15 people, a thorough audience analysis can be a key to success. Within both the writing and the presentation processes, your audience analysis is a key preparation step that will you clarify your goals and objectives. Most books on public speaking describe audience analysis in terms of demographics-how many males versus females in a workgroup, ages, cultural background, and so forth. We don't find the demographic approach to be very helpful in the small group settings that are common in business. We suggest that you approach audience analysis by answering seven simple but key questions and keeping those answers in mind as you prepare your document or presentation.

AUDIENCE

The first thing you want to know is who will be at the meeting. Who will be reading the document? What is my relationship to and history with this group of people? Are they peers, supervisors, or subordinates? What do I know about them from our past meetings together? To the extent that you know the people and something about the way they work and think, you can predict their responses to your message and plan your appeal accordingly. For example, you know that one person in your workgroup always objects to new proposals with the argument: "We've always done it this way. Why change?" Knowing the nature of the objections that will arise will enable you to be prepared with a line-by-line comparison of how the new procedure will be superior to the old procedure.

WHAT DOES THE AUDIENCE KNOW ABOUT ME?

An essential concept for a business executive is the idea of credibility. Do people believe you when you speak? Are they confident that you know what you're talking about?

If you are totally unknown to your audience, it will be helpful for them to have some background information about you-knowing your level of expertise on the topic can lend credence to what you have to say. You can provide this information or, preferably, someone the audience respects might introduce you. Even though boasting is not considered polite in our culture, you should not be modest about your credentials if it helps improve the strength of your message.

Aristotle called it ethos. We call it speaker image or credibility. (Even the ancient Greeks were concerned about a speaker's credibility!) While many have written on the subject of establishing credibility, we have narrowed the concept to three main components.

Knowledge of the topic. The speaker must be genuinely knowledgeable about the topic under discussion. The audience must perceive that the speaker knows his or her subject matter and is truly an expert. Barring national recognition, you can boost your credibility by using highly credible sources and disclosing those sources to your audience.

Trustworthiness. The speaker must be perceived as trustworthy by the audience. Generally, audiences seem to trust a speaker unless they are given a reason not to. Credibility is destroyed when the speaker is caught in a lie and, once damaged, is almost impossible to rebuild. (Remember Danny Nixon? Reverend Jim Bakker? Linda Tripp?) Speakers may also be rated low on trustworthiness if they make wild, unsubstantiated claims or are unable to support their points in the question-and answer session.

Charisma. A speaker is perceived as more credible to the extent that he or she is dynamic and personable. Good public speaking skills are important; and appropriate appearance and an outgoing and likable personality are also part of the mix.

Experts generally weight these three components of credibility as follows: knowledge, 60 percent; trustworthiness, 30 percent; and charisma, 10 percent. However, in the real world, it doesn't always work that way. For example, although leaders of infamous cults can be considered charismatic, if their behavior leads to the untimely deaths of their followers, they could hardly be considered trustworthy. Similarly, politicians who aren't skillful communicators are at a distinct disadvantage in this television age. In the 1984 presidential debates, Ronald Reagan outshone challenger Walter Mondale in spite of Mondale's better grasp of facts and issues. Reagan's dynamic personality overshadowed his challenger's best intellectual efforts.

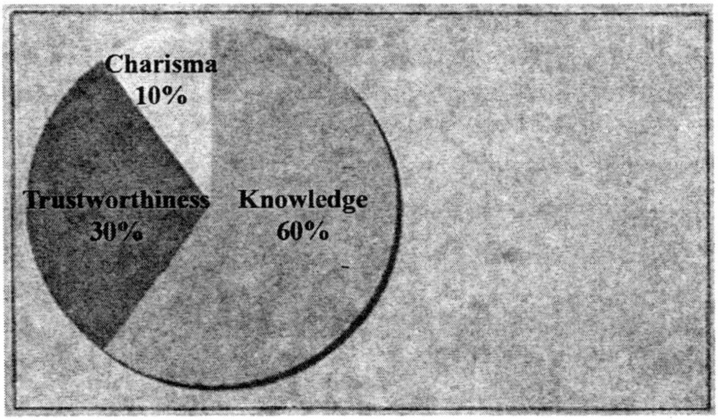

Figure: Components of credibility.

So what is the lesson for business speakers who want to earn a reputation for high credibility? First, know your subject matter. Second, do not do anything to make your audience question at your trustworthiness. And third, practice your public speaking skills to improve your presentations.

An issue that some of our business students face has been known as the "Y&I factor"-young and inexperienced. If you are younger than your business associates, you may have to work harder to establish your credentials.

WHAT DOES MY AUDIENCE KNOW ABOUT THE TOPIC?

One of the most important factors that will guide a speaker or writer is the level of expertise of the audience. This is a significant factor as you prepare your message, because you should gear your information and appeal to the level of your audience's understanding. For example, typically, a highly technical R&D project would need to be put into layman's terms for a financial group that is deciding whether to support the project. However, that same R&D group would probably present its findings at a much higher technical level at a scientific conference.

A frequent consideration for business executives is the use of jargon in documents and presentations. You need to know your audience's knowledge of the topic in order to know how much jargon you can use. If your message is aimed at too high a level, you run the risk of losing your audience. If your message is aimed too low, they will be insulted and bored, and they will tune you out. Speakers frequently ask what to do if it's mixed audience, with varying levels of expertise on the topic. Generally, the talk should be aimed either at the level of the decision makers in the group, or at the most common denominator.

AUDIENCE OPINIONS ON THE TOPIC

It is the defined advantage for a speaker or writer to know if his or her audience has formed an opinion on the topic under discussion and, whether that opinion is firm or flexible. In a persuasive appeal, writers and speakers plan their messages differently for supportive, hostile, or apathetic audiences. The pattern or organization, the types of supporting materials, and the nature of the appeal all vary, depending on the audience's predisposition toward the topic. Clearly, if you know that most of your listeners-and especially the decision makers-support your ideas, you will have an easier task than if you know that they will be antagonistic. But perhaps the most frustrating situation is one in which the audience just doesn't care about the topic or the message. Then you really have your work cut out for you.

AUDIENCE MOTIVATION

Motivation underpins our behavior, so it's important for the author of a document or the speaker in a presentation to know what factors might persuade the audience to accept a message. While the list of motivators could be quite long in theory, in the business world, much of the motivation comes down to the bottom line. Does this proposal help your company to save money or to make money? Can this new initiative allow employees to use their time more efficiently?

This is not to say that the corportate world is motivated only by greed and profits. However, you need to consider what factors are important to your listeners and incorporate them into your message. Only then can you motivate your audience to pay attention and, hopefully, to accept your message.

AUDIENCE KNOWLEDGE NEEDS

Another important factor in your audience analysis is understanding what your audience needs to know and wants to know. Do your logistics people want to know about what the manufacturing people are doing? They do if they're interested in supply chains, but they might be more immediately interested in other factors. Tailor your speech to what they want to know.

AUDIENCE RESPONSE

This often comes down to knowing what you (or your managers) want to accomplish as a result of your presentation. Your audience should leave with a clear understanding of what they need to do and what you are planning to do.

Rely on Situational Analysis

Audience analysis should include situational analysis-for both presentations and documents. There are the following variables:

- Recent developments in the business environment (e.g., rumors of acquisition by a larger company)
- Recent developments within the immediate workgroup (e.g., a new reporting line through a financial group)
- Workgroup stress due to a deadline for a major project
- Workgroup satisfaction (or dissatisfaction) due to success (or failure) of a recent project
- Factors involved in the physical work environment, which can even involve conditions in the presentation room (too cold or too warm can distract people from your message)

SUMMARY

Analyzing your audience is a crucial step in preparing your presentation. It often pays to find out ahead of time what people really think about your proposal or what motivates them toward achieving a particular goal. You may need to take the time to talk to coworkers in order to gain the information you need. However, you will find that the time and effort you expand will help produce the desired response to your message.

Note: "General Motors Corporation" is the best example of "Analyzing your Audiences". For more detailed information reader can visit www.gm.com

13

Support Materials for Presentations

The extent to which you can justify your point, support your position, and make your case often determine the success of your presentation. The successful communicator knows that strong support for ideas can often determine the audience's perception of your credibility on the topic as well as the outcomes after the speech is over.

Many managers and executives probably haven't given much thought to the idea of formal supporting materials, such as you would use for a college research paper, because data and information are so readily available within their work environment. People working in business often use materials, such as financial reports, market research, and projections, to construct their written documents and presentations.

The topic is set, the data is available, and they use that data as they plan the message. What they lose sight of is how important it is to translate data and projections into information the audience can use. Part of gathering supporting materials involves building a unique point of view that adds new meaning to what was previously thought of as mere data. We will cover two major topics relating to supporting your ideas. First, we examine the types of supporting materials that are available to use in documents and presentations. Second, we offer guidelines for the effective use of supporting documentation.

QUANTITY OF SUPPORTING MATERIAL

Gathering supporting material is an important task in both the prewriting step and in the preparation step of the presentation process. Experts recommend that you gather three times as much material as you need. Doing so enables you to:

- Choose only the best evidence to help youin making your case

- Have extra background information in the question-and-answer session
- Feel more confident with a higher level of knowledge on the topic
- Relieve any speech anxiety you may experience

TYPES OF SUPPORTING MATERIALS

There are five types of commonly used supporting materials:

- Statistics
- Definitions
- Examples
- Comparisons and contrasts
- Testimony and quotations

STATISTICS

Numbers and data are most likely going to be an integral part of any business presentation. Unfortunately, many managers think that if they have some statistical data, they automatically have a presentation. One Eastman Kodak executive told us he spent six hours in a meeting looking at charts and graphs. Merely showing data is not the same thing as delivering a presentation. You should be judicious in selecting the data you wish to use. If you present only those numbers that are crucial to the central idea of your message, they will stand out as persuasive and will increase the impact of your verbal message. Additionally, you should be sure that any data you present is well designed so the message is may be instantly crystal clear.

DEFINITIONS

How you use definitions in your presentation will depend on your audience analysis. There are two types of definitions: literal and stipulated. You may use a literal definition if you are using jargon or technical language with which your audience may not be familiar. For example, novice investors may not know the difference between a load and a no-load mutual fund. Alternatively, you might use a stipulated definition when the usage in a particular field may differ from the norm-for example, Stephen Covey uses the term ecological balance to describe an organizational environment. This stipulated definition varies significantly from the way biologists might describe a balanced ecology.

EXAMPLES

The use of examples is an excellent technique for showing the application of your presentation material to your audience. Examples can make your presentation come alive and break up the monotony of a long presentation. They may be real or hypothetical. Real examples have the advantage of being verifiable. Your audience knows that it happened and that your information has validity.

At the same time, hypothetical examples can be equally helpful for the speaker. They can be used to draw the audience into the material and to make the presentation really hit home. This can be especially true if you use audience members for your examples. A speaker might say something like this: "Let's say Joe needs to verify his data. He could contact anyone in Mary's department and they would have the information if they were hooked up to the network." This hypothetical example draws both Joe and Mary into the presentation (it's difficult to let your mind wander when the speaker is talking about you!), and it also demonstrates how the information can be applied to this particular workgroup. If the situation is somewhat informal, a speaker may also use the classroom teacher's technique of asking an audience member to provide an example. But don't try this unless you are confident you have a responsive group!

CONTRASTS AND COMPARISONS

This type of supporting material works well when a speaker is explaining something new to an audience. Comparing new information to something familiar makes it easier to understand. You might explain how to operate a VCR by comparing its control buttons to those on an audiocassette recorder. Or you could describe an updated version of PowerPoint by describing the ways in which it is similar to the earlier version and the ways in which it is different.

TESTIMONY AND QUOTES

Even if you are an expert in your field, it is nice to have the support of others who agree with your position. These experts could be as prominent as Federal Reserve Board members or Harvard economists, or they may be supervisors and colleagues who have provided you with information. Either way, you should acknowledge anyone who has contributed to your presentation. You may simply say, "Steve's department provided these figures on sales revenue." Not only does that give the credit where it is due, but (assuming Steve is highly regarded by his colleagues) it can improve your own credibility on the topic.

GUIDELINES FOR USING SUPPORTING MATERIALS

The following guidelines pertain to the accuracy of your materials, giving credit for ideas and sources, using a variety of materials, and being creative. Be sure your supporting material is accurate. People in your audience who are be familiar with your topic will find any errors in data, procedure, process, or sources. Check your document and presentation visuals for typos and accurate figures. Simply spell checking is not enough. You should proofread your material and ask a colleague to proof it also. Give credit where it is due.

You help your own credibility as a speaker and avoid the appearance of plagiarism when you cite your sources for information. Whether your source is a Stanford research study or a colleague who supplied figures on inventory, letting your audience know where you got your material will go a long way toward improving the impact of your message. In a formal report, you might do this by using footnotes. In a presentation, often a passing mention will suffice. If the information is important and has been supplied by a team member or a member of another group who made a special effort to obtain it for you, make certain that you clearly acknowledge your source. It is the right thing to do, and it will help build teamwork and your image as a team player.

If you do not give a source (a publication or data set) during your presentation, make sure you know where you got the information in case the issue will come up in the question-and-answer session. Try to use variety in your supporting materials. As we mentioned earlier, many managers tend to rely too much on graphs and data and not enough on other aspects of organization and support. Your listeners will be more responsive and will find it easier to pay attention if you use a variety of ways to support your ideas.

For example, after you have shown a numerical table or graph, give an example of what it might mean: "We plan to have every high school student in Los Angeles familiar with our new software package by the year 2000." Or you might make a comparison with a familiar reference: "Finding this information was a task even Sherlock Holmes would find daunting."

Don't be afraid to try some creativity in your supporting materials. Think of ways in which you can make the facts, data, and ideas come alive for your audience. Find an example that supports your point-or make one up yourself. Find experts who agree with your viewpoint and quote them directly or in paraphrase.

We recently saw the creative use of supporting materials by the chairperson of a Parents Athletic Advisory Committee, who went before the local board of education to discuss the need for a new pool for the district. First, the presenter used colour photographs of deteriorating masonry and corroded pipes to dramatize the problems with the old pool. Second, rather than simply saying, "The pool is used constantly during the day," the speaker used a slide to present a detailed list of the school and community groups using the pool from 6:30 A.M. through 9:30 P.M. This simple tactic served to show the board members the faces of real people who are affected by their decisions.

SUMMARY

While you may not generally think about supporting materials when planning your presentations, making this a routine part of your preparation will increase your credibility with your audience and your confidence with your material. Gathering your material before you begin drafting your ideas or outlining your talking points is a key part of your presentation process, as well as the prewriting process. Collecting thorough documentation enables you to select the best and most significant material for your presentation, which in turn will increase your credibility as a presenter and reduce your anxiety.

Once you have the supporting materials you need for the presentation, you are ready to begin organizing your main ideas. You have completed the first three steps of the prepresentation process: defining your purpose, analyzing your audience, and gathering your support.

Note: For complete information and understanding on Gathering Supporting Materials, reader can visit www.pg.com

14

Organizing Ideas

A good presentation is like a good story: It has a beginning, a middle, and an end-in that order. In material on writing and editing in a previous chapter, we imparted the "Army approach" to giving messages:

- Tell them what you're going to tell them.
- Tell them what you've told them.

These straightforward statements also describe a sound, basic approach for organizing presentations. In this chapter on organization, we'll discuss the introduction, body, and conclusion of a presentation, and we'll make the case for using a thesis or purpose statement. We've organized the material in this chapter in the order in which you will actually deliver the presentation, but these individual parts-introduction, body, conclusion-do not necessarily need to be prepared in that order. If you have just thought of a great idea for an introduction or a great quote that will work well in the conclusion, set it aside for later. You should begin by writing your thesis or purpose statement. Next, you should organize your main ideas. After you have done the major work on these two sections, you will have a clearer idea of the most appropriate way to introduce and conclude your presentation.

INTRODUCTIONS

Introductions tell your audience, very clearly and concisely, what you are going to tell them. This is a crucial point in your presentation because you are giving your listeners a template, an organizational structure, that they can use to anticipate your points and, most important, to see how your ideas pertain to them. This is where you help them in anticipating the so-what factor that lurks in the minds of most people who sit down to listen to a presentation. You can be more effective when you answer their most basic questions: "Why am I sitting here, and what do I need to do after we leave?"

When novice public speakers are confronted with introducing a presentation, they often think of beginning with a joke. While jokes may be appropriate in some settings, we recommend you begin by thinking about the purpose of your introduction. A good introduction should accomplish four key tasks:

Inform the audience why it is there? To improve the likelihood that you will be successful, you need to help people understand why they've come to hear you, what they are going to hear, and what they are expected to accomplish after they leave.

Capture the audience's attention. People don't pay attention well. There may be distractions in the room. People may be thinking about their own presentations or perhaps daydreaming about lunch. You need to do something to get your audience to focus on you. However, if you begin with your all important thesis/purpose statement, those who are not paying attention will miss the reason for the presentation.

Focus on the topic. In the introduction, you should begin to get people thinking about the topic you will be discussing, and you should appropriately reflect the tone of the topic. That is why an irrelevant anecdote or humor simply for humor's sake doesn't work.

Establish your own credibility. The audience will be making a snap judgment about your abilities as a speaker and your expertise on the topic.

First Impressions

You need to make a good first impression with your content and delivery. If your audience is unfamiliar with your credentials, you should introduce yourself and your background. This is no time for undue modesty: Be candid about your experience and expertise. If an audience is unfamiliar with your back- ground, you must show them why they should listen to you and pay attention to your message. Under no circumstances should you do anything to hurt your credibility. For example, do not insult the audience, even as a joke. While this may work for stand-up comedians in a comedy club, it rarely helps your image in a business presentation. Other common errors occur when people jest about their credentials or the fact that they don't know why they were chosen to present. Making such statements establishes a barrier that you will then need to overcome.

Beginning a Presentation

Among many choices, we offer five excellent ways to begin a presentation:

1. Begin with humor. If your opening comment is light, sensitive to your audience, and relates to the topic, then use humor. Audiences like to laugh; they can let off a little energy after being forced to sit in one place for a while. Humor may also serve to bond you with the audience. Self-deprecating humor on the part of the speaker works particularly well because few can take offense if you poke fun at yourself.
2. Begin with a question. This is often an effective way to involve audience members in your presentation. This might be an actual question to which you would like a response ("How many of you have used catalog shopping in the last 30 days?"), or it might be a rhetorical question ("Have you ever thought of what it might be like to navigate the halls of this building in a wheelchair?"). Questions can be extremely useful as conceptual organizers if you phrase them to help your listeners anticipate where your presentation is going. If you use the question technique, be sure to clarify whether you want a response. The audience generally likes to cooperate, but no one wants to be the first to make a mistake. And be careful of using this technique for potentially sensitive issues ("By a show of hands, how many of you have ever answered a personal ad in a newspaper?").
3. Begin with a narrative. You can tell a story that relates to your topic and illustrates the purpose of your presentation. Journalists doing feature stories often use this technique. Instead of merely describing health care legislation, for example, a reporter may find a family that cannot afford health insurance and open with a profile of that family.
4. Begin with a startling statement to get attention. "According to the Port Hope Police Department, you have a 25 percent chance of being the victim of a violent crime in this city. That means that out of the 20 people in this room, 5 of us could be victimized in the next 12 months." If you dramatize, make certain that your figures are accurate.
5. Use a concrete example. Other techniques, including real-life examples of a key point, can also be used as an engaging

opener. For example, in one of our undergraduate classes, a student discussing teen pregnancy brought in her three-year-old daughter. Another speaker began a presentation on violence in the movies by showing videotaped clips from films. Each was a very effective, attention-grabbing start.

CREATING THE THESIS STATEMENT

It would be nice to think that a good introduction will get your audience to listen intently to your presentation. But, because people are generally poor listeners, we recommend adding a fourth component to our three-part organizational pie. In addition to the introduction, body, and conclusion, we recommend using a thesis statement.

Many people think of the thesis, or purpose statement, as part of the introduction, and it does, indeed, come at the end of your introduction. However, we are discussing it separately here in order to stress its importance in successfully setting the agenda of your presentation from the outset.

Your thesis should be stated immediately after you introduce your presentation. It not only gives your audience a clear sense of your direction and plan, it also helps them comprehend and retain your message. For longer presentations (those exceeding five minutes), we recommend that you follow your thesis sentence with a preview of your entire presentation. This is also a useful tool if you are doing a presentation with multiple speakers because it allows you to both introduce your team and to identify who will be doing what?

Here's an example of how to preview your entire presentation after giving your thesis statement:

INTRODUCTION: Fire. We are fascinated by fire. We enjoy warming ourselves by a roaring fire in the winter, and yet fire can be terrifying when it is out of control. As a member of the Fire Safety Team for XYZ Company, I've had training in many aspects of fire safety.

THESIS: Today, I would like to discuss fire safety in the workplace and offer some tips you may use at home as well.

PREVIEW: I plan to discuss three major areas: the kinds of fires we may encounter, what to do if you encounter a fire at work or home, and ways that these fires may be prevented.

In this example, the speaker introduces the topic, clearly lays out a purpose, and then previews the scope of the presentation.

Table: The Development of a Thesis Sentence

Topic: Using ACME Outplacement Services	
General purpose: To inform	*General purpose*: To persuade
Specific purpose: To let the audience know what services are available to them	*Specific purpose*: To convince the audience that they should contract with our firm for downsized employees
Thesis sentence: Today we will review the services offered by our office.	*Thesis sentence*: Today you'll understand why we're the first choice among outplacement firms to service your needs.

(Note that the speaker has also established credibility by giving personal credentials on the topic.) More examples of thesis statements can be found as follows:

Examples of Thesis Statements

- This afternoon we'll be going over the new procedures for appraising your employees and answering any questions you might have about the changes in the compensation system.
- Today we'll review the suggestions that have been made to deal with the inventory crisis and ask for your input about which one is most likely to solve our problem.
- I'll be showing you just how easy it is to enroll in our Executive MBA program and earn your degree in two years without interrupting your career.
- This merger will bring great changes to our company, and today we'll look at how it will specifically impact each of your departments.
- There are a number of ways to reduce the cost of your health insurance, and this morning we'll review several of the new options being offered.

DEVELOPING THE BODY

To continue our "Army" analogy, the body of the presentation is where you "tell them"-where you impart your content. When you begin to organize the body of your message, you are, in a sense, drafting, just as you would in the writing and editing process. Your goal is to get your main ideas down. You're thinking about logic and structure, just as you do when you're preparing a written document.

To develop the body (the content) of your presentation, your need to focus on two main areas: (1) organizing your ideas for maximum impact and (2) using transitions to link your ideas effectively.

ORGANIZING IDEAS

The ideas within the body of the speech must be put forth in an organized way. Most of us are familiar with common patterns of organization: chronological, spatial, topical, and so forth. For example, a presentation about budget forecasting will generally proceed in a chronological format. Indeed, the organizational patterns of most messages are frequently very obvious-after you have been listening for a few minutes. Our goal is to make certain that you don't lose your audience for those first few minutes.

If you have a clear pattern of organization, much of your strategy is set. In the preceding example on fire safety, the speaker makes it easy for the audience to follow the message by previewing how the presentation is organized. If you do not have a clear pattern of organization, you need to develop one so that the point of your message may become clear. Deciding how to organize the body of your presentation sometimes depends on your topic; other times, it depends on your audience. For example, if you are planning a persuasive appeal but your audience has no knowledge of the topic, you'd probably choose to begin in a more informative way. On the other hand, if you're making a presentation to an audience that already knows about the topic, you probably should begin more subjectively, appealing to your best talents of persuasion.

When one speaker we know was presenting a plan for a multilevel marketing company, he found out that few members in the group were familiar with the concept of multilevel marketing. Therefore, he began by teaching the concepts, and only then was he able to pitch his particular product in a way the audience could understand. By finding this out beforehand through careful audience analysis, he was able to avert what could easily have been a disastrous presentation.

OUTLINING WITH SOFTWARE

While many writers and presenters still like to sit down with a pad of paper or note cards to outline their ideas, more and more people are using their computers. Most word processing programs now come with an "outline view" mode that enables you to organize your main points, subheads, and transitions right on the computer screen. These are helpful because they provide you with a structure to follow and a way to keep your ideas organized. However, you must still do the conceptual work of pulling out the main and subordinating points and fitting them into the pattern that matches your presentation.

Many presentation software programs include templates that actually give you an outline for organizing ideas according to the type of presentation you are creating. For example, Microsoft PowerPoint provides "Auto Content Wizards" for such presentations as Motivating a Team, Recommending a Strategy, Reporting Progress, and Introducing a Speaker. Such templates may be helpful to the novice who has little company support in the area of business communication. However, most managers find the templates cumbersome to use and too confining in terms of breadth and depth of content.

If you are familiar with your topic area and have a clear purpose and solid audience analysis, you will probably find it more expedient to prepare your own pattern of organization.

While you're organizing the ideas in your presentation, don't forget about the supporting material you have worked too hard to gather. Your data charts, examples, comparisons and contrasts, definitions, and testimony from others can be key variables in making your point. For some presentations, the supporting material will be the main point-for example, figures on turnover and absenteeism might be a main topic for a presentation on improving the quality of work life in an organization. In other circumstances, you may want to place supporting material where it will help buttress a specific point. For example, in explaining a new billing system, you might find it helpful to use contrast and comparison-showing similarities and differences between the old and new systems. This linkage will help your audience follow your message and understand how to use and apply the new system.

TRANSITIONS

An important yet often overlooked step for your presentation planning involves paying particular attention to the transitions that you use to link your ideas together. For audiences, transitions serve as signposts, and guides that help them navigate the points of your message. Transitions are crucial: If you ignore them, your audience can be left floundering, even if you have created a well-organized document or presentation. Transitions can be as simple as a single word (such as therefore) that denotes you are making a concluding statement based on your preceding ideas. Transitions can also be internal summaries: "Now that we've outlined our cost overrun problems, let's look at possible solutions." Another very effective transition is to number your points: "Today I'd like to describe three key ideas: Number one..." With such a quick lead-in statement, you can help your audience anticipate where you're going and guide them to the desired outcome.

You don't want to add your transitions too early in the presentation preparation process. As you edit, you'll no doubt change ideas around. This can happen even during the practice sessions. If you work on transitions too early in the process, you will spend valuable time on a step that will probably be changed later.

Making a Conclusion

A key summary step in delivering your presentation is "telling them what you told them." Once you have gone through the main points of your presentation, you are ready to conclude. You need to accomplish two main tasks with your conclusion:

- Reinforce your topic, purpose, or main points.
- Provide closure or completeness to your presentation.

When you are done, it should be clear to the audience that you are finished speaking and that it is time for the question-and-answer session-or for applause! To be effective, tailor your conclusion to the audience and reinforce the points that you want them to take away. For most speakers, this involves one or more of the following:

- A summary of the main points of the presentation
- A restatement of the thesis
- An appeal or challenge to the audience

Example of a Good Ending

Our earlier example of a fire safety speaker lends itself to showing a well-thought-out transition for concluding: There are few things in life more tragic than being the victim of a fire. Hopefully, I have given you some insights on how you can both avoid becoming the victim of a fire and protect your coworkers or family. Remember, there is no substitute for prevention and preparation: Check the batteries in your smoke alarm; have an escape route planned; and leave being a hero to the professionals.

SUMMARY

Having well-organized thoughts is the key to a great presentation. A clear, logical, and tight presentation can help your listeners in comprehending your message and enhance your credibility as a speaker.

When you organize your materials, you will probably find it helpful to return to your thesis statement, your audience analysis, and your supporting materials as you develop your strategy. You may find, for example, that you need more data to support your point or that you need more information on how strongly your audience favors your proposal.

When you are confident of the structure and organization of your presentation, you also will be able to convey your message-and your credibility- clearly and effectively.

Note: Pepsico is the best example in Organizing Ideas. For more information reader can visit www.pepsico.com

15

Planning Visual Support

A key element in the preparation of any business presentation is the use of visual aids. Often, your decisions regarding visuals happen when you prepare for your presentation and conduct an audience analysis. You'll evaluate who will be in your audience analysis.

You'll evaluate who will be your audience and decide what kinds of information will be of most persuasive. While colourful PowerPoint slides and fancy projection systems have become all the rage in many business settings today, computer-generated visuals may not be appropriate in every situation. Indeed, there are times when you may want less sophisticated visuals-or no visual aids at all.

For example, local health clubs often have their fitness instructors conduct seminars for community groups. For those seminars, the instructors create a stronger visual impact by using themselves as demonstrators and distributing handouts.

In a recent survey in Presentations magazine, 96 percent of the respondents agreed that, in general, technology enhances presentations. However, 54 percent also agreed that technology can detract from a presentation.

In a previous chapter, we provided examples of how to improve the layout and design of visuals that you use in written documents. These basic examples are also pertinent to the design of visuals in presentations; however, there are key modifications (for example, font size, colour, and complexity) that need to be made.

We demonstrate some of these differences by providing before-and-after examples in this chapter to show the characteristics of good visual aids. You'll learn how to plan and improve the visual supports for your presentation.

We cover four primary topics in this chapter:

- Why use visual aids?
- Types of visual aids
- Characteristics of good visual aids
- Guidelines for using visual aids

REASONS FOR USING VISUAL AIDS

In his early work, Business and Professional Speaking, Eric Skopec, now Regional Director for Business and Management at Learning Tree University in Los Angeles, maintains that there are two main reasons to use visual aids: to make ideas memorable and to display complex relationships.

As Skopec discusses, it's important to help your audience remember information, and you can do this by giving them more than just an oral presentation. Research on learning supports the idea that stimulating more of our senses (e.g., both seeing and hearing information) improves comprehension and retention.

Eric's second point is equally important-visuals can help explain relationships and ideas that are too complex to understand easily by just listening. For example, it is easier to understand sales forecast figures when you talk about them at the same time you present them graphically. Beyond Skopec's basic rules, the following are additional reasons to insert visuals into your business presentations:

- They break up the text of a long presentation.
- They help to alleviate speech anxiety because you focus the audience's attention on something other than the speaker.
- They demonstrate your skill with newer technologies.
- Your efforts look more professional than those of competitors who don't use visuals.

Sometimes it is not advisable to use sophisticated visuals. For example, if your company is downsizing or cutting costs, it would not be advisable to spend thousands of dollars on a professionally created presentation about ways to save money and decrease costs.

Similarly, an audience without much experience listening to presentations might be distracted by elaborate visuals and slick transitions. They might spend more time looking at the visuals than really listening to your message. These decisions are often part of your audience analysis during your preparation.

TYPES OF VISUAL AIDS

There are many types of visual aids, and your selection will depend on your purpose, your audience, your own skills, and your budget. Generally, visual aids that take more time to design and create are the easiest to use during a presentation, but they can often be the most expensive.

Some visual aids, like flipcharts and actual objects, work best with small groups, while others, such as slides, work well with groups of any size. With very small groups, users often display visuals right on the screen of a notebook computer.

Again, your selection of the type of visual to use will be made during your presentation preparation process. You need to decide which type of visual will:

- Best support your goals and the audience's requirements
- Work within your time, space, and budget limitations
- Be accepted by your audience
- Be the most comfortable for you to use

Your corporate culture will also frequently dictate the type of visuals that you can use. Some companies routinely expect PowerPoint presentations and have all conference rooms wired for easy use of the computer projection system. Others prefer lower-tech overheads or even handouts.

PRESENTATIONS MAGAZINE

Computers and audiovisual technology are changing quickly in the information age. Material written for this book may be outdated six months after it's published. We have found that good visual aids for presentations have five general characteristics:

- Visible (easy to see)
- Errorless
- Easy to use

Table: Types and Characteristics of Visual AIDS

Visual Aid	*Cost*	*Equipment Rental*	*Technical Skill Needed*	*Advantages*	*Disadvantages*
Computer-created and projected slides	High initial investment in computer and software	Computer and projection system needed	Competence in visual design and equipment use	Professional image, flexible design, special effects	Cost and equipment; may distract listeners
Overheads or transparencies	Relatively low; prepare on computer or copy machine	Overhead projector, generally available	Competence in visual design; must learn to center and focus	Easy to use; can use and connect with audience	Needed equipment
Photographic slides	Moderate cost for camera and processing film	Slide projector	Low; projectors work with remotes	Projects large and attractive images; works well with audio	Must darken room; lose contact with audience
Posters	Relatively low; cost of posterboard and makers	Easel to support poster	Some artistic or computer design ability	Easy to use	Too small for large group
Handouts	Relatively low copy costs, unless using colour	None	None	Helps listeners remember ideas	Can distract from message and speaker
Objects	Low	None	None	Demonstration	May be too small to see
Flipcharts (easels)	Low	Chart, easel, marking pen	None	Good to record group ideas	Often messy and unprofessional
Whiteboards	Low	Board and marking pens	None	Flexibility to write spontaneously	Often messy and unprofessional
Chalkboards	Low	Board and chalk	None	Flexibility to write spontaneously	Often messy and unprofessional; must turn back on listeners
• Attractive					
• Relevant					

A GOOD VISUAL AID IS VISIBLE

If your audience can't see your visual, it cannot be effective. However, we still see visuals that are too small (overall) in size, have fonts that are too small, and incorporate poor colour choices.

Visuals that are Too Small

You cannot create a good visual by simply typing up a list of ideas and using the list as a visual. Nor can you take a chart from a report, copy it onto a transparency or scan it into a software presentation package, and expect it to be visible to your audience. You have to anticipate the general size of the group you will be addressing and the general dimensions of the room you will be using in order to size your visuals appropriately. If the overall image is too small, it won't be effective.

Table: Characteristics of Good Visual Aids

Visual Characteristic	*Audience Concerns*	*Don't*	*Do*
Is the visual aid visible?	Can they see it?	Use type smaller than 24-point, combine too many colours, use dark backgrounds with dark lettering	Check your visual aid in the room you will be using and with the equipment you will be using
Is the visual aid errorless?	Are they distracted by typos and inaccuracies?	Forget to proof, grammar and spell check	Proofread; get a colleague to proof; spell check; grammar check
Is the visual aid easy to use?	Are they distracted by the user's ineptitude?	Use a visual you aren't familiar with and technology you haven't practiced with thoroughly	Use the easiest and most convenient visual in keeping with your audience needs
Is the visual aid attractive?	Can they understand the point of the visual? Is it nice to look at?	Put too much on one slide, use complete sentences, use too many colours, use fluorescent colours	Use a simple design; use key-word bulleted text; use a few primary colours; use a consistent template or company logo
Is the visual aid relevant?	Does it tie directly to the topic and enhance their understanding of the message?	Use irrelevant pictures or clip art, use humorous images without careful consideration	Use only the best supporting materials to enhance your argument

Visuals with Small Fonts

Another common, avoidable problem is the use of fonts that are too small. For most rooms, a good rule of thumb is that the smallest font on your visual should be 24 points, with appropriately larger sizes to emphasize the differences among your heads and subheads. However, be aware that even some fonts that are recommended in some computer software templates may not be large enough or clear enough when used in a projector.

Visuals with Poor Colour Choices

Choosing the specific colour(s) to use in your visuals is a complicated task. You need to consider, among other factors, your company or corporate image. Are there specific colour combinations that are identified with your company (e.g., red for the Xerox logo; yellow for Eastman Kodak's film boxes; green for Fuji film)? You also need to consider your audience's cultural background. In some cultures, white is a sign of happiness and celebration; in others, it is a sign of mourning.

We know of one major multinational company that had to repackage a product line because it used the wrong colours; the same thing can happen to your presentation. It can fail simply because you didn't choose the right colours or because you chose colours that didn't work well together. For example, red letters on a blue background might look cool on your computer screen, but the combination is hard to read on a projection screen.

Be sure to test your materials before your presentation.

A GOOD VISUAL AID IS ERRORLESS

You need to do more than just run your slides' text through the spell checker. A spell checker typically doesn't highlight misused words. You must proofread carefully, more than once, and ask a colleague to proofread for you, too. It is very hard to pick up your own errors, and these become magnified when shown to a group on the big screen. Any numbers or charts should be double-checked for accuracy, and confirm that your percentages add up to 100 percent. We guarantee that someone in every group will notice and point out such errors, casting doubt on your credibility.

A GOOD VISUAL AID IS EASY TO USE

Choose a medium with which you are comfortable and that is readily available in your business settings. Using readily available overhead projectors might make more sense than renting and setting up a computer projection system.

A GOOD VISUAL AID IS ATTRACTIVE

We have found that some visuals are easier to look at than others. An attractive visual that combines a few primary colours in an appropriate way is preferable to using all 16 million colours on your palette. Stay away from florescent shades that scream "Look at me!" and distract from the message.

Beyond colour, the design should be clear, uncluttered, and consistent (for example, your company logo might appear in the same location on each slide). What you are trying to show on the visual should be immediately apparent to your audience. The diagrams and figures should not be so complex and convoluted that your audience is confused or has trouble following the idea.

Additionally, you should not try to get too much on one visual. Rather than four pie charts on a single visual, show them separately to focus the audience's attention. If you want to show a comparison of the four, introduce them individually and build a slide to bring them together later.

GOOD VISUAL AIDS ARE DIRECTLY RELEVANT

Your visuals should be directly relevant to your topic, and they should not distract from your purpose and focus. Even if you spent hours in collecting data, you don't have to show every statistic if it doesn't directly support your point or if your audience doesn't need to know about it.

There are several things your visuals should generally avoid, including cartoons, humor, and irrelevant photos or clip art. Cartoons and other humorous materials can be effective under some circumstances, but they can also be offensive.

Use them judiciously. Resist the urge to scan irrelevant photos and clip art into your presentation just to jazz up a text slide. If a piece of art or a photo doesn't have a direct link to your topic, it will distract the audience from your presentation. Although you may have the world's cutest kitten, Muffin's picture doesn't belong in your presentation-unless, perhaps, you work for Purina.

GUIDELINES FOR USING THE VISUAL AIDS

There are three basic guidelines for using visuals effectively: Practice with visual aids, show your visual at the right time, and maintain maximum eye and voice contact with the audience.

Practice with Your Visual Aids

Before you stand up to deliver your presentation:

- Know how to use the audiovisual equipment.
- Know what to do if the equipment isn't working.
- Have a backup plan if you can't run the audiovisual technology or it cannot be repaired

Also, keep in mind:

- When you will put up each visual
- When you will take it down

How to do so without blocking the projection of the visual or your audience's view of it

SHOW YOUR VISUAL AIDS ONLY AT THE RIGHT TIME

Audiences are easily distracted, and they tend to look at visual aids, so you need to be sure your audience's attention is on an appropriate, relevant visual. When you (and your audience) are done with a visual, take it down, and don't put up the next visual until you are ready. Correct timing of your visuals is essential if you are going to retain control of your presentation and keep your audience focused on your purpose and message. When using overheads, it is acceptable to leave the screen blank in between transparencies; on a computer system, insert a blank slide or a title slide into the presentation. Don't use the automatic timer on your computer projected visuals. It may be tempting to use this technology tool to have your visuals advance automatically. However, in an extemporaneous presentation, you may change your phrasing, add new examples, or change the pace of your talk. It's always better for you to control the timing of the slides.

MAINTAIN MAXIMUM EYE AND VOICE CONTACT WITH THE AUDIENCE

A competent speaker has control over his or her audience. In order to maintain this control, you should keep your eyes and voice focused on the audience as much as possible. This is why the chalkboard is a poor visual aid: It requires the speaker to turn away from the audience to write, and thus contact with the audience is lost. Even if you stand sideways, you are still seeing and connecting directly with only half your audience.

Many people make this same mistake with overheads and slides. They turn their backs to the audience and point and talk to the screen. Use a pointer and touch the transparency/overhead in order to identify key areas. With a projection system, learn to use the cursor or program's pointer. You might also use a laser pointer, but don't try these without sufficient practice, as they are tricky to control properly. Avoid the "slow reveal" with overheads. You've no doubt seen people try to do a "slow reveal." When displaying a list of points on an overhead, they cover up the list with a piece of paper and reveal key points one line at a time.

Not only is this process awkward and distracting, it is also extremely patronizing to your audience. If you truly think your complete message will distract your listeners, try one of the following:

- Build the final visual by adding overlays.
- Use separate visuals.
- Use a computer program (for example, PowerPoint) to display slides in a sequential and timely fashion.

SUMMARY

Visual aids can greatly enhance your message and help your audience in comprehending and retaining that message. Before you get up in front of your audience, remember to check your visuals by putting them up and testing them. Make certain you can see them from the back of the room, or a similar room, with the lights set at the appropriate level. You, the speaker, need to consider your visuals throughout the phases of the prepresentation process. Use audience analysis, supporting materials, and your own experience and corporate culture as guidelines for choosing the most effective visual. Be sure to practice your presentation with your visuals, so you can be certain they support and advance the points you are trying to make. As you practice, you can also double-check your visuals for visibility, accuracy, attractiveness, and ease of use. Finally, have a backup plan in the event you experience an audiovisual breakdown. These guidelines for the design and use of visual aids will help to improve your presentation and add impact to your message.

Note: For detailed information and understanding, reader can visit www.virgin.com

16

Delivery Skills

When many people think about public speaking and business presentations, they think primarily of delivery skills. Indeed, many speakers initially think their biggest concern is how they look, sound, and act in front of a group of people. In truth, while delivery skills are important, they're secondary to defining your purpose, analyzing your audience, and organizing your ideas. At the same time, we recognize that competent delivery skills are essential to getting your message across to your audience. In this chapter, we discuss some of the more common concerns about delivery:

- Types of delivery
- Avoiding distractions
- Using your voice effectively
- Using posture and gestures to enhance your message
- Practicing your presentation

TYPES OF DELIVERY

Table: Types of Delivery

Style of Delivery	*Advantages*	*Disadvantages*
Manuscript	Precise wording, phrasing	Creates barrier with audience; limits eye contact/connection
Memorization	Precise wording, phrasing	Sounds recited; a disaster if you lose your train of thought
Impromptu	Helps you think on your feet	Not enough preparation for major presentation
Extemporaneous	Sounds conversational; allows adaptation to time/situation	Requires planning and rehearsal

There are four basic styles that you may use to deliver your presentation. We'll discuss each, and you'll find a brief summary of them in Table below.

READING FROM A MANUSCRIPT

While manuscripts for speeches may be acceptable for heads of state and Supreme Court justices, who must be precise in their content and wording, they are taboo in your everyday business presentations. Reading the text of a speech sets up a barrier between you and the audience; it limits the connection you can make personally with the audience; and it is generally frustrating to listeners, who would rather read the report themselves than hear you read it.

Having said that, we also recognize that high-profile speakers (heads of state, national newscasters, and corporate CEOs) can be effective when they read prepared scripts because of their control over the presentation context. They can position their audience and the TV cameras. They also use sophisticated TelePrompTers that project the text onto transparent viewing screens. The audience doesn't see these screens, so the speakers seem to make continuous eye contact. For the business presenter with a face-to-face live audience, however, we find that reading usually appears unprofessional and can damage the speaker's credibility.

SPEAKING FROM MEMORY

You might choose to memorize your presentation. There are two pitfalls: First, your presentation can sound stilted, as if you were reciting to the audience; and second, if you forget even one word or phrase, your mind can go blank and you will be lost (and, unlike your school play in second grade, there won't be a teacher in the wings to prompt you!). If you do choose to memorize, make sure that you work on the phrasing and intonation to avoid making your presentation sound like a recitation, and make sure you have a set of notes to back you up.

IMPROMPTU SPEAKING

There are times when you will be called upon to speak off-the-cuff. You may be in a meeting and be asked to update the group on the status of your project, even though that wasn't on the agenda. Or you may feel compelled to speak up at a meeting when you have a strong opinion on a particular topic.

Keep the following tips in mind:

- Know your goal.
- Think quickly about the sequence of your points.
- Jot down one or two key words.
- Be concise.

- Make certain this specific setting is where you can most effectively make and sell your point.

About Writing Speeches
Many public speaking texts and instructional videos use the term "writing your speech" to describe the process of preparing and delivering a presentation. You won't find that term used here. We find that the most successful presenters do not write out a speech word for word and read it to the audience. Rather, the successful presenters research and organize their material, then speak extemporaneously, working from key-word notes and aiming for more conversational phrasing.
When are speeches written out and read?
Under some special circumstances, speeches are written out. For example, major policy and political addresses must be precisely worded and require a more formal delivery style. Similarly, keynote addresses at conferences may be successfully written out and read to a large audience. But most business presentations are delivered in the context of small meetings, often with fewer than 15 people present, and reading these presentations would be disastrous to your professional image because it would create a barrier between you and the audience.
Ghostwritten Speeches
Sometimes, CEOs and high-level executives have someone else write their speeches so that they can allocate their time to more pressing business concerns. However, as a good speaker, you still need to guide the writer by clearly defining your key objectives and sharing your analysis of the audience. After receiving a draft of a ghostwritten speech, it is important to review, edit, and rehearse it, not only to be sure that the message accurately reflects your feelings and positions, but also to make certain that the words and phrasing match your personal style.

Avoid an impromptu approach to major presentations. Your major presentations need to be planned, organized, and rehearsed before delivery. Even the best speakers need to plan ahead.

The Value of Impromptu Speaking
Sometimes in public speaking classes, presentation skills workshops, and seminars, participants specifically practice impromptu speaking. Typically, speakers suggest topics and then draw them out of a hat or choose them on the spur of the moment. Each person stands up in front of the group and speaks for a minute or two on that topic. The results are often humorous and the content is rarely meaningful. One speaker might describe "my most embarrassing moment." Another might instruct the group on "how to brush and floss your teeth." Still another might offer thoughts on "who will win the Super Bowl this year." (This last one is particularly funny when the speaker knows nothing about the game of football.) But this exercise is not done just for laughs. The experience of speaking on an impromptu basis helps speakers learn to think on their feet and to practice speaking quickly and effectively.

SPEAKING EXTEMPORANEOUSLY

When you speak extemporaneously, you will be relying on a plan and key-word notes. This is the delivery style that we recommend. To do it successfully, you have to plan, determine your purpose, analyze your audience, and establish supporting materials. Rather than scripting your presentation, organize your ideas in a key-word outline, and then deliver your presentation from the outline or note cards. Aim for a conversational style, as if you were speaking to your audience in a one-on-one setting. The unique feature of an extemporaneous presentation is that, if you were to deliver it several times, it wouldn't come out exactly the same way each time. With an extemporaneous delivery style, you can feel free to add thoughts and examples that occur to you during the presentation-or even eliminate some points if there's a time crunch. You have flexibility, and you can better involve and make connections with your audience. It's far more effective than reading, memorizing, or speaking in an impromptu manner, and your message will have maximum impact.

AVOIDING DISTRACTIONS

In Business and Professional Speaking, published in 1983, and still very relevant today, Eric Skopec advocated a style of delivery that he called "mechanically adequate." A mechanically adequate speaker does nothing to distract the audience from the message. So, rather than coming up with a long list of dos and don'ts for presentation delivery, each speaker can examine his or her own attributes and abilities in order to eliminate any distractions.

Extemporaneous Speaking

Extemporaneous speeches are:

- Prepared
- Outlined
- Researched
- Rehearsed
- Conversational
- Flexible

Advantages of extemporaneous speeches:

- Personal connection with audience
- Adapt to time limits
- Flexibility with audience feedback

Unique features of extemporaneous speeches:

- You can deliver it any number of times and it won't come out exactly the same way each time.
- You, the presenter, have control over the presentation situation.

For example, many people find they speak more quickly when they are nervous, as one might be in a public speaking situation. Speaking too quickly can distract from your message because your articulation can suffer and audience comprehension can be diminished if you don't allow time to let the ideas sink in. Eliminating such a distraction from your delivery allows the audience to focus on the message. It is important to identify and eliminate common distractions, including those associated with your appearance, gestures or repetitive actions, and posture (videotaping and peer critiques work wonders!). A busy combination of colours, an open fly, too much makeup and jewelry, and an unkempt appearance can all distract the audience from your message. Playing with your pen and jingling the change in your pocket may not be noticeable to you, but they are to the audience. Even a stiff posture with no movement can call attention to itself.

It's helpful to think about network news broadcasters. While there may be a few exceptions, we generally don't know where they're from by their dialects; we don't recall specific outfits; and we don't remember if they used any special posture or gestures. Broadcasters avoid distractions so that you, the audience, can focus on the news story. And that is the goal in presentational speaking. You don't have to try to be John F. Kennedy, Barbara Jordan, or James Earl Jones. Your job is to be yourself, to deliver your message, and to avoid distracting your audience from that message.

USING VOICE EFFECTIVELY

Most people are rather surprised when they first hear themselves on tape. "Do I really sound like that?" We don't have a good sense of how we sound to others because the structure of the ear and its vibrations interfere with how we perceive our own voices. If you don't like your voice, there isn't a whole lot you can do to change its quality. You can, however, make sure that your voice doesn't distract from the message.

PRACTICE

Practice your presentation, or even read a passage from the newspaper, using a cassette recorder. (Don't use a video camera, because you might be distracted by your appearance and other aspects of nonverbal communication.) Listen to your tape for the following:

- Is your articulation crisp and sharp, or do you drop endings and run words together? The appropriate use of a simple -ing ending (for example, speakin' versus speaking) can make the difference between sounding competent or unprofessional.

- Is your tempo appropriate for easy listening, or do you speak too quickly or too slowly? Is your voice too loud or soft for the size of the room and the audience?
- Does your voice sound expressive? Are you demonstrating that you understand the meaning of the message, or are you speaking in a monotone, as if you're just reading or reciting something of no interest?
- Do you use vocal "fillers" that might distract from the message? Once the audience starts counting your "ums," you're in trouble and probably don't even realize it.
- Your own self-analysis, or that of a close friend or coworker, can help you identify one or two areas to improve before your next presentation.

One way to solve a pesky delivery problem is to exaggerate the solution while practising practice. Let's look at two examples:

- Speaking too quickly. If you speak too quickly and run your words together, a potential solution is to practice speaking very slowly and distinctly.
- At first, make your speech agonizingly slow. Force yourself to slow down and articulate each word. As you start to speak more distinctly, gradually speed up to a more normal pace.
- Speaking in a monotone. If you sense that your voice is too monotone and expressionless, try emulating a dramatic actor. For a few minutes, get crazy with your message. Have some fun. Exaggerate the changes in your pitch and intonation. Then gradually calm it down and use your audience analysis information to determine what changes will improve your presentation style.

Make certain, however, that you eliminate these extreme "practice exaggerations" from your actual presentation style. We have encountered one exasperating and pretentious presentations instructor who gains attention in groups, meetings, and presentations by using overly dramatic intonations. Not only are such exaggerations aggravating, they are also distracting and counterproductive. When you are delivering your presentation, avoid being egocentric, and pay attention to feedback from your audience. They'll know the difference between your acting a dramatic role and just being yourself.

GETTING RID OF THOSE VOCAL FILLERS

Eliminating vocal fillers (for example, um, uh, well, like, and ya know) can be the toughest challenge facing some speakers. Typically, the best technique is to spend time consciously trying to get rid of them. You should not wait until the day of the presentation and write yourself a note:

"Don't say um!" It won't work.

Get rid of the ums by consciously eliminating them during casual conversations at the dinner table or with friends. By eliminating these fillers from your casual conversation you will be able to get rid of them in your business presentations.

USING POSTURE AND GESTURES TO ENHANCE MESSAGE

Now it's time for you to get out that video camera or stand in front of a mirror. Deliver your presentation or do an impromptu self-introduction while watching your behaviors. A good presenter maintains eye contact with the audience and presents pleasant facial expressions, has an upright but not stiff posture, and uses gestures to emphasize points. For most business presentations, your audience is relatively small, and you don't need the dramatic gestures and movement that would be appropriate on a stage in front of thousands. To enhance your message, use these two guides:

- Appear natural and relaxed, as you would in most business discussions. Remember, it's okay to smile.
- Use nonverbal communication cues to add emphasis to your message.

Because your gestures, posture, and even voice intonations can affect the quality of your presentation, it's important to be aware of how you're projecting to your audience. The following suggestions can help you to do this.

MAKE EYE CONTACT

You want to maintain eye contact with the audience by looking at one person for several seconds, then moving on to another person. Don't read from your notes, although it's okay to glance down at them occasionally. If you try to avoid looking at your audience by looking beyond them (to the clock on the back wall, for example), people will notice and become distracted-and to you the audience will seem like an intimidating mob. If you quickly glance around the room and do not maintain eye contact while you make your point, you're using the "scared rabbit" approach. Darting eyes make you appear to be extremely nervous.

Remember, you are under no obligation to look at everyone in the audience. If it works better for you, choose to focus on the friendliest faces, such as people who are nodding in agreement with your message. However, don't ignore people who are starting to frown or look bored. They are giving you extremely important feedback, and you need to be aware of them before you get into questions and answers.

USING APPROPRIATE POSTURE

Your posture should be professional and confident. In most situations, this means that you should stand firmly on two feet and not shift your weight from side to side or lean on a table or podium. Don't appear stiff and unnatural. Incorporate some movement into your delivery style, but don't pace or wander.

You might move toward the overhead or computer in order to display visuals, or you might take a step toward your audience to emphasize a point. Use natural movements as you would when you are engaged in animated conversations.

Taking a step toward a listener who is starting to look bored (or worse, nodding off) can help that person become more attentive, and it can eliminate a major distraction to others who are trying to listen.

MAKING GESTURES WORK

Like your posture, your gestures should be natural and seem like a normal extension of your body language. One effective technique is to use your hands for emphasis, to punctuate your discussion, and to refer to your visual aids. To help structure three points in your presentation, hold up one, then two, then three fingers to emphasize the sequence. If the gesture feels like a natural part of your presentation, it is probably appropriate.

Avoid distracting, nervousness, repetitive, and meaningless movements-for example, tapping on the podium, playing with your ring or watch or pen, jingling the keys or coins in your pocket, or stroking your beard. Speakers can generally identify their own distracting gestures after a brief encounter with a mirror or a few minutes of videotape. Again, you need to practice in order to get rid of those distractions.

PRACTICING FOR PRESENTATION

"Practice? Who has time to practice?" We hear that comment too often from managers, executives, and students when it comes to preparing for a presentation. Many executives feel such time pressure that they barely have time to gather their data and make a few slides before speaking. However, if you ignore this crucial step in the preparation of your presentations, you will surely find some surprises-and may even experience some of our "presentation disasters". Practice alleviates speech anxiety, and being prepared is a courtesy to your audience members. The people listening to you are spending their valuable time, and you need to help them use it effectively. Often, presenters don't know how to use successful techniques for practicing their speeches. Instead, they frequently take their note cards into a conference room and review them, sometimes quietly muttering the phrases they intend to use. This is rarely helpful because it is a setting and rehearsal very far removed from the actual presentation situation.

The following guidelines can help you more effectively practice your presentation:

- Duplicate, as closely as possible, the conditions under which you will presenting. Try to practice your presentation in the room where you'll be delivering the speech. If that's not possible, be sure to stand (unless your presentation calls for you to sit) and project your voice as if you were speaking to the number of people you expect.

PRESENTATION DISASTERS

We've seen enough presentations in our years of teaching and consulting to get a good sense of what does and doesn't work with an audience. Here are some of our more memorable "presentation disasters."

- Factual errors. One group of MBA students who served as consultants to a local business not only got the name of the company wrong, they misspelled it on every slide. It should go without saying: Proof once, proof again, then get someone else to proof visuals for you. If you miss something as basic as the company name, your audience will start to wonder what else you might have missed.
- Inappropriate attire. We've seen everything from project engineers in scruffy jeans to executives in too-trendy clothing

that included loud colours and short skirts. There is no single correct way to dress, but you should always appear professional and in sync with the rest of your team and with the audience. (If you mowed the lawn in those pants, they probably aren't right for a presentation.)

- Really, really bad slides. We thought we'd made the point about good visual aid content and design, but some people still insist on typing things up on a word processor, putting them on an overhead, and covering, then revealing, one line at a time to the audience. This drives us-and others -crazy! We were totally distracted from the content presented by a physician whose overheads were out of focus and caused eyestrain. If you want to use visual aids, be prepared to do it right. Make sure they are visible and that they enhance your presentation.
- Condescending attitude. Sometimes this happens because people really are smarter than the rest of us, and their impatience shows; more often, it's to make up for feelings of inadequacy or lack of confidence in the content. Either way, it puts off the audience and lessens a speaker's credibility and impact. If you're not sincerely interested in getting your message across, you are doomed to fail. Every single audience deserves respect.
- Lack of preparation. This is one disaster we've seen all too often. The audience resents lack of preparedness as an intrusion into their busy time. As a consequence, your image suffers. Even if you have great charisma, you can't charm your way out of a poorly prepared presentation. Black out the time you need to prepare and practice so you do your professional best.
- Practice with your visual aids. Nothing tries the patience of an audience as much as technical problems with visuals, and there is nothing more certain to heighten a speaker's level of anxiety. Use your visuals when you practice to make sure they work properly. Confirm that you have matched the timing and placement of visuals to the talking points of your presentation.
- Practice with a tape recorder or a video camera. Using a tape recorder or a video camera will give you an opportunity to hear how you sound and to critique your content and phrasing so that you can make any necessary adjustments ahead of time.
- Practice in front of an audience, if possible. It can be extremely helpful to have a coworker, colleague, friend, or spouse listen

to your and comment on your presentation. People close to you want you to succeed and will be brutally honest in their evaluations if you ask them. Furthermore, if you can give your presentation to a family member with all the distractions of home about you, you should have no problem when it comes to the real thing.

SUMMARY

Delivering a presentation well is a matter of planning and practice. If you understand the types of delivery available and aim for an extemporaneous style, you will establish rapport with the audience and improve the likelihood of accomplishing your goal. Concentrate on avoiding any behaviors or mannerisms that would be distracting to your audience. Use your voice and gestures to enhance your message. Practive is the key to improving your delivery style, enhancing your confidence, and increasing your chances of success. Even if you need to improve in a few areas, don't panic. Work on one or two areas at a time. Major improvements seldom come overnight. Remember, your initial goal is be mechanically adequate, to do nothing that distracts from your message.

Your goal is not to have people leave saying, "What a great speech!" Your goal is to have them saying, "What great ideas!"

Note: For detailed information on Delivery Skills, reader can visit www.basesystems.com

17

Handling Questions and Answers

The presentation is over. You've delivered your sure-to-win-them-over conclusion, and you heave a big sigh of relief. Not so fast. How you handle the question-and-answer (Q&A) session following a presentation can be as important as what you do during the presentation itself. By preparing for your listeners' questions and maintaining control of those questions, you can add impact to your presentation. Without adequate preparation, you can undo everything your speech accomplished. Preparing for questions occurs at several points during your preparation process.

Even during the preparation step, when you analyze the audience and set your goals, you should anticipate questions that might arise. For example, if you know that one of your colleagues always raises objections to proposals based on long term implications, you can be sure to project your data to cover the future impact. If your presentation depends heavily on explaining quantitative figures to non-quantitative people, you can test your figures and charts on a colleague beforehand. Not only will this give you the opportunity to prepare answers, you also can test those answers when you rehearse. This chapter describes common pitfalls associated with answering questions and provides suggestions for using Q&A sessions to add strength and credibility to your presentation. We'll address the following:

- Preparing for questions
- Taking questions in a business presentation
- Listening effectively to questions
- Responding when you don't know the answer
- Maintaining control of the Q&A session
- Planting questions: Is this a good strategy?

PREPARING FOR QUESTIONS

Competent speakers prepare for question-and-answer sessions by anticipating questions during their preparation process. Politicians sometimes prepare for debates and press conferences by having their aides them the toughest questions they might face. If you are having trouble anticipating questions, try running your presentation past a colleague, or check with someone who will be attending the presentation and ask about their major concerns. By anticipating questions, you can be prepared not only to reply but also to have any needed backup information or data.

Although anticipating questions can be helpful, there is no substitute for thoroughly preparing your content. Public speaking textbooks often recommend that you gather three times as much information as you need for a presentation. Some of that added preparation will give you more knowledge and a higher comfort level on your topic, and much of it can be useful support in your question-and-answer session. Even if your presentation does not specifically cover the topic of a question, you might be able to use a piece of background information to satisfy your listeners and to demonstrate your competence on the topic.

TAKING QUESTIONS IN A BUSINESS PRESENTATION

Should you have the audience hold questions until the end, or should you take them during the presentation? There are pros and cons to both approaches. Obviously, if you are doing an instructional presentation and your audience's understanding of subsequent material will depend on their understanding of earlier material, then you need to answer questions as they come up-or at internal summary points during your presentation. When you use this technique, you need to make certain your audience is not diverted from your main purpose and doesn't lose the thread of your message. Additionally, if you have strict time constraints, answering questions during your presentation may prevent you from completing the presentation.

By holding questions to the end, you may run the risk of not being able to address major concerns during the presentation. However, it may be worth the trade off for a smooth, flowing talk delivered within your time constraints. Let your audience know at the outset if they should ask questions along the way or hold them to the end of the presentation. Only you can decide which strategy works best, depending on your topic, audience, purpose, and time limits.

LISTENING EFFECTIVELY TO QUESTIONS

Many times, a speaker's listening skills suffer because of anxiety about delivering a major presentation. It's important to listen to questions carefully and to be prepared to respond with a quick, accurate, and appropriate reply. When you are asked a question, make direct eye contact with the questioner and focus on the key words in the question. If you don't understand the question, ask for clarification (for example, you might say, "If I understand you correctly, you're asking..."). Be certain that you stay tuned in to the nonverbal communication that is associated with the question. A questioner's gestures, facial expression, and tone of voice can help you interpret the substance and tone of the message. Do not fall into the trap of using rehearsed party-line responses. Politicians who answer every question with a rehearsed answer sound shallow. Be respectful of all questioners, and offer them an intelligent response.

Be certain to monitor your own gestures, facial expressions, and other nonverbal cues when you are both listening to questions and answering them. If you are on a team or panel, be attentive when others are speaking. Your inattention, even if you are preparing your own points, might be seen as an unintended sign of disrespect.

RESPONDING WHEN YOU DON'T KNOW THE ANSWER

If you haven't anticipated a question or you don't have the information, don't fake it. It is not worth the risk to your credibility as a speaker or as a manager to take a chance on information that might be wrong. The best approach is to indicate that you don't know the answer, and if it is important, tell the questioner you will find the answer and share it. If you believe someone else in the group has the information, you may refer the question to that individual; however, we recommend that you do so with caution-it is extremely easy to lose control of your presentation. Remember, it is appropriate to point out, politely, that a question is not relevant and that the group needs to focus on the issues at hand.

MAINTAINING CONTROL OF THE Q&A SESSION

When you're the presenter, you're in charge, during both the presentation and the Q&A session. Several techniques will help you maintain control:

- Answer questions succinctly and nondefensively.
- Be informative rather than persuasive.
- Stick to the facts.

- Do not allow yourself to be drawn into a debate with a member of the audiences.

The trick is to remember that when a question is asked, focus on the questioner, and when you respond, speak to the entire group. By including everyone in the reply, you will discourage the disruptive sideline chats that can occur while you are engaging one member and inadvertently excluding the rest of your audience. This technique can also help diffuse tension in a hostile situation. When the allotted time is ending, or after you have answered major concerns, signal the close of your presentation: "We have time for only one more question." "My time is just about up."

There are two common mistakes speakers make during Q&A sessions. The first is to forget in monitoring the amount of time left. The second is failing to leave time for a brief concluding statement that will wrap up the session.

ENDING THE Q&A

In closing, you should shift the question-and-answer session back to your presentation topic in order to refocus your audience. Here's an example:

Thank you for your attention. I appreciate your interest in the new laser printer we have been developing, and I trust you'll continue your enthusiastic support of this venture. Please feel free to contact me with any additional concerns or ideas for strengthening the project.

SUMMARY

To a novice speaker, a question-and-answer session may seem like an intimidating situation, akin to a firing squad or an inquisition by a grand jury. It shouldn't be. A question-and-answer session is a positive opportunity for a speaker to advance the points made in the presentation and to clarify any areas of confusion. With the proper preparation, most speakers learn to welcome the Q&A and even enjoy the challenge.

Note: For detailed information, reader may visit www.infosysblogs.com

18

Speech Anxiety

It's not all in your head. Speech anxiety is real. Survey after survey has found that the fear of public speaking is the most common fear that people have. More people fear giving a speech than are afraid of flying, spiders, or even death. If you are one of those who would rather visit the dentist than give a speech, you are not alone. A little anxiety before a big presentation is normal, especially for high achievers, executive personalities. You can use that adrenaline to add energy and excitement to your message. Although too much anxiety can get in the way of your doing a great job, our goal in this chapter is to help you understand and control speech anxiety by addressing the following two themes:

- Why are we afraid of public speaking?
- What can we do to reduce or control our speech anxiety?

WHY ARE WE AFRAID OF PUBLIC SPEAKING?

You may have your own individual reason for being afraid of public speaking, but we can generally group the source of speech anxiety into one of three areas: fear of the unknown, a bad experience, and a social norm.

FEAR OF THE UNKNOWN

Think of your first day on a new job. You don't know what the work environment is like, how you'll be treated, or the sorts of responsibilities that you'll have. Once you become familiar with your work situation, a lot of those first-day jitters usually disappear.

It's the same way when you are making a presentation or giving a speech. Many people simply haven't had the opportunity to prepare and present speeches during their education and work experiences, and they are unfamiliar with the process and the outcome. They have not learned the steps involved in preparing for a business presentation, and they are unsure of how they should proceed. Additionally, since they have never delivered an oral presentation to a large group of people, they don't know how they personally will react to the situation or how it feels to have all those eyes staring at you.

A BAD PAST EXPERIENCE

A top MBA graduate student at the Simon School once related a personal experience in her Presentation Skills class. This student remembered the exact circumstances and even the exact words her fifth-grade teacher used to tell her she would never be a competent public speaker after one disappointing performance. For over 15 years this student had carried the stigma that she was a failure as a public speaker. She went on to overcome those self-doubts and become one of our finest speakers and a student government leader, but the sad truth is that many are not so fortunate.

Managers and executives often report that they had a defined bad experience in high school, a time when self-images are fragile and the need for peer acceptance is high. A single bad past experience may keep people from choosing professions or seeking out jobs that require professional communication skills. Similarly, long-held fears may cause an individual to miss chances for promotion to more responsible jobs that require presentations.

A SOCIAL NORM

If you watch young children performing a musical or dance number, they seem completely uninhibited. Flower girls in weddings rarely appear nervous, and children seldom ask you to turn off your video camera. We do not appear to be born with a fear of performing in front of others; on the contrary it appears to be something that we learn somewhere along the way. Perhaps we learn it from a parent who is nervous about a presentation at work, or from a teacher who tells her class, "Don't be nervous" as they get ready to put on a play for the school. It gets passed along when our college students tell their friends they have to give a speech and are greeted with, "Aren't you nervous? I could never do that!" In many ways, our culture has taught us to fear this event we call public speaking.

IS SPEECH ANXIETY REALLY A BAD THING?

In most circumstances, a little speech anxiety is good for you. It means that you are concerned about doing a good job and that you are conscientious about the message you need to deliver. A little anxiety gives you some adrenaline, some energy to put into your performance. People who are completely relaxed about giving a presentation tend to do a ho-hum job with their delivery. We need a little nervous tension in order to connect effectively with our audiences.

Conversely, when you have too much nervous energy, your anxiety can interfere with your presentation delivery. We next discuss strategies for overcoming your speech anxiety.

REDUCING OR CONTROLLING SPEECH ANXIETY?

We believe that speech anxiety is real and there are five excellent techniques for controlling or reducing it: knowing your material; practicing, practicing, practicing; knowing how you react; using visual aids; and reconceptualizing the situation.

Know Your Material

You don't have to have a Ph.D. to understand that people feel more comfortable talking about a subject they know well. Ask students who come unprepared for class and pray their teachers won't call on them. Even college professors will tell you they feel more comfortable discussing the subjects they know best rather than those that are less familiar and less frequently covered. The more you know about your topic, the more comfortable you will feel in your presentation. When you are preparing a presentation and have the opportunity to pick your own topic, pick something you know and feel confident about. Be certain that you also choose a topic that relates to your audience.

If you can't pick your own topic, make sure you learn as much about it as you can during your preparation and drafting steps. Experts recommend gathering three times as much information as you need for your presentation. This will enable you to (1) pick only the best supporting material, (2) have a supply of backup information for the question-and-answer session, and (3) lessen your anxiety.

Practice

This step, which is part of your prepresentation process, is probably the single most important factor for alleviating speech anxiety. The more you practice, the more you practice, the more you will become familiar with the material and the more you will relax. But it isn't enough to simply review your notes or go through your prepared slides.

A good practice session needs to duplicate as closely as possible the circumstances under which you will give the presentation. This means practicing in the same room, or a similar room, in which your speech will take place, standing, and using the appropriate visual aids.

Know How You React

Everyone has a different response to the pressure of a presentation situation, and only experience will teach you how you will react. For the novice speaker, it may be startling just to stand at a podium with all those eyes looking at you. Others may find they have sweaty palms, a dry mouth, or trembling hands. Identifying your own reaction is half the battle. Next, you need to take clear, logical steps to manage it. For a dry mouth, keep a noncarbonated beverage handy, and perhaps some hard candy or cough drops to suck on before you begin your presentation. For those of you who suffer from quivering hands, no one will notice unless you use your hand to point to a visual on the overhead projector, in which case, the image on the screen will magnify the shaking! To circumvent this problem, use a pointer or pen and place it firmly on the visual. As for sweaty palms, well, they won't really matter unless you shake hands with someone in the audience.

After you have taken steps to deal with your personal reactions, put them aside. Remember, an audience will only rarely perceive your level of anxiety. They are there to hear your message.

Use a Visual Aid

Visual aids (used judiciously, of course, as we suggested earlier) can also help reduce anxiety. While your audience is looking at a visual aid, they are not looking at you. If you feel pressured when you are the center of attention and have all those eyes staring at you, use a visual to focus their attention elsewhere momentarily and appropriately.

Reconceptualize the Situation

Most speakers become very self-oriented when they prepare for a speech. They worry about how they will look, how they will sound, how they will appear before the audience. The average business audience is not there to critique your public speaking style; they are there to hear your message. To be successful and to help you ignore your nervousness, remind yourself: "I have a message I want this group to hear." Do not focus on the idea that you have to "perform" for this group. Your audience analysis and the other steps you used to prepare your presentation will help you concentrate on your audience and how your message relates to them. When you do so, you will stop worrying about yourself and stop being nervous. Similarly, you can think of the situation as an extended one-on-one conversation. Picture yourself sharing information with two or three key people in a casual conversation or small group discussion. Don't imagine the audience in their underwears. One of the most common tips you'll find in other books on public speaking is to relieve speech anxiety by imagining the audience in their underwear. This is not one we recommend.

The theory behind it is that if you can imagine the people in your audience looking silly, you won't feel so intimidated by them. We can't recommend this line of thinking because we work from the premise that good speakers need to respect their audiences and put those audiences first when conveying a message.

SUMMARY

Most people with speech anxiety will respond well with practice and thorough preparation. If, however, you feel that your own speech anxiety is more severe and that you require help beyond the tips provided here, we urge you to seek out an anxiety-reduction program. The success rate of these programs is excellent. Many speech departments and counseling offices at larger universities provide programs that generally use relaxation techniques and visualization skills to help you learn to relax before and during a presentation.

Table: Resources for People with Speech Anxiety

- Courses offered through local community and high school continuing education
- Toastmaster's International-available in companies and communities (check the phone book)
- Dale Carnegie Effective Speaking Programs
- Courses offered through local colleges for credit or noncredit
- Anxiety-reduction programs offered through universities or hospitals
- Private therapist or counseling
- Support groups for all types of anxiety disorders

Try one of these programs. It might make a difference in more than just your ability to make presentations!

Note: Reader can find more information on www.InformationR.net

19

Assessing Your Presentation

As you're packing up your notes and visuals following your presentation, you probably feel a great sense of relief-and hopefully, a sense of accomplishment for a job well done. However, you shouldn't let these fleeting emotions be your final contact with this presentation. The best presenters add a final step to the process: a post presentation evaluation. In this step, you evaluate each aspect of the presentation process and plan for future improvement. You need to do this specifically in three key areas: purpose, audience analysis, and delivery.

DID YOU ACHIEVE YOUR PURPOSE?

Early in the presentation process, you specified your general purpose, your specific purpose, and what you would like to have happen as a result of this presentation. Now you need to examine the outcome of your presentation: Did you achieve your purpose? Did you accomplish your goals for the presentation? If you did, why were you successful? If not, why not? What factors contributed to the audience's acceptance or failure of your proposal?

AUDIENCE ANALYSIS

If you followed a systematic presentation process, you probably spent a good bit of time doing audience analysis. You looked at what your audience knew, what you wanted them to know, and what they needed to know. How successful were you in reaching this particular audience? If you didn't reach them, why not? Go through the questions we asked you to explore to identify the source of the communication breakdown. Did the audience know more than you realized they knew? Were they bored by your presentation? Did they know less than you realized? Were they lost during your presentation? What might you have done differently to better connect with this group of people?

DELIVERY

This is probably the area most frequently used for a postpresentation evaluation. In this step, you evaluate the verbal and nonverbal communication that contributed to the success or failure of your presentation. Did you use your voice, posture, gestures, and facial expressions to maximum effectiveness? Did your visual aids work smoothly and enhance your presentation? Did you control your anxiety? Did you seem knowledgeable and confident in the question-and-answer session?

You may not be able to complete the post presentation evaluation totally on your own. If you have a videotape of the presentation, this may help in your self-assessment. However, you may need to enlist the help of close colleagues to give you guidance on how well you met your objectives in the presentation. Certainly, if you are involved in a team project, team members should be open to constructive comments for improvement from others on the team.

One of our most memorable examples of thorough self-evaluation comes from a former MBA student at St. John Fisher College. Alan was an excellent presenter with a high-visibility job in county government, and he was always looking for ways to improve his performance. During his final presentation, he used a large poster board on an easel as a visual aid. When he was through referencing the chart, he took it down, as is appropriate.

However, he hadn't decided what he was going to do with the chart. He held it awkwardly for a few moments and then laid it down on the floor. For a few moments, the audience could hear Alan's voice, but we saw only his back as he leaned down to lay his visual on the floor. It wasn't a major issue in what was otherwise an excellent presentation. However, when Alan saw the videotape, he was appalled by what he had done. Not only had he not planned how to remove his visual, he kept speaking while he lost visual contact with the audience. His written self-evaluation included two pages on the correct use of visual aids.

We aren't recommending that you get overly scrupulous about every aspect of your presentation delivery. However, you can be sure that Alan will never make that same mistake again. He evaluated his performance, didn't like what he saw, and developed a strategy for dealing with it in the future.

SUMMARY

Unless you evaluate your preparation and performance after the presentation, you won't be able to adjust your strategy for the next presentation. You may be condemned to repeat fatal errors or annoying distractions that can test the patience of your audience. Even if your presentation was successful in achieving your purpose, it is good to know just what you did correctly so you can capitalize on those strengths next time. Doing a presentation without systematic evaluation afterward is like not calling the doctor to find out if your child's throat culture is positive for strep: It leaves too much to chance and allows mistakes to multiply. The evaluation doesn't take long, and the insights will be well worth the effort.

Note: For detailed information and understanding reader may visit www.Ige.gov.ok/Ige

20

Writing and Presenting as a Team

Because of the growth of teamwork and cooperative cross-functional projects in most business settings, managers and executives frequently find themselves working on group rather than individual projects. In this chapter, we show you how to manage group writing projects and team presentations, and we offer ways to apply both the writing and editing process and the presentation process to successful teamwork. The Total Quality Management (TQM) movement and other leadership initiatives demand efficient group and team efforts. Executives need to manage group writing and presentation processes so that these processes consume less time and fewer resources. Managers also need to make decisions on the adoption and support of computerized software packages and tools designed for use by groups. The proper software tools and the right conceptual tools provide a team with an excellent structure for accomplishing its task.

Writing a document and organizing a presentation as a team can be a frustrating experience, especially for those who prefer to write and present on their own. At the same time, an effective team can exploit the resources of its members and produce documents and presentations that are stronger, more coherent, and more persuasive than any one individual might produce alone.

When you are initiating team or workgroup projects with written products (for example, reports and proposals), it is important to start by implementing a writing and editing process parallel to the process described in first few chapters. You need to focus on establishing a team process, evaluating team member's skills, and evaluating your written products.

STEP 1:EVALUATE THE TEAM PROCESS

Planning ahead, anticipating barriers, and analyzing strengths will help teams avoid wasted, redundant effort, which is a major reason that team projects exceed timelines and budgets. Does planning ahead sound simple? It is not. In fact, one of the first barriers that a team faces is the need to rein in compulsive team members who are driven to get their "real" work started, immediately! For various team members, that "real work" might be writing down basic goals, developing a budget, designing research, allocating space for designing a prototype, or some other individual hot button.

Our hot button is saving time and eliminating redundant efforts, especially those related to writing up materials and developing databases. The quickest way to create work that will need to be redone is by having to rewrite. For a team project, these tasks range from the simple (deciding which word processing software to use) to the complex (establishing responsibilities, processes, and procedures for the complete project).

For writing projects, use these steps to improve the success of your team:

- Clarify the following:
  - What needs to be done?
  - Who is doing it?
  - When they are doing it?
  - How they are doing it?
  - How long it will take?
  - What it will cost?
- Use computers and software tools, such as:
  - Word processing software
  - Grammar and spell checkers
  - Project management software
  - E-mail
  - Presentation software
- Edit drafts sequentially.
- Create a final document.
- Proof that final.
- Obtain appropriate releases (from content experts and managers).
- Plan how to reproduce and distribute the material.
- Distribute and reproduce the material.
- Follow up.

Begin by selecting a word processing package and a document template. Why? The minute that two or more people start to independently write up ideas, establish independent guidelines for project management, or choose different ways to handle data, the team will develop inconsistent products that will require revision after revision. Believe us! We have been there many times, and it is a monstrous headache and one common reason that team members end up working nights and weekends, editing and reediting, trying to get projects completed. Prewriting steps will help you determine what you need to accomplish. We developed information on prewriting steps in our previous discussion, and we shared related information on defining your purpose. Audience analysis is one of several prewriting steps, which include identifying your:

- Objectives or goals
- Users or readers (audience analysis)
- Users' objectives or goals
- Users' existing knowledge
- Users' questions and needs

Prewriting steps help you in determining if writing is the appropriate or best technique to use in your situation, as well as what to include or exclude. To the extent you know what to include, who your audience is, and your goals, you will be able to avoid common initial writing errors and writer's block.

STEP 2: EVALUATE YOUR TEAM

Evaluate and use team members' skills. We are assuming that the composition of a team has been determined and that you know what needs to be done. The next major step is evaluating who does what. A common problem that teams face is that people try to do tasks they are afraid to admit they cannot do. Not only is time wasted, redundant effort is needed to fix new problems that arise. Keep in mind that people are often embarrassed to admit that they have weak writing skills, and sometimes they aren't even aware that there may be room for improvement. To expedite projects, have the skilled team writers "write" and the skilled team editors "edit." Have team members complete tasks that best utilize their skills.

For projects with a major writing (and/or related presentation) component, we recommend that you follow these guidelines:

- Use a project leader and/or a study group leader.
- Know and share your own individual strengths and weaknesses.

- Anticipate personal and work-related problems and commitments (family, sanity, etc.) that may interfere.
- Summarize actions to be taken; assign responsibilities.
- Arrange useful, focused working sessions and times.
- Come prepared for work sessions.
- Follow through on assignments.
- Monitor and facilitate individual participation.
- Establish specific goals and timelines.
- Determine the format, layout, and templates for your written products first!

These simple yet often overlooked steps will greatly enhance your team productivity.

Use project managers. It is important to use project (or group) leaders to do the following tasks:

- Identify goals, products, and outcomes.
- Establish and coordinate timelines.
- Identify skill sets and other resources needed, such as content experts.
- Identify strengths and weakness of participants.
- Schedule and track the components of a project.
- Monitor progress and process concerns.
- Negotiate the changes.
- Facilitate delivery of the project requirements and the products.

Gantt and PERT charts are excellent tools for project management. We strongly urge you to use Gantt and PERT charts to identify and avoid conflicts related to allocation of resources (people, money, facilities, etc.) for specific projects and among multiple projects. Resolving conflicts among projects (and deciding which manager or senior vice president to please or put off) is a major headache. Gantt and PERT charts are extremely useful for tracking related costs and testing what-if scenarios related to resource allocation. Problems often result from inadequate allocation of time and resources for completing research; writing and editing; printing and distributing materials; and preparing and practicing presentations. In addition to Gantt or PERT charts, you may choose from a number of computerized project management software products (e.g., Microsoft

Project). One problem, however, with project management software is that learning to use it is often a time-consuming task, and when a team is trying to ramp up a new project, that time is often not available. Managing team projects is becoming more sophisticated due to the number of new options in word processing and project management software packages. It's useful for all managers to look at groupware packages (for example, Lotus Notes, Microsoft Project, Timeline) to determine how to share schedules and documents. It is seldom cost-effective to have your technical staff format documents and presentations. Avoid having highly paid executives or managers doing these tasks. In fact, after your content experts complete their initial drafts, hire a consultant or assign a highly skilled staff member to edit and format the materials.

STEP 3: EVALUATE WRITTEN MATERIALS

In addition to evaluating your process and team members' skills, you will be more successful in developing useful written materials if you have the following:

- An executive summary that can be used to make a decision
- A clear, logical organizational structure
- Visually emphasized key points
- Graphics, tables, and figures that advance your arguments and decrease text
- The substance of your report in body of the report, not in the appendixes
- A good conclusion
- Report(s), handouts, and visuals that are coordinated for your presentation

SUMMARY

If you follow the straightforward steps in this chapter, your written materials will be improved. To save time, develop a presentations based on your materials after you finish your written project. Having a finished document before you start to develop a presentation will lead to coordinated materials and fewer revisions of your presentation.

Note: For detailed information and understanding more, reader may visit this site: http://www.infosys.com/instepweb/

21

Presenting As a Team

Team presentations may derive from written documents or they may be initiated solely as stand-alone projects, without previously written documents as guidelines. Obviously, preparing a presentation from an existing document will give you a head start.

TEAM PRESENTATION WITH WRITTEN DOCUMENTS

If your assignment is to present a written document as a team, you've already tackled the biggest part of the job: And you have probably worked on the layout and design of visuals where appropriate. So the first four steps of the presentation have already been completed. However, as a team, you need to review these steps to make sure everyone is working from the same game plan. Once you have done this, you need to do some very specific work to transform that document into an oral presentation. Some of the issues you need to work through with your team are as follows:

- What material will we select for presentation? A team presenting a report or proposal can rarely cover the entire document in an oral presentation. If you were to assume the audience members would also be reading the document, what are the most significant things that you would select to highlight during the presentation?
- What format will we use to present the material? Sometimes, past experience and/or corporate culture will tell you how to present the material. At some companies, presenters rarely stand in front of a group, but rather sit around a conference table, often with a built-in projection system. In other situations, a presenter would be expected to stand in front of a group that sits in formal rows of chairs. If your team has the option to

choose a delivery style, discuss how you might be most effective. Many excellent presenters feel more comfortable on their feet, since they can move around and put more physical energy into their presentations. Others might find more receptive listeners with a less formal style. Your goal for your team presentation should help to guide you in this decision.

- Who will present this presentation? The temptation for many teams is to select the team member who is the best speaker and nominate that person to do the entire presentation. This is, of course, one option, but it is rarely one that works best. If this is truly a team effort, the whole team should be involved in the preparation of the material, and, unless it's a very large team, all team members should speak during the presentation and/or the question-and-answer session.

  Even though presentation skill levels may vary considerably within your team, the expertise that each individual brings to the project can generally compensate for less-than-perfect delivery skills. Furthermore, demonstrating the commitment of all team members to the presentation can enhance team and message credibility.

Some of our international students and clients have been reluctant to participate in team presentations because they feel their language skills are not good enough for an American audience. We have always encouraged these people to participate fully in their team presentations, usually with excellent results. We have found two interesting things to happen:

- First, most managers and executives today are becoming familiar with Asian, European, and South American dialects because corporate culture in general is becoming so international. Once an audience becomes used to the differences in pronunciation of a speaker, it generally is not a distraction.
- Second, a business audience is there to hear the content of your message. With the exception of speech instructors or consultants, listeners are rarely there to critique a speaker's delivery skills- they want to focus on your message. Unless an individual's skills are so poor as to make him or her unintelligible, international speakers rarely present a problem for business teams.

TEAM PRESENTATION WITHOUT WRITTEN DOCUMENT

Obviously, if you are beginning a presentation from scratch, you will need to do a considerable amount of work in planning the presentation before you get to the aspects of team delivery described in the preceding section. We recommend that you go back to previous chapters and work through the seven steps in the presentation process, from defining your purpose to handling questions and answers. While some of the work may be divided among members of the team, you need to keep all team members informed and involved through each step of this process. This ensures that your presentation can be supported by everyone and that everyone can participate fully.

GENERAL PRESENTATION GUIDELINES FOR A TEAM

Following are the guidelines for presenting as a team:

- Practice the presentation together as a team. While you may be familiar with the material, especially if you are presenting from a team-written document, the team presentation should appear as a unified whole-not as a series of minipresentations. Additionally, practicing team presentations helps you to revisit the content of the presentation for accuracy, as well as to identify any areas of overlap or redundancy. It gives you a chance to make sure your visual aids work well from a mechanical standpoint (e.g., "Can this computer projection system read my PowerPoint disk?") as well as a visual standpoint ("Oops, the fluorescent colours really don't look too professional, do they?"). You can also use rehearsal time to help one another on delivery skills (as in, "Joe, be sure not to block the screen with your body when you show that slide.") and improve overall comfort level within the team.
- Introduce yourself and the members of the team. Unless you can be 100 percent sure that everyone in the room knows each presenter, this step is essential. It will establish some familiarity with the team and enhance your credibility as speakers.
- Use the introduction to preview the content of the presentation and how the team will present it. This preview will give your audience a framework demonstrating how you will proceed, making it easier to follow. The preview could be something as simple as this: "First, I'll be describing some background

information on the project and how we approached our study. Then Joe will described the data we collected and our forecast for the next year. Next, Mary will discuss some of the liabilities of going along with this project. And I'll be back at the end to talk about some of our recommendations."

- Plan clear transitions between speaker segments. Transitions serve as signposts for your listeners so they can follow the presentation more easily. A common team transition is the internal summary, where the speaker might say something like, "Now that I have shown you how the data supports this project, I'll turn this over to Mary, who will discuss some concerns about liabilities."
- Visual aids used in the presentation should all follow the same format. Many speakers today use Microsoft PowerPoint, and if you do, the presentation slides should be done in a consistent template, as a package. We have seen teams where each speaker did his or her own visuals, and the results generally appear unprofessional and uncoordinated. If this is indeed a team presentation, then there needs to be consistency among medium, format, and appearance to help tie the parts of the presentation together.
- All team members should be available for the question-and-answer session at the end of the presentation. In addition to following the guidelines for handling the Q&A, the team members should discuss ahead of time who will handle questions in specific areas. It is helpful to have all team members participate in the Q&A, but they should be neither competing to answer questions nor reluctant to respond to a concern.
- As with individual presentations, the team presentation should not drift lamely to a close at the end of the Q&A. One team member should signal when time is up and offer an appropriate closing comment on behalf of the group.

GUIDELINES FOR SPECIAL-OCCASION PRESENTATIONS

While most managers and executives spend most of their presentation time in informing or persuading audiences and workgroups, there are times when you will be called upon to deliver a special-occasion presentation. These kinds of presentations include:

- Speeches of introduction
- Speeches to pay tribute or to present an award
- Speeches of gratitude or to acknowledge an award
- Eulogies at funerals and memorial services
- Toasts at recognition banquets and weddings

While each of these occasions is different and special in its own right, the general guidelines for all of these presentations are the same.

1. For special-occasion presentations, you should still go through the presentation preparation process. The early steps are the most important-determining your purpose and analyzing your audience. You need to know these things in order to determine what kinds of remarks are appropriate for the occasion and what your audience would like and needs to hear.
2. Your role as the speaker is to focus on two specific tasks: reflecting the tone of the occasion and making a connection with the audience. Your remarks should appropriately reflect the feelings evoked by this occasion (for example, jubilance at a colleague receiving an award for outstanding sales performance, solemnity at the untimely death of a junior executive in a car crash). It is also your job to connect the occasion to the audience, to draw them into the spirit and feeling of the event (for example, an amusing anecdote that reflects how this salesperson achieved her success, a few lines from a poem that the executive kept on the wall of his office for inspiration).
3. Keep your remarks short. Most special-occasion presentations should take not more than 2 to 3 minutes. Most often, you are not the main focus of the occasion, so let your audience appreciate your remarks as a supplement to their overall listening experience.
4. Here are some basic guidelines specific to each type of special-occasion presentation.

Introductions: Avoid the trite, "Here's a person who needs no introduction..." in favour of a well-prepared and thoughtful speech. Be sure to get some background information on the person you will be introducing, and use that information in the most glowing terms. While light humor may be appropriate if your speaker is somewhat humorous or fun-loving, it is inappropriate to make fun at the speaker's expense (unless this is a "roast"). You don't need to give a person's complete history, but outline the points most relevant to the talk, state why the individual is an appropriate speaker for this group, and introduce the speaker's topic or the title of the talk.

Paying Tribute or Presenting an Award: These speeches are very focused. You are there to acknowledge the accomplishments of a colleague and present some recognition of those accomplishments. You should definitely gather information about the person's background as it relates to the recognition he or she is receiving. It is also appropriate to personalize the attributes of the award recipient for your audience, perhaps by relating a personal experience you had with the recipient or an anecdote related to you by a colleague.

Giving Speeches of Gratitude or Accepting an Award: When you are the recipient of an award, you should thank the group or organization sponsoring the award. You should also thank coworkers, team members, or even family and friends in some cases-those who supported you and made it possible for you to win this recognition. You can also go beyond the standard thank-you remarks and share a lesson, an idea, or a brief inspirational story that will connect you with the audience.

Eulogies at Funerals and Memorial Services: These can be among the most difficult presentations to plan. There is generally so much emotion involved in the death of a close family member or coworker that many find it difficult to speak publicly at these times. If you have accepted the invitation to deliver a eulogy, you should spend much of your preparation time reflecting on the deceased and on the words that would bring most comfort to your audience. The eulogy is one place where the sincere speaker is always appreciated, even if the delivery is not the most articulate or polished.

Toasts at Recognition Banquets and Weddings: Most of us have been to enough banquets and weddings to see examples of how not to deliver a toast. Some of the most common don'ts are as follows:

Don't deliver a toast with no preparation: "Here's to Harry and his lovely bride what's-her-name..."

Don't deliver a toast after you have been partaking of the open bar with great enthusiasm.

Don't deliver a toast with private jokes and references that only a few people in the audience can understand. A corollary: Don't deliver a toast in a language only a few attendees can understand.

You should consider it an honour to be asked to deliver a toast, and you should put as much thought and preparation into this speech as you would other presentations.

Once again, you should think of the person or couple who is receiving the toast and the reason for the occasion. Consider the special attributes of the people involved and consider the audience and what they want to hear.

Special-occasion presentations are often not a routine part of an executive's speaking calendar, and yet they can be significant in your personal and professional development. With the proper preparation and practice, they can become a natural part of your professional portfolio.

SUMMARY

While many business professionals are still responsible for giving individual presentations, the team presentation is becoming an important part of today's corporate culture. Understanding how to approach the task of working as a team and working through the steps in a systematic way will ensure the success of your writing and presentation projects. And while many busy executives find the time involved in teamwork can be demanding, the results of the effort are generally thought to be worthwhile.

Note: For further detailed understanding, reader can visit www.members.microsoft.com

22

International Business Communication

Customers, shareholders and the media soon lose faith and interest in a company that projects a confused or inconsistent image. Which is why every business strives to present itself to the outside world as a united entity with a single set of beliefs. The trouble is, the bigger a company becomes and the more national borders it crosses, the harder it has to work to preserve the united front that is so vital for its continued prosperity and growth.

For many multinationals, developing everything centrally - such as the messages they want to broadcast and the brands they market - is the only answer. This central norm or party line is then disseminated throughout the organization. This can work if the people at HQ are prepared to adapt the party line to suit local needs - and if their colleagues in the foreign subsidiaries are willing to keep an open mind. All too often, however, everyone assumes that their own attitudes and beliefs are universal, right and normal. It doesn't even occur to them (the idea doesn't enter their heads) that people from other cultures might see things from a different perspective.

It's only natural to regard your own view of the world as the right one; and to believe that anyone who doesn't share it is strange or unusual. But there is, in fact, no such thing as normal. Which is why party lines can cause so much misunderstanding, conflict and stress - both for the people who are trying to disseminate them, and for those on the receiving end. The people at head office jump to the conclusion that the subsidiaries are being deliberately difficult or obstructive; and the people in the subsidiaries automatically assume that their foreign bosses are arrogant megalomaniacs who simply don't care about the problems their directives are causing.

Clearly, there will be times when your international colleagues are indeed being arrogant or deliberately obstructive. Often, however, they will simply be trying to do what they genuinely believe is best for all concerned. It's easy to jump to negative conclusions about other people's motives if you measure what they do and say against your own cultural norms. But not everyone looks at mission statements and corporate initiatives in the same way as you do; another culture's working rhythm may be very different from yours; and your natural communication style could well seem brusque - or excessively indirect.

MISSION STATEMENTS

At its most general and abstract, the party line is often declared publicly in the company's mission statement. As you might expect, however, not everyone interprets it in the spirit that head office intends:

When three large engineering firms - two from Northern Europe and one from the USA - merged, they invested a lot of time, money and resources in producing the new company's mission statement. At a seminar designed to bring middle management together, the top directors invited delegates to explain how they had disseminated the new core values among their local employees.

Each of the Northern European countries involved (Germany, Finland, Sweden) had presented the statement to their teams at a series of short meetings held during working hours. The teams had discussed the core values briefly, and that was that. To their embarrassment, very few of the managers on the seminar could remember them in any detail.

The Americans, on the other hand, had met regularly, outside working hours, to discuss what the new core values meant to each of them. They had translated the abstract aims into concrete guidelines which they could relate to their daily work. Everyone carried a copy of the statement with them at all times and consulted it regularly.

Each side had been very surprised to hear the other's approach. After a few beers in the bar at the end of the day, one of the Finns leaned across to one of the Americans and said: 'What you said about the mission statement - that was just bullshit for the board, wasn't it?' The American was astonished. 'No', he replied, 'why would you think that?'

It was unthinkable to the Northern Europeans that the Americans could take the mission statement so seriously. Equally, it was unthinkable to the Americans that the Northern Europeans could dismiss it so casually. Of course, the two firms had only recently merged; so these two groups of managers were bound to be influenced by their premerger ways of doing things. But that doesn't explain why there was such a wide gap in their perceptions on this particular issue. It's highly likely that cultural conditioning was also playing a major part here.

Mission statements often say things like:

We believe that the Zoetica brand must represent a positive force in the world. We will act in line with this belief at all times.

or

We believe in the integrity of human beings, and will treat our employees, customers and anyone coming into contact with Zoetica accordingly, inviting all to be part of the Zoetica family.

These are, of course, honourable sentiments that no reasonable person could object to it. The trouble is, they're framed in very abstract terms. But then, of course, they have to be. A company can't make a concrete and meaningful statement of intent and values without losing flexibility. And flexibility is what businesses need if they are to survive. They've got to be able to take decisions quickly, and act upon them right away. They've got to retain absolute flexibility to diversify, downsize, grow, and so on.

The American managers in this situation would probably lean towards the theoretical end of the scale. They took the abstract values expressed in the mission statement very seriously and were prepared to spend their own time discussing them in depth. They had no trouble translating these general theories into concrete, practical guidelines that they could relate to their daily work. If you like using abstract concepts to solve problems, you may well respond to your company's mission statement as positively as these American managers did.

If, on the other hand, you lean towards the empirical end of the scale, you may find it hard to take this kind of abstract theorizing seriously. The Northern European managers discussed the core values briefly and dismissed them as meaningless. What possible relevance could they have to their daily working lives? We recently asked the German HR manager of a large multinational how she felt about her company's mission statement.

She said: 'Well, we have to have one. It's good PR. But, in practical terms, it isn't worth the paper it's written on.' The Northern Europeans would probably share her view. That's why they couldn't even remember in any detail what the mission statement said; and why the Finnish manager was convinced that the American managers' explanation of how they had disseminated the new core values was just bullshit for the board.

We're not trying to suggest that all Americans would lean to the left of this scale; nor that all Northern Europeans would fall to the right. But there's no denying that attitudes towards mission statements do vary considerably from culture to culture. And when an empiricist meets a theorist there's considerable scope for misunderstanding. The idea that anyone could take all this abstract theorizing seriously didn't even occur to the Finn, while his American colleague was astonished to learn that there were people in the world who didn't take it seriously.

CORPORATE INITIATIVES

There's no way you can undo a lifetime's conditioning. But, when you're working internationally, you have to make some effort to understand and adapt to the way different cultures seeing things. If not, the company's attempts to project a consistent and harmonious external image will lead to considerable conflict and disharmony internally:

The American HQ of an international chemicals company produced a'quality chart' which included the following statement: 'Each and every one of us will take responsibility for the quality of our products.' They sent the chart to the Indian, French, Chinese and UK subsidiaries, and asked them to sign it and send it back.

The Indians, the British and the Germans complied with the request straight away. But nothing was received from the French. Several e-mails were sent to chase it up, but these remained unanswered. Finally Edward (the American boss) called Viv (the French manager) to find out what was going on. The conversation went something like this:

Edward: I'm calling about the quality initiative. Did you get the chart we sent you on the last month?

Viv: Yes.

Edward: Oh you did get it. Good. So could you get everyone to sign it and send it back to us? By the end of the week, if you can.

Viv: Well, no, I'm afraid of I can't. I've discussed it with the team and none of us is willing to sign it.

Edward: Not willing? Why not?

Viv: We don't agree with it.

Edward: You don't agree with it?

Viv: No.

Edward: But it isn't a question of agreement. All we're asking for is your buy-in.

Viv: Yes and, as I said, we can't do that. It's not logical. Production and quality control are in Belgium.

Edward: What difference does that make?

Viv: How can we be held responsible for something we don't have no control over?

Edward: No one's going to hold you responsible. We're just asking you to pledge yourselves to the global quality initiative.

Viv: But the document clearly says: 'Each and every one of us will take responsibility for the quality of our products.' We can't possibly sign it.

Edward and Viv discussed this question again several times, without success. Viv and his colleagues refused to be moved and their relations with the Americans grew increasingly hostile. Eventually (finally), the Indian country manager intervened and suggested a compromise that both sides were prepared to accept. Viv and his colleagues would sign the quality chart if Edward gave them a written assurance that they wouldn't be held contractually responsible for the aims that were stated in it. Edward thought this was obvious and couldn't understand why they were being so difficult. The French were equally perplexed: 'In that case', they said, 'the chart is meaningless. So why are you issuing it?' Relations between the two countries remained hostile for some time.

There's no doubt in our minds that Viv and his team were as committed to product quality as Edward was. So why did this corporate initiative lead to so much misunderstanding, frustration and resentment? At first sight, the whole situation is very puzzling. The USA is famous for having an extremely litigious culture: few business deals are finalized until the lawyers have drawn up a detailed contract that covers every possible eventuality; people will usually only sign a contract if they're confident it is watertight (comprehensive and impossible to misinterpret); they will tend to consult it regularly throughout the life of the deal; and partners who fail to honour their contractual obligations will most probably be threatened with legal action. So why didn't Edward understand Viv's reluctance to sign the quality chart?

Well, most of the international business people we work with would agree that the USA also has a forward-looking culture where taking an optimistic, upbeat approach is the norm; and where people feel fairly comfortable stating their beliefs, hopes and intentions both openly and publicly. When Edward was at school, for example, he and his classmates started each day by putting their hands on their hearts and pledging their allegiance to the flag of the United States of America. For him, publicly confirming your commitment to quality is similar to pledging yourself to 'one Nation under God, indivisible, with liberty and justice for all'. So it simply didn't occur to him that anyone would regard the chart as a legal contract.

That's why he was so puzzled when Viv said he didn't agree with it: 'But it isn't a question of agreement. All we're asking for is your buyin'; and 'We're just asking you to pledge yourselves to the global quality initiative.' But, of course, Viv isn't a native English speaker and the subtle vocabulary differences meant nothing to him. As far as he was concerned, Edward was asking him to agree to take responsibility for something he had no control over.

Viv tried very hard to explain his position, but Edward didn't seem to register what he was saying. As soon as they received the quality chart, the analytical French immediately tested the logic of what they were being asked to do. The wording was clear and unambiguous: 'Each and every one of us will take responsibility for the quality of our products.' Clearly, then, if they signed the chart, it would have the force of a contract. If there were a quality failure, they would be in breach of that contract. And Viv and his team could end up losing their jobs as a result. But quality control was in India. So there was no way they could be held responsible. Straight Cartesian logic. And because Edward refused to acknowledge their argument, the French immediately suspected his motives. This was obviously a devious head office plot to cut headcount without making redundancy payments.

Edward's approach to the quality chart was far more intuitive. Committing yourself to product quality was unquestionably the right thing to do. Sure, production and quality control were in India. So obviously the French couldn't be held responsible for problems that arose there. But that didn't prevent them from monitoring customer satisfaction and responding fast and efficiently to complaints. And that was all he was expecting from them to do.

The two colleagues are viewing the situation from opposite poles. And both of them assume that their own view is the norm. As a result, it doesn't even occur to Edward that there is any other way of interpreting the quality chart than his own. Similarly, it doesn't occur to Viv that the Americans would bother to issue such a chart - and ask him to sign it - if they didn't intend to enforce it.

So what could Edward have done to avoid all this unnecessary drama and ill-will? Well, have another look at the way he handled the phone call to Viv. He didn't make much effort to find out what Luc's concerns really were, did he? He was far too busy concentrating on himself and what he wanted. As a result, he pushed all the wrong buttons.

According to American anthropologist, Edward T Hall:

The essence of effective cross-cultural communication is more to do with releasing the right responses than with sending the right messages.

In other words, you've got to push the right buttons. To do that, you need to keep an open mind, try to put yourself in the other person's position, ask perceptive questions, and really listen to what they are saying and how they sound when they say it.

If Edward had done that, the conversation might have gone very differently:

Edward: I'm calling about the quality chart. Did you have a chance to discuss it with your people yet?

Viv: Oh yes. We've discussed it in a great detail.

Edward: OK ... And how do they feel about it?

Viv: It has caused quite a few problems here.

Edward: Really? What kind of problems?

Viv: Well, we don't see how you can hold us responsible for something we have no control over.

Edward: But ...You know, Viv, I think there's some kind of misunderstanding here. Tell me, what is it you feel you have no control over?

Viv: It's not a feeling. It's a fact. The Indians are responsible for product quality, not us. So we can't sign a contract that says: 'Each and every one of us will take responsibility for the quality of our products.' It isn't logical.

Edward: You mean your people see this chart as a contract?

Viv: Yes, of course. Isn't what it is?

Edward: Well, no. There's nothing legally binding about it. It's just an acknowledgement of what I hope we all believe in anyway.

Viv: So why do you want us to sign it?

Edward: Well, it's what we normally do here in the States. It's a kind of symbolic gesture. You know, a way of pledging support for the company's aims ... But I guess you guys thought there was some kind of sinister motive behind it. Right?

Viv: Well, yes. People are very worried about losing their jobs, through no fault of their own.

Edward: Losing their jobs? Well, Viv, let me assure you that simply isn't going to happen ... Listen, how about if I come over and ...

In the first conversation, Edward concentrated on his own agenda. This time he focuses on Viv and his team. Did you have a chance to discuss it with your people yet? elicits a much more useful response than Could you get everyone to sign it and send it back to us? From what Viv says, and probably his tone of voice too, Edward realizes that something is wrong.

So he follows up with a couple of open questions (ones that start with who, what, why, where, how etc) to try to find out more: And how do they feel about it?; What kind of problems?

Luc's reply surprises him and, at first, he instinctively wants to contradict him - But no one's going to hold you responsible - as he did in the first conversation. Fortunately, he stops himself just in time, acknowledges that there may be a problem of interpretation here, and probes further with another open question: You know, Viv, I think there's some kind of misunderstanding here. Tell me, what is it you feel you have no control over?

In his reply, Viv refers to the quality chart as a contract. This is just what Edward needs to know. But he's very surprised. So he asks a closed question (one that invites a Yes or No answer) to check that he has understood Viv correctly: You mean your people see this chart as a contract?

Because Edward shows interest and a willingness to understand, Viv is beginning to feel less defensive and now asks a closed question himself: Isn't that what it is? Negative questions - Don't you like it? Can't you do it? Didn't it work? - are often used to show surprise. So what Viv means is: I'm very surprised to hear you say it isn't a contract, because that's certainly what we all think it is.

When Edward reassures Viv that there's nothing legally binding the chart, Viv asks: So why do you want us to sign it? Edward could get angry or exasperated here. But he didn't. He tries to work out where Viv is coming from. This is a key moment in the conversation. It's when the fog really starts to clear for Edward. He explains what the chart means to him as clearly as he can. And then asks a closed question to check that he has correctly deduced how the French feel about it: But I guess you guys thought there was some kind of sinister motive behind it. Right?

Once Edward knows that Viv and his colleagues are worried about losing their jobs, he realizes how much damage this seemingly uncontroversial corporate initiative has done to morale in the French subsidiary. And he can start trying to put things right.

Implementing corporate initiatives is never easy. And there's no magic formula that will guarantee success. But because Edward was prepared to question his own assumptions and make an effort to put himself in Luc's position, the two colleagues now understand one another much better than they did before. And there's a good chance that harmonious relations between head office and subsidiary will be re-established.

WORKING RHYTHMS

The need to present a united front makes life difficult for everyone: the people like Edward who are trying to disseminate a party line; and the people like Viv who are on the receiving end. If you work as a subsidiary, you may end up regarding the people from HQ as corporate seagulls: they fly in, shit on you from on high, and fly out again. It's hard enough to resist HQ diktats when they are imposed from afar. It's even harder when the corporate seagull builds a nest in your workplace. This is exactly what happened at the Irish production facility of a Swiss multinational:

When the head of the Irish plant resigned, the Swiss decided to parachute in one of their own people. The new Swiss manager's office was very close to the canteen and he was disturbed to note that the Irish employees were going for frequent and extensive coffee breaks. Instead of taking just one 10-minute break in the morning, and one in the afternoon - which was what happened in Switzerland - they seemed to go to the canteen whenever they felt like it, and to sit around laughing and joking with their friends for 20 minutes at a time.

The new Swiss manager decided that something needed done to stop all this time-wasting. So he made a unilateral decision to install coffee-making equipment in every department; and announced that, in future, the canteen would only open at lunchtime.

The Irish employees were not impressed by the new party line. Far from wasting time under the old regime, they had spent their coffee breaks sharing departmental news, asking advice and generally networking. When this forum was closed down, interdepartmental communication started to deteriorate. It wasn't long before productivity at this, the company's biggest plant, started to go down.

The Swiss, of course, are famous for their attachment to time. If you're from a monochronic culture too, you may find that you instinctively do one thing after another, in a linear fashion. And you probably feel that unless each moment is used for a specific purpose, it's wasted. If, on the other hand, you lean towards the polychronic end of the scale, you may well regard time as more elastic, and you could even find yourself doing several things at the same time.

The Swiss Germans (and, indeed, the Germans) tend to plan their time in a very structured and ordered way - and, in this respect, it's their master. As they work out Die Tagesordnung (the Daily Order), they will often allot a specific and precise amount of time to each task - including their coffee breaks. So, while the Irish are not particularly polychronic, they certainly lie to the right of the Swiss on this scale. As a result, their working rhythms are more relaxed. That's not to say they get less done than their Swiss counterparts. They just use their time in a different way. And that was probably the underlying cause of this misunderstanding.

But there is a puzzling aspect to that situation. Business hierarchies in both Ireland and Switzerland are relatively flat. And in flat business cultures, bosses tend to consult widely, and subordinates generally feel free to express their own views openly. So why didn't that happen here? Why did the new Swiss manager behave in such an autocratic way? And why didn't his Irish subordinates challenge his decision?

Maybe the Swiss guy simply panicked. It's not easy taking over as manager of a foreign subsidiary. When you first arrive in a new country, everything strikes you as very strange. The way people do things seems completely different from the way you do things back home. You can feel so dislocated that you fail to notice the many similarities between where you are and where you come from. What the Swiss manager saw was an undisciplined workforce who seemed to be blatantly (very openly) taking advantage of the management's goodwill. While he wouldn't have behaved so autocratically back home, he probably felt it was the only thing he could do under these strange new circumstances.

But what about the Irish? Why didn't someone try to explain how useful the coffee breaks were? Well, perhaps they regarded HQ with suspicion and resentment. People in an overseas subsidiary often do, as you will know if you have ever worked in one. Complaints like: They have no idea of the conditions over here, and they're not interested; all they ever do is to issue instructions; they never ask us what we think are common place. If this was how the Irish employees felt, they would have seen no point in challenging the new boss's diktat. He was just doing what people from HQ had always done: shitting on them from on high.

The lack of communication in this situation had a damaging effect on all concerned: the Irish, the Swiss boss and the company. The moral to this tale is clear: if you are being asked to accept a party line that conflicts with the way you do things in your part of the world, don't just assume that HQ's motives are sinister, or that the sole purpose of the directive is to make your life difficult. Try to find out what's behind it. Ask some questions, and listen to the answers with an open mind. However hard it may be, try for a moment to put yourself in HQ's position. And then, as clearly, calmly and objectively as you can, explain your own position and the impact that the new directive will have on you and your colleagues. This won't guarantee success, of course. But it has to be more productive than keeping quiet and letting things go from bad to worse.

COMMUNICATION STYLES

It's a problem that confronts the corporate seagull all too often. You arrive at the subsidiary, issue your instructions, and then later discover that everyone has completely ignored them:

A large French company decided to introduce a new global purchasing policy. In the past, subsidiaries had sourced many of their supplies locally. In future, they would be expected, where possible, to use the same suppliers as the French parent company. The French purchasing manager visited the subsidiaries one by one to explain the new arrangements. In each case, she presented the facts and figures very clearly, and made sure the purchasing teams were fully aware of the considerable cost savings that would be achieved.

She had been expecting a certain amount of resistance from the Japanese subsidiary. So she wasn't particularly worried by the surprised glances and exhalations of breath that greeted her announcement. Nor was she unduly concerned when one of the team said: 'This will be very difficult for us.' After all, they were bound to say that. The important thing was that no one rejected the proposals. She went home feeling relatively pleased with herself.

Six months later, she was surprised to see that the Japanese had not made one single purchase through the new system. She phoned Tokyo to find out what was going on. Her colleague said: 'We made it very clear, when you were here, that we couldn't use this new system.'

It's hard to believe that they were all present at the same meeting, isn't it? So what went wrong here? Were the Japanese being deliberately two-faced and underhand? Did they think that if they pretended to go along with the joint purchasing project to the French woman's face, they could simply ignore it once she had gone back to France? And what about the French woman? Was she being arrogant, or just incredibly obtuse? Well, in all probability, both sides were behaving in what they regarded as a professional and straightforward way. The Japanese thought they had made it perfectly clear that they couldn't source their supplies from France. The French woman was equally sure that the Japanese had no serious objections to the new arrangements. It was just that their understanding of the word difficulty was not the same.

The Japanese impulse is to preserve harmony. For them, consensus rather than open disagreement or conflict is the name of the game, and their communication style reflects this. In this cultural context the word difficult, accompanied by eye and body language that every other Japanese would immediately understand, means: This is absolutely out of the question. There's no way we can agree to this. But when the French say difficult they mean: Not easy, but not impossible either.

Have a look at this pair of statements:

Edward T Hall - the American anthropologist - divides the cultures of the world into low context and high context communicators and a number of cross-cultural experts have adopted his terminology. Low context communicators tend to express themselves in explicit, concrete, unequivocal terms. There's little cultural baggage or 'context' attached to the words they use and you can usually take what they say at face value. If you are, for example, American, German, Scandinavian, or Finnish, you will probably fall into this category. And when you're doing business with other low context communicators, you will probably find their communication style reassuringly straightforward and comprehensible.

High context communicators, on the other hand, tend to communicate more implicitly. They expect you to be able to interpret what they mean from your knowledge of the cultural values that lie behind the words, what they're actually talking about at the time, their tone of voice and, of course, their eye and body language. Interestingly enough, both the French and the Japanese would fall well to the right of this scale. But, of course, their cultural contexts are different. You may be a high context communicator yourself, but that won't necessarily make it any easier for you to understand a high context communicator from another culture.

It didn't occur to the French woman to check that she had understood her Japanese colleagues correctly. As a result, a lot of time and money was wasted and HQ's relations with their subsidiary were disrupted. If you're a corporate seagull, you can learn from her mistake. Don't take what the people in your subsidiaries say at face value. Watch their body language too. If she had taken notice of those surprised glances and exhalations of breath, the French woman would have realized that her Japanese colleagues weren't prepared to accept her proposals.

Making sure you understand exactly what the other person means won't guarantee for the success. But at least you will know where you stand. In this situation, for example, the Japanese refused to accept the party line because they were worried about quality. If this concern had been brought out into the open, the French could have discussed it objectively with their Japanese partners, and tried to find ways to overcome their concerns.

In Working rhythms above, we looked at the difficulties a Swiss manager had when he banned coffee breaks in an Irish plant. The Irish clearly have a more relaxed attitude towards time than the Swiss. And this may well have been one of the reasons the problem arose. But the misunderstanding was most probably compounded by their differing communication styles.

The Swiss are low context communicators. In fact, they generally fall to the far left of this scale, while the Irish (along with the British) would lean towards the right. And when a low context communicator meets a higher context communicator, they may both misinterpret the signals the other is sending. When the Swiss guy gave the Irish the bad news about coffee breaks, he probably did so in very frank and explicit terms:

You are wasting too much time laughing and joking in the canteen when you should be working at your desks. This is completely unacceptable. In future, the canteen will only open at lunchtime. You will find coffee-making equipment in your department. Please remember that you are allowed one 10- minute break in the morning and one in the afternoon.

But this approach would have come across to the Irish as autocratic, impersonal and cold. When we described this situation to Padraig, an Irish business acquaintance of ours from Dublin, he told us that if the Irish have bad news to give, they generally try to sugar the pill (sweeten the medicine). He illustrated his point by telling us the following joke:

A tourist approaches two fellows and ask them how far it is to the town. The first fellow assures the tourist it's just two miles down the road. The tourist thanks them and goes off. The second fellow then says: 'Why did you tell him that? Don't you know that it's four miles?' To which his friend replies: 'Sure I know, but the poor man is walking.'

SUMMARY

There are those who will tell you that a process called 'globalization' is creating an environment in which companies can operate virtually anywhere in the world under identical conditions to those back home. This is a dangerous belief. It leads people to assume that there is one norm, one way of doing things, one way of looking at the world. As the people in the situations we have looked at discovered, there is no such thing as normal.

When you are doing business with different cultures, there will almost certainly be a gap, of one kind or another, between your perceptions and theirs. This need not stop you from presenting a united front. The key to success is to acknowledge that there is a gap and to make genuine attempts to bridge it. The most successful cross- cultural communicators are those who are instinctively able to push the right buttons. To follow their example, you need to:

- Keep an open mind;
- Try to put yourself in the other person's position;
- Ask carefully chosen open questions (ones that start with who, what, why, where, how etc);
- Really listen to the answers;
- Ask closed questions (ones that invite a Yes or No answer) to check that any deductions you've made are correct.

Note: Reader can find more information on www.novozymes.com

23

Knowing Your Place

The multinational organization may need to present a united front to the outside world, but in your daily business life you will be dealing with people who work behind that front. A dynamic company is similar to that of a healthy political system. If it is to move forward and grow, it needs internal diversity and competition. But, of course, these diverse individuals and competing groups have to be kept on track; synergies have to be achieved; consensus has to be reached; and final decisions have to be taken. Which is why virtually every organization - no matter how small - has some kind of chain of command.

Most companies make an attempt to show how the hierarchy works by producing an organization chart. This will certainly show you who is nominally responsible for what, and who reports to whom. But how accurately does it reflect what happens on a day-to-day basis? Does it tell you, for example, what the balance of power really is, how far an individual's authority or responsibilities extend, how much autonomy the people involved enjoy? Can you see, at a glance, how decisions are made, where an individual's loyalties lie, who you should talk to when you want to get things done and, most importantly, how your colleagues expect to be treated? In our experience, it does not.

Of course, a lot will depend on how big your company is and on how well you get on with the various personalities involved. But the way you instinctively answer these questions will also be strongly influenced by where you come from. When you're on home territory, you will usually know your place, and be aware of how your colleagues expect you to behave. But once you step outside your own corporate and national culture, you may well find people whose expectations and behaviour are very different from yours. Once again, there's no such thing as normal. Attitudes towards handling the hierarchy, taking responsibility, monitoring performance and getting colleagues to play ball (cooperate) will vary from culture to culture.

HANDLING THE HIERARCHY

How you handle the hierarchy will, to some extent, depend on that where you would place yourself on the following scale:

Flat Hierarchy										**Vertical Hierarchy**
Leaders should share power										Leaders should hold power
50	40	30	20	10	0	10	20	30	40	50

If you expect your leaders to hold rather than share their power, you may well believe that when 5A wants to get 5B to do some urgent work for her, she should refer to her boss (4A). He can then ask 4B to tell his reportee (5B) what to do. If, on the other hand, you believe your leaders should share power, you would probably expect 5A to speak directly to 5B without getting the bosses involved.

When you're working with people whose culture seems to have little in common with yours, there's always a temptation to believe that they will do everything differently. But, as some of our clients have discovered, that's not always the case: being the same.

Since 2000, Canning has been working with the Renault-Nissan alliance - first in France and later in Tokyo - to promote greate cultural understanding between French and Japanese colleagues. In the early days of the alliance, a group of French engineers in Paris told their Canning cross-cultural consultant that it wasn't always easy to get their counterparts in Tokyo to play ball.

The Japanese would listen carefully to what the French said and assure them that action would be taken; but then weeks would go by and nothing would happen. A little later, during a cross-cultural seminar in Tokyo, a group of Japanese engineers made very similar comments about their French counterparts. In both cases, our colleagues responded by sketching this diagram on the flipchart:

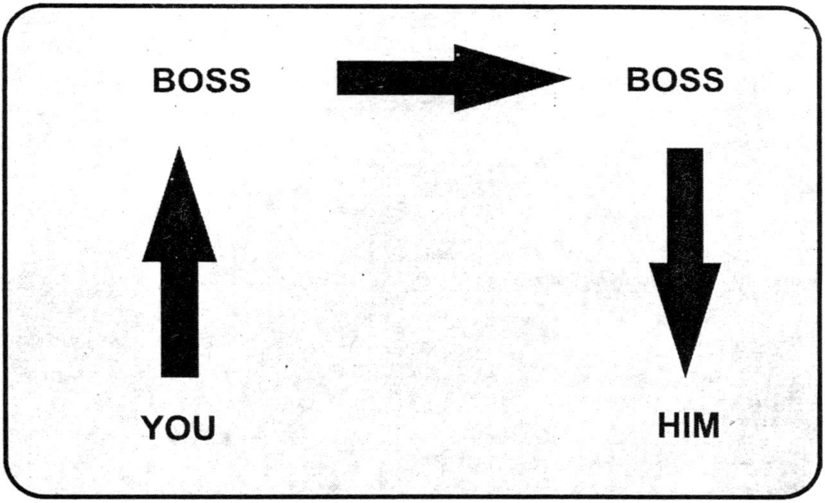

Both the French and the Japanese engineers immediately understood what they meant. 'Ask your boss to speak to 5B's boss.' In other words, handle the hierarchy in just the same way as you do at home. Both groups were equally astonished: 'Why on earth didn't we think of that?'

Well because, in many respects, the culture gap between the French and the Japanese is fairly wide. So it didn't occur to them that, on this particular issue, their approach would be so similar. But the French and the Japanese - along with people from Spain, Latin America, South-East Asia, India and Africa - would lean towards the right of the hierarchy scale. And if you want to get a counterpart to play ball, you will probably need to get the bosses involved.

If this French automotive giant had entered into a joint venture with some fellow Europeans - Brits, Scandinavians or Dutch, for example - it probably wouldn't have occurred to them that their new partners' approach to the hierarchy would be any different from that of theirs. But, in fact, business hierarchies in the UK, Northern Europe and the USA tend to be fairly flat; people are used to being able to challenge their leaders' decisions; they expect their boss to consult them, not issue diktats from on high; and if their colleagues are being troublesome, they tend to tackle them directly. If one of our colleagues in Canning UK played the hierarchy in the French or Japanese way, your two British writers would probably be pretty upset. That's because, in flatter business cultures, running to the boss every time there's a problem is often seen as bad form (socially unacceptable). And colleagues who make a habit of it are likely to become very unpopular.

Of course, France and Japan are not the most vertical cultures you will come across. There are some countries - like India, for example - whose social conditioning places them at the very far right of the hierarchical scale. A British business acquaintance of ours has vivid memories of the first time he went to India on business; he was running his own company in the UK at the time:

I was in the middle of a meeting with a customer in Bombay (now called Mumbai) when my fountain pen fell off the table and on to the floor. As I bent down to pick it up my customer shouted 'Peon!' at the top of his voice. I was so startled, I left my pen where it was. A few seconds later, a small barefoot man rushed in and my customer started to reprimand him: 'My guest's pen has fallen to the floor. Why were you not here to pick it up? This is inexcusable. This must not happen again.' Much to my embarrassment, the poor man apologized profusely to me, picked the pen up, and placed it carefully on the table. When I tried to thank him, my customer said: 'There's no need to thank him. That is his job.' I felt very uncomfortable indeed. In the UK, a boss who spoke to his subordinates in this way would probably be taken to an industrial tribunal.

That's not to say the UK has the flattest business hierarchies you will find. Danny Pooley, an English colleague of ours, has equally vivid memories of the first time he went to Sweden in the early 1980s to run a presentation skills course:

When the participants had finished preparing their first short presentation, I said: 'Now I'd like each of you in turn to stand up in front of the group and deliver your speech. Sven, why don't you go first.' Sven smiled, turned to the rest of the group and said something to them in Swedish. I didn't understand a word of the short discussion that followed. But I noticed that everyone contributed to it. Sven then turned to me, smiled again and said: 'Actually, Danny, if you don't mind, we think Erik should go first.' At the coffee break, I asked the group why they had been so surprised when I asked Sven to go first. They explained that, in Sweden, teachers were always careful of not to do anything that would make them appear authoritarian. They realized that who should make the first presentation was a relatively minor issue, and reassured me that my innocent suggestion had not in any way offended them. 'But, you see,' said Sven, 'I couldn't possibly go first without consulting the others. I would have felt that I was pushing myself forward. And that kind of behaviour is totally unacceptable in Sweden.'

Swedish business hierarchies tend to be very flat indeed. In fact you could probably spend several days in a Swedish office without even realizing who the boss is. That's because, as Sven explained to Danny, they are taught from an early age that no one should believe they are better, or worth more, than anyone else. Along with the Danes and Norwegians, the Swedes tend to feel instinctively suspicious of people who push themselves forward, behave extravagantly, or boast about their achievements. Modesty is the personal quality that these three cultures seem to value above all else; and if you describe one of them as 'ordinary', they will probably regard it as a compliment.

Some say that this attitude has its roots in the social code that evolved among Scandinavia's small rural communities. The peasant farmers soon discovered that, if they were to survive the harsh conditions of the late Middle Ages, they needed to work closely together as a group. Such inter- dependence required considerable equality of effort and reward: a farmer who thought he was better than his neighbours might believe he deserved more than them in return for less effort. Such behaviour would destabilize the community and clearly could not be tolerated. The Lutheran reformation, which was embraced by the Nordic countries in the course of the 16th century, must also have played a significant part in reinforcing the Scandinavians' dislike of immodesty, extravagance and self-glorification.

Whatever its origins be, this centuries-old, unwritten social code still exerts a strong influence throughout Scandinavia. In 1933, Danish author Aksel Sandemose published a novel ('A Fugitive Crosses His Tracks') condemning the negative impact these values could have. Unable to accept the petty jealousies and narrow-minded behaviour he perceived in his own home town, he moved to Norway. Jante - the imaginary small Danish port featured in the novel - is based on the home town Sandemose left. Jante's small-minded, envious inhabitants live by their own 'TenCommandments' - or 'Jante Law' - which include: 'You shall not think you are special; You shall not think you are cleverer than us;' and 'You shall not think you can teach us anything.' Few young Scandinavians today actually read this novel; but most will refer to the 'Jante Law' to explain their culture. As our colleague Danny discovered during the presentations seminar in Sweden, people still think it's wrong for individuals to push themselves forward; and many ex-pat Swedes will claim that it was the 'Jante Law' mentality that drove them out of the country.

Australia is an another country that celebrates its horizontal power relationships. The Australians have their own version of the 'Jante Law'. They call it 'Tall Poppy Syndrome': because it's the tallest poppy in a field that will be picked first, it's the tallest poppy that is the most vulnerable.

In other words, if you behave in an immodest or egotistical way, you will be punished. The Australians have little respect for people who think too highly of themselves. And, in 1999, they showed quite clearly that such feeling runs very deep:

John Howard, who was Prime Minister at that time, wrote a new introduction to the constitution. In that he included the following statement:

'We value excellence.'

It's a line that many countries include in the preamble to their constitution, and that most companies expect to see in their mission statement. But it provoked enormous controversy among the Australians. The media immediately attacked Howard for trying to undermine the 'Tall Poppy Syndrome'. And when, during a radio interview, he said: 'If there's one thing we need to get rid of in this country, it's our Tall Poppy Syndrome', then the nation was outraged. In a subsequent referendum, the vast majority voted against the new preamble to the constitution.

To the Australians, striving for individual excellence implied pushing yourself forward or trying to be better than others. And in a society where everyone is equal, such behaviour can be perceived as very divisive. So if you're managing a team of Scandinavians or Australians, remember the 'Jante Law' and 'Tall Poppy Syndrome'. Don't play the heavy-handed (autocratic) boss; consult them frequently; and don't be surprised or offended if they challenge your decisions.

Many Indians, on the other hand, have a strong sense of their place in the order of things. The Hindu caste system has resulted in a rigid social stratification which still exists, despite Mahatma Ghandi's best attempts to break it down. And, as the Bhagavad Gita dictates, they believe that it's better to do the job you are born to do than the job another was born to do - even if you might do it better. The vertical hierarchy is naturally determined and should not be interfered with or ignored. In the mid- 1990s, Canning ran a series of courses for the Steel Authority of India. We worked with a number of different groups of Indian managers. But in each case our brief was the same: to help the participants create and deliver more dynamic and effective in-house training programmes. During the early part of each course, their Canning trainer asked each group a vital question: 'What, in your view, is a manager's job?' All the managers in every group - men and women alike - gave exactly the same unequivocal reply: 'A manager's job is to tell people what to do.' And they were genuinely surprised, and even a little puzzled, when our colleagues suggested that there might be other ways of defining the role. So if you're managing an Indian team, don't expect them to challenge your decisions, or come to you with suggestions of how you might do things better. As far as they're concerned, you're the boss and making decisions is your job.

Most societies believe that there's a natural, almost predetermined, order of some kind and their business cultures reflect this. And when someone from outside interferes with this natural order, people don't like it at all:

When Pieter, a South African businessman, secured a major infrastructural contract in Japan, he put together a team of locals from his firm's Japanese subsidiary to run the project. One night he had dinner with the team leader, Yoshinori, a man in his late forties. The conversation was rather flat, so Pieter started talking about the performance of their respective teams in the recent rugby World Cup. 'Your team was absolute rubbish', he said jokingly, and then waited for Yoshinori to make some similar comment about the South Africans. But Yoshinori just nodded and smiled. So Pieter tried again: 'But I guess that's normal. I mean, you don't exactly top the league in any sport, do you?' Again Yoshinori nodded and smiled. Pieter was very frustrated: all red-blooded males enjoy making fun of other people's sporting ability; so why didn't this guy start mocking the South African team? As he left the restaurant, Pieter was beginning to wonder whether Yoshinori was the right kind of person to run such an important project.

The next morning, he decided to replace Yoshinori with Takashi - an MBA graduate (in his late twenties) from a top American university - who was working in a junior position on the project. Pieter spoke first to Yoshinori and then to Takashi. The former reacted to the news that he was to be moved sideways with extremely good grace. But, when Takashi was told about his promotion, he seemed both dejected and terrified. Over dinner that evening, a puzzled Pieter discussed Takashi's reaction with a close Japanese friend. His friend nodded wisely and said: 'The nail that sticks up will be hammered down.' Pieter frowned: 'What does that mean?' he asked. 'It's a well-known Japanese proverb', his friend replied. He then went on to explain that moving someone ofTakashi's age so quickly and so publicly up the hierarchy was rather unusual. Takashi was probably embarrassed to be pushed forward in this way. And he would find it hard to earn the respect of his team members. Next day, much to Takashi's relief, Pieter reinstated Yoshinori as a team leader.

The fact is, Pieter knew all about vertical business cultures - after all, he came from one. And he assumed that, like his South African compatriots, Takashi would be flattered and encouraged by such an early and rapid promotion. But it isn't enough to know whether a culture is flat or vertical. You also need to know where it falls on the following scale:

Individualist My first duty should be to myself									**Group-oriented** My first duty should be to the group I belong to	
50	40	30	20	10	0	10	20	30	40	50

If you come from an individualist culture like Pieter, you probably think it is perfectly normal to reward an individual's effort with public praise or rapid promotion. But, as his experience with Takashi shows, people from group-oriented cultures will often feel embarrassed to be treated differently from their peers.

TAKING RESPONSIBILITY

Where you fall on the individualist-group-oriented scale that will also affect your attitude towards taking responsibility.

A colleague of ours was running a workshop for a Japanese multinational. The participants were all Europeans, apart from one Japanese guy called Makoto. The Europeans were given the opportunity to ask Makoto about aspects of Japanese culture that puzzled them. And Makoto was encouraged to ask similar questions of the Europeans. His first question was very revealing:

Why do Europeans always make excuses? And why do they never really say sorry?

The Europeans were incensed, and demanded examples. Makoto said:

If a European misses a deadline, he will say it was because there were bugs in the software, or a delivery didn't arrive. If a European has made a mistake, he will say it was because he was given the wrong figures, or the database hadn't been updated. These are excuses. Why doesn't he simply apologize? Or better, why doesn't he try and solve the problem?

The Europeans all argued that it was important to explain why a task had not been completed. From Makoto's perspective, however, they were simply blaming someone else for their own shortcomings. In Japan, people's responsibilities traditionally tended to be far less compartmentalized than in Europe. And, even today, the idea that this is not my job is still relatively uncommon. It doesn't matter what your job description is, if something needs to be done, you deal with it yourself.

Several years ago, Canning ran a course for some senior European managers from a well-known Japanese multinational. At the beginning of the course, one of the company's top Japanese managers gave the Europeans a 40-minute presentation explaining how he expected them to behave. Below is the text of one of the many slides he showed:

Take every responsibility. Never give excuses. Think only how to recover the situation. Forget your job description. Communicate with your manager frequently. You can perform your manager's job. Your manager's job is possibly your job. Do not refuse it because of job description. You are responsible for your subordinate's job. The job itself must be the aim of life.

Though many younger Japanese would say that this is now an old-fashioned view, most accept that it still exists inside their companies. And few Japanese would disagree with what this senior manager said next:

If somebody conflicts with others and is excluded from the community, he cannot survive. No prima donnas (people, like the main woman singer in an opera, who demand special treatment) are welcomed. No strong leaders are needed.

While leadership courses are now very popular in Japan, the Japanese definition of leadership is not the same as it is in, the UK and the USA. A colleague of ours recently asked two British managers to draw a very simple picture that would illustrate their idea of leadership; he then asked two Japanese managers to do exactly the same thing. The results were fascinating. On both pictures, the leader was slightly larger than the team members. But the British had placed the leader to the far left of the page - in other words, in front of the team - and he or she seemed to be waving the team members forward, like an officer with a group of soldiers. The Japanese, on the other hand, had placed the leader to the far right of the page - in other words, behind the team - and he or she seemed to be trying to persuade the team members to 'go forward' to the left of the page. When asked to explain their pictures, the British managers talked about leading by example, arguing their case well and motivating by both praising and criticizing. The Japanese managers, on the other hand, talked much more about coaching and teaching.

In a vertical culture that is also individualistic, you might expect the boss to make the decision and hand it down. But Japan is a vertical and group- oriented culture where harmony must be preserved at all costs, and individualist leaders are not appreciated. Strategic or policy decisions are only taken after a long and thorough consultation process called nemawashi.

During nemawashi, managers have a series of one-to-one consultations with their team members. These often take the form of informal chats in the bar or spontaneous conversations in the office. People discuss as many options as they can think of. All the implications are examined - time, money, people - and all the subtleties of face-saving are considered. So, by the time the decision is finally taken, everyone's commitment to it is guaranteed.

The way in which more individualist cultures challenge and disagree with one another at so-called decision-making meetings comes as a terrible shock to most Japanese business people. For them, a round table meeting is just a formality - to rubber stamp (ratify) what has already been agreed during nemawashi.

MONITORING PERFORMANCE

How far do you expect your subordinates to work on their own initiative? And how closely do you expect your boss to monitor what you're doing? Again, expectations can vary considerably from place to place, as Renate - a German businesswoman - found when she first moved to Paris to work for a French company:

I had always assumed that most Western Europeans worked in a similar way. However, a few weeks into my first project, my new boss saw me in the corridor, drew me to one side and said: 'I don't seem to have received any weekly reports from you.' I replied: 'Well, no. There's nothing of any interest to tell you yet. I'm still doing the groundwork.' My boss gave a typical French shrug and said: 'But that's no reason not to write a report.

This project is my responsibility and I need to have regular feedback from every member of the team. It's normal.' I was astonished. When you're running a project in Germany, your boss just lets you get on with it. You only write a report when you've got something to say.

A French boss isn't just the manager. He is le responsable. Everyone in the department and everything that happens there is his responsibility.

Which is why Renate's boss felt the need to keep a close eye on what she was doing. This was very different from Germany where, as Renate said, your boss usually leaves you to work on your own initiative. And it took her some time to get used to the French way of doing things.

Her boss's attitude towards responsibility also affects the way he inter- acts with his fellow managers. He will often be far too busy running his own little empire to concern himself with what's happening in another department.

Whereas German, British and American managers usually feel fairly free to pop into one another's offices to offer suggestions or proposals, Renate's boss would probably regard such behaviour as unwelcome interference.

As we saw in earlier, culture clashes can be particularly painful when HQ tries to impose its own cultural norm on all its subsidiaries. Many of the new management techniques that companies adopt to try to create some kind of competitive advantage originate in the USA. After all, it was the Americans who turned management into an academic discipline. But the USA, for the most part, has an individualist and hierarchically flat business culture. And some of their management strategies are simply not suited to more vertical societies:

Sarah worked at the London HQ of an American investment bank. As HR manager, it was her job to ensure the smooth introduction of a new 360- degree appraisal system in all of the bank's offices in Europe. But the Spanish were refusing to play ball. While their managing director and HR manager both claimed to be in favour of the system, the other senior managers were not.

Sarah had sent numerous e-mails to the two men suggesting ways in which the system could be implemented, and had also spoken to each of them several times on the phone. But their message was always the same: 'We agree that the system should be introduced. But our senior managers are resisting it strongly. They say it simply isn't right for Spain.'

A 360-degree appraisal means that your performance is assessed not only by people above you in the hierarchy, but also by your peers and subordinates. In some cases, the company's clients are also invited to submit their comments. So why did the Spanish find this idea so hard to accept? Well, Spain certainly has a strongly vertical business culture. But that's not the only reason. It's also because Spain would probably fall to the right of the following scale:

Acquired Status	**Given Status**
People should be judged on what they do, not who they are.	Other factors – such as family, class, nationality, race, education, age, sex, religion – should also be taken into account.
50 40 30 20 10 0	10 20 30 40 50

The idea that businesses should run along meritocratic lines is becoming more and more common. So, at first sight, you may well place yourself to the left of this scale. But is that how you really feel, or how you believe you ought to feel? If you're a man in your fifties, for example, how happy would you be to report to a woman in her early thirties? If you're from a fairly mono-cultural society, how would you feel if your company appointed a foreigner as CEO? If you and most of your colleagues went to one of the top universities, how would you all react if the company recruited someone with no academic qualifications as your new boss? This scale probably raises more issues than you think.

In given status cultures, how fast you work your way up the hierarchy doesn't just depend on how well you perform. For the Spanish bankers in the situation above, age and gender were also important factors. In Spain, and other vertical/given status cultures, managers often treat their subordinates in a paternalistic way. They look after them much as a father looks after his son. Not only will they champion them for promotion or the best jobs, and protect them from intra-company disputes, but they will also advise them on personal matters.

How could a subordinate possibly be asked to anonymously appraise such a father figure's performance? The idea was completely incompatible with the Spanish managers' cultural values. Their attitude was quite clear: I look after my employees and if they're not happy they will find some way to tell me - just as a son would tell his father. And what about their daughters, you may well ask? Well, unfortunately for Sarah, many older Spanish men - brought up in the highly conservative years when Franco ruled the country - still find it difficult to accept that women should be treated as equals in the workplace. That's not to say a woman manager can't do business perfectly effectively in Spain or other paternalistic cultures. But she needs to be aware of their values and expectations and, if necessary, adapt her behaviour accordingly.

In Spain and Italy, it's not unusual for a senior manager who has retired to retain considerable influence over the staff in the company he used to work for. Many Northern Europeans are amazed when they discover this. Sarah was no exception. But when, during an informal chat, the Spanish bank's HR manager suggested that their retired CEO might be able to help her, she was perfectly willing to try playing the game the Spanish way. She called the influential 65-year-old and arranged to have dinner with him. Naturally, she let him choose the restaurant and pay the bill. And, even though it went against her feminist principles, she dressed and behaved to charm. During the meal, they discussed a wide range of different topics, but none of them related directly to business. It wasn't until the coffee and liqueurs arrived that the retired CEO briefly mentioned the 360-degree appraisal system. He knew all about the problems Sarah had been having. But he was sure the managers would accept the idea once he had spoken to them. A few months later, Sarah was able to report that the Madrid office had agreed to implement the system provided it was modified to suit local conditions.

The highly sophisticated former CEO had obviously been able to suggest a compromise that would satisfy Head Office and suit the Spanish managers' leadership style. If Sarah had not been prepared to seek his help, the outcome might have been very different. Trying to impose an appraisal system that was designed by an acquired status culture on managers from a given status society can cause serious long-term damage to the relationship between head office and subsidiary - as a number of our clients have discovered.

GETTING PEOPLE TO PLAY BALL

Wherever you come from, you're unlikely to have much respect for colleagues who embarrass you in front of others, betray the confidence, fail to do their fair share of the work, or break their word in some way. When they come from the same culture as you, at least you have some common point of reference to measure their behaviour against. Even so, it's not always easy to work out what their motives really are, or how far you can trust them. And when they're from a different country, it can be harder.

An international company appointed two high potentials - Jean-Claude from France, and Toshiyuki from Japan - to run a project together. They seemed to get on well and, after much discussion, worked out a modus operandi and detailed schedule that they and their teams could agree to. Toshiyuki went back to Japan and submitted a written report, outlining what they had agreed, to his boss. A few days later, Jean-Claude had a brilliant idea. There was a much more efficient way of handling the project. Jean-Claude discussed the proposal with his French team and, before long, everyone concluded that it would work perfectly. A delighted Jean-Claude submitted a revised schedule to the French steering committee. He then called Toshiyuki:

Jean-Claude: I've got some good news. We've managed to streamline the schedule. I'll mail you the details in a minute. But, basically, it means we'll be able to complete the project a couple of months earlier than we thought.

Toshiyuki: You've changed the schedule?

Jean-Claude: Yes. I suddenly realized that if we split the teams into eight work groups rather than six, we could overlap phases two and three, and run phases five and six concurrently.

Toshiyuki: You've changed the work groups?

Jean-Claude: Yes. It's so simple, I don't know why we didn't think of it before.

Toshiyuki: I see... But I told my boss that the schedule had been finalized. I've already submitted my report.

Jean-Claude: Well, just tell him we've had a better idea.

Toshiyuki: It will be very difficult for me to explain the changes to him.

Jean-Claude: I don't see why. I mean, changing the schedule is going to save a lot of time and money. I'm sure he'll be very pleased.

The project went ahead, but the relationship between the Japanese and French teams deteriorated fast. Toshiyuki and his colleagues weren't openly obstructive, but Jean-Claude got the impression that they were somehow 'working to rule'. Before long, the project had fallen seriously behind schedule, and the group's HR director was asked to find out what was going wrong. He asked Canning to run a series of cross-cultural workshops.

The first one was with the Japanese team. Our consultant asked them to role play a few typical business situations and then discussed the various cultural issues that arose. During one of these discussions, Toshiyuki suddenly exploded: 'But that's just typical of the French! They never stick to an agreement. Jean-Claude changed the project schedule after I had submitted it to my boss. This is totally unacceptable. How can I ever trust him again?'

Jean-Claude certainly didn't cynically set out to renege on (break) an agreement, or to make Toshi's life difficult. Quite the reverse. His motives were honourable, and he behaved in a way that his French colleagues would probably regard as normal. But his actions caused fatal damage to the relationship. Once again, it's all down to differing cultural values. From the Cartesian Jean-Claude's perspective, if there was a more efficient way of scheduling the project, then it was only logical to adopt it. For him, taking decisions like this is part of a manager's job. It's normal. How could anyone possibly object?

Well Toshiyuki could, and did. From his perspective, a final agreement had been made. In his consensus culture, managers don't behave in such an individualist way. Strategic and policy decisions are only taken after long and careful nemawashi. And if you want to change them, there has to be another equally thorough consultation process. When he changed the plans, Jean-Claude had not only broken his word. He had also put his Japanese colleague in an embarrassing position. Toshiyuki would lose face with his Japanese boss and probably with his Japanese team members too.

Jean-Claude was completely unaware of how Toshiyuki felt. He had learnt a lot about Japanese culture before joining the project team, and always made a genuine effort to see things from his Japanese colleagues' perspective. But, on this occasion and on this issue, it didn't even occur to him that there was a culture gap. Unfortunately, it's occasions like this that can present the greatest danger to the international business person. Stereotypes can be reinforced and relationships irrevocably damaged without your even realizing it.

Clearly, learning how your international colleagues expect to be treated and why they take time. And no matter how carefully you do your homework, there will always be some cultural gaps which you're not aware of. So does that mean misunderstandings of this sort are inevitable? Well, no. Not necessarily. It's all a question of how sensitively you communicate.

In fact, it was the way Jean-Claude communicated with Toshiyuki that caused most of the trouble. You see, he focused exclusively on himself and his own agenda. And, in our experience, that is a major cause of misunderstanding and conflict, not only between people from different cultures, but between compatriots too. No matter where you go in the world, you'll come across some people who seem to be natural born communicators. Everyone respects them; everyone likes dealing with them; everyone seems to be prepared to make an extra effort to help them. You can probably think of one or two of your own colleagues who fit this description. And if you analyse what these successful communicators do, you'll find that they have one thing in common. Whoever they're dealing with, whatever they're talking about, however committed they are to their own views and values, they show empathy with the other person.

Empathy is the ability to put yourself in someone else's position; to see the world through their eyes; to imagine how they're feeling. Clearly, the more you have in common with someone, the easier it is to show empathy. But if you want to be a successful international communicator, you have to develop the ability to empathize with everyone - even people who seem to look at the world from a completely different perspective.

The trouble is, if you try to work out how these people show empathy, you end up with a list of practices that are so obvious they sound simplistic: keep an open mind; find out how people feel and what kind of pressures they're under; imagine why they find it hard to accept your proposals; ask questions and really listen to the answers. All of this is plain common sense, isn't it? Well yes, it is. Unfortunately, when you're under stress, common sense can be one of the first things that goes out of the window. If you've got a deadline to meet and your colleagues are refusing to play ball with you, empathizing with their problems is often the last thing you feel like doing. And if, like Jean-Claude, you're totally convinced that your proposal is the right one, it may not even occur to you that Toshiyuki sees things differently. But if only Jean-Claude had used a bit of imagination, if only he had kept an open mind, asked a few perceptive questions, and really listened to what Toshiyuki was saying, the conversation might have gone very differently:

Jean-Claude: I'm calling about the project schedule. I think I've found a way to save some time - and quite a bit of money too.

Toshiyuki: Really? How?

Jean-Claude: Well, if we split the teams into eight work groups rather than six, we could overlap phases two and three, and run phases five and six concurrently.

Toshiyuki: Oh! Very big changes.

Jean-Claude: Yes. It would mean reworking the whole schedule, I'm afraid of that. How would you feel about that?

Toshiyuki: It would be very difficult for me.

Jean-Claude: Difficult? In what way?

Toshiyuki: I told my boss that the schedule had been finalized. I've already submitted a formal report.

Jean-Claude: Right... What would he say if you told him we wanted to change it?

Toshiyuki: It would be very difficult for me. Everyone has been consulted. The final schedule has been agreed.

Jean-Claude: I see... Well, obviously I don't want to cause you any problems with your boss. But as I said, it would save the company a lot of time and money... What would you and your colleagues usually do in this kind of situation?

This time, Jean-Claude had tried to put himself in Toshiyuki's position before he picked up the phone. Of course, given his cultural conditioning, it would have been hard for him to anticipate his Japanese colleague's reluctance to tell the boss that everything was going to be changed. But it didn't take much imagination or common sense to realize that Toshiyuki might not be very enthusiastic about revising the schedule. After all, they had just spent several weeks planning the project together. So Jean-Claude was careful not to present his colleague with a unilateral decision. Instead, he:

- Made a tentative proposal

  I think I've found a way to save some time - and quite a bit of money too.

- Acknowledged that it would involve making substantial changes

  It would mean reworking the whole schedule, I'm afraid of.

- Asked a series of open questions and really listened to the answers

  How would you feel about that?

  Difficult? In what way?

  What would he say if you told him we wanted to change it?

  What would you and your colleagues usually do in this kind of situation?

By showing empathy, Jean-Claude kept all the channels of communication open. As a result, at least he stands some chance of getting the schedule changed without damaging the relationship. Maybe Toshiyuki will suggest that Jean-Claude should ask the French boss to speak to the Japanese boss. Maybe he'll have some other proposal. Or perhaps he'll simply repeat that the whole situation is very difficult for him. It's anyone's guess. But whatever he does say, Jean-Claude is in a much stronger position than he was at the end of the first conversation. He now knows that this is a delicate issue, and that he and his French colleagues will have to think very carefully about the best way to handle that issue.

It's hardly a rocket science, isn't? And yet a lot of the international business people we work with (rocket scientists included) are frequently astonished at how much difference asking a few questions and showing a bit of empathy can make:

An Italian lawyer, who had just started a one-year secondment with a law firm in London, came to Canning for a few days' one-to-one training. When James, her trainer, asked how she was getting on with her British colleagues, she said that she was finding it very difficult to make friends: 'I try to be friendly and converse with them, but they are very cold; very closed. It's always the same. After a few minutes, they find some excuse to bring the conversation to an end.'

James was rather puzzled and suggested that they role play one of these conversations. The Italian woman agreed, and started talking... about herself. Ten minutes later, she was still talking. And she would probably have gone on a lot longer if James hadn't interrupted her. 'Why', he asked 'didn't you try to find out something about me?' The Italian woman said: 'In Italy, when you want to show that you are open and friendly, you do it by telling people a lot about yourself.' James explained that the reverse was true in the UK: 'If you want to make friends with your colleagues here, you need to show interest in them. And that means asking questions.' The Italian woman looked doubtful, but agreed to try to follow his advice when she got back to her office. A few weeks later, she called James: 'You were right. Asking questions has really broken the ice. I've now made friends with several of the women in the office. And the other day they invited me to join them for dinner.'

It isn't only countries that have their own way of looking at the world, and their own way of doing things. Different professional groups have their own 'culture' too. It's a question of whom or what you identify with. An American medical doctor, for example, may feel she has more in common with a doctor from Syria than she does with the administrators in her own hospital. Inside every company there are always certain groups or individuals who seem to look at things from completely opposing perspectives:

Financial control: You're obviously going to cut your direct costs. Otherwise there's no way you're going to meet the profit target.

Profit centre: Quite frankly I'm not even prepared to discuss my direct costs until you can justify the HQ charges we had to pay last year.

Financial control: It's simple enough. Untracked costs have to be paid for by the profit centres. They're allocated on the basis of headcount, office space and the volume of tracked costs. How else can we work it out?

Profit centre: Good question. How else could we work it out? And, more to the point, what steps are you taking to bring your own costs down?

It's a familiar situation, isn't it? These two colleagues come from the same national and corporate culture. They know their place in the hierarchy, who's responsible for what and how people expect to be treated. But there's still a 'culture' gap between them. The financial controller is one of the cops (policemen); one of the people - accountants, auditors, compliance officers, quality control executives, HR managers even - whose job it is to make sure that everyone follows the rules, and that overall corporate objectives are achieved. The profit centre manager, on the other hand, is one of the risk-takers - the people who go out into the market and bring back the business that pays everyone's salary. Clearly, both groups perform a vital role. The company couldn't survive without either of them. But the nature of their jobs means that they often find it hard to identify with each other.

The trouble is, they're never going to bridge this 'culture' gap if each of them persists in focusing exclusively on himself and his own agenda. Take the financial controller, for example. He went to the meeting with a specific message to deliver: You've got to meet the profitability target. And to do that, you'll have to cut your direct costs. Which may be perfectly true. But the profit centre manager went to the meeting with an equally specific and clear message to deliver: The HQ charges we had to pay last year were unacceptably high. If you don't reduce your costs, we won't meet our profitability target. They started out on opposite sides and they stayed there.

Of course, there may not be any alternative to cutting the profit centre's direct costs and, if so, the financial controller will need to show steel (be firm); at the same time, the profit centre manager will certainly want to communicate his dissatisfaction with the HQ charging system and demand adjustments to it. But that doesn't mean the conversation has to turn into a battle. Instead of starting off with: You're obviously going to have to cut your direct costs. Otherwise there's no way you're going to meet the profit target the financial controller could have:

- Asked an open question - one that starts with who, what, why, where, how;
- Really listened to the answer;
- Acknowledged the profit centre manager's difficulties and shown genuine empathy with him;
- Probed the profit centre manager's attitude to cutting his direct costs with a closed question - one that invites a Yes or No answer;
- Answered his concerns calmly and reasonably.

If he had, the conversation might have gone very in a different way.

Financial control: How do you feel about the new profitability target?(open question).

Profit centre: I don't think we stand any chance of achieving it, to be honest. I mean, we're still trying to build up the market.

Financial control: Yes, I can see that it's going to be much harder for you than for the more established units. (empathy) But your headcount is quite high in relation to turnover. Do you see any scope for cuts there? (closed question)

Profit centre: To be honest, laying off a couple of people isn't going to cause more difference. My major problem is the HQ charge. It accounted for nearly 30 per cent of our total operating costs last year. I mean, that can't be right, can it?

Financial control: Well, I'm sure we've only charged for the services you used. But 30 per cent is very high, I agree. (answer) Why don't we go through the figures together and see if we can work out where...

This approach won't guarantee success. But at least the two colleagues are listening to each other. At least they are trying to understand one another's point of view. And that has to be better for the relationship than talking at each other from behind well-established battle lines.

SUMMARY

Once you step outside from your own corporate and national culture, you'll find people whose attitudes towards power and authority are very different from that of your own. And if you measure the way they behave against your norms, you could end up misinterpreting their motives: a Brit would probably suspect his French colleagues of duplicity if they went behind his back to the boss; a French responsable might think his German subordinate was trying to cover something up if she failed to report back to him regularly; and a Japanese manager might think his European counterpart was being a prima donna if he made a policy change without consultation.

The modern business world is complex, diverse and stressful. And there's no panacea that will magically cure all these communication problems. But if you try to show a bit of genuine empathy you'll find that, at least, it can be an effective painkiller. So remember:

- Ask plenty of open questions - ones that start with who, what, why, where, how;
- Really listen to the answers;
- Probe for more information by asking closed questions - ones that invite a Yes or No answer;
- Acknowledge the other person's position;
- Answer their concerns calmly and reasonably.

Note: For indepth and detailed knowledge, readers can visit www.pepsico.com

24

Knowing the Limits

It's easy to see why you need to try to adapt to the way your international partners interpret the party line or handle the hierarchy. But what can you do when you come up against beliefs or practices which seem to go against everything that you believe to be right?

People who cynically set out to break the law, or behave in a way that they know is morally reprehensible existing in all the cultures.

When an accountant in a subsidiary presented the annual report she had prepared, the parent company CFO said: 'You'll have to rework these figures. The bottom line is four million below the number we want.' 'Reworking' the figures to produce the bottom line the CFO wanted would have meant deliberately disobeying accountancy conventions and breaking the law. So the accountant refused. Several weeks later, the company made her redundant. As she didn't want to get involved in a lengthy and possibly career-damaging court case, she decided not to take any further action.

A sales manager was sent by his company to an emerging market country to negotiate an important contract. On the first evening, his hosts took him out to dinner and kept refilling his glass with wine and liquor. The sales manager got very drunk. So much so, that when he was invited to spend the night with one of the four beautiful girls who had suddenly appeared on the scene, he acted completely out of character and accepted the offer. Next morning, his hosts presented him with the contract and asked him to sign it. 'But we haven't negotiated the terms,' said the sales manager. 'Yes we have,' said his hosts. 'The negotiation took place last night. Don't you remember?' When he still refused to sign, his hosts started to threaten him. After an extremely uncomfortable half hour, the sales manager eventually managed to leave without signing anything. When he got back home, he overcame his embarrassment and told his bosses exactly what had happened. He then phoned the prospective partners and arranged to meet them on neutral territory to negotiate the deal. He went to the next meeting with two colleagues and, this time, none of them drank anything stronger than mineral water.

By anyone's standards, presumably even by their own, the CFO and the 'negotiators' in these two situations were doing the wrong thing. In deciding how best to deal with them, all our two business people could do was follow their own conscience.

The accountant refused to break the law; on the other hand, she wasn't prepared to take the company to court for fear of damaging her long-term career prospects. The sales manager was stupid to get drunk, and even stupider to accept the offer of sexual favours. But he followed his conscience once he had sobered up (was no longer drunk) - even though telling his bosses what had happened must have been embarrassing, and could even have lost him his job.

Though there's plenty of malpractice in the world, there's plenty of honourable conduct too. The advice below is as relevant today as it has ever been:

Exercise caution in your business affairs, for the world is full of trickery. But let not this blind you to what virtue there is; many persons strive for high ideals, and everywhere life is full of heroism.

On home ground, you will have a pretty good idea of what you should or shouldn't do; and you will usually be able to distinguish between those who are resorting to trickery (being deliberately dishonest) and those who are trying to be virtuous. But when you're dealing with people from different cultures, it's not always easy to work out whether they're over- stepping the limits of what their society regards as acceptable behaviour or not. That's because no two cultures draw the line between what is right and what is wrong in exactly the same place.

Some may believe that rules, regulations and the laws of the land should be followed to the letter (literally), whatever the circumstances; while for others, there are situations where bending the rules, or finding ways round complex and seemingly senseless legislation, is perfectly acceptable. What one person regards as a gift, another may see as a bribe. One culture's idea of fair competition may be perceived elsewhere as sharp practice. Your attempts to be discreet may be interpreted by some as dishonesty.

Rules, Regulations and the Laws

Where do you stand on bending the rules?

Whether you believe rules should be followed to the letter, or interpreted according to the circumstances, you will find that not everyone shares your view:

Fixed Truth								**Relative Truth**		
There are clear rights and wrongs.								What is right or wrong depends on the circumstances.		
50	**40**	**30**	**20**	**10**	**0**	**10**	**20**	**30**	**40**	**50**

Thomas, a Swiss businessman who had just moved to Italy, needed some legal advice. Gianni, an Italian friend, gave him the name of a good lawyer in a reputable firm. 'He's not a partner,' said Gianni, 'but he's very competent, and he won't overcharge you.' Though the firm's hourly rate was, in fact, fairly high, Thomas was very impressed with the young Italian who welcomed him into his office the following day, and decided to engage his services.

The matter was quickly resolved and Thomas asked the lawyer what the final bill was, and how soon he would receive it. The lawyer said: 'Well, that depends on how do you want to pay; and, of course, on whether do you require an invoice.' Thomas looked puzzled. 'It's up to you, to decide,' the Italian added. 'But a cash payment would save you quite a lot of money.' Thomas had heard that plumbers, electricians and even hairdressers in Italy sometimes asked for cash to avoid paying value added tax. But he couldn't believe that a firm of lawyers would be prepared to break the law in this way. His response was instinctive: 'I'd like an official invoice, please.'

When he left the lawyer's office, he called Gianni and told him what had happened. His friend was rather surprised: 'But why did you do that?' he asked. 'You could have saved yourself some money, and helped the lawyer to supplement his income. Non-partners don't earn very much, you know.' It was only then that Thomas realized that the lawyer would have kept the money for himself. 'But that's completely illegal,' he said. 'Well, technically, I suppose it is,' replied Gianni. 'But everyone does it. I mean, what harm does it do?'

Thomas clearly comes from a fixed truth culture where rules are supposed to be followed by the letter, whatever the circumstances. People from North America, Australia, and northern Europe tend to lean this way. Gianni, on the other hand, comes from a relative truth culture where the circumstances dictate the way you behave.

He gives his loyalty to his family and the people he is close to rather than to a set of abstract rules. People from much of South/South-East/ East Asia, Africa and around the Mediterranean tend to lean this way. And when someone from a fixed truth culture comes up against someone from a relative truth culture, they may well have trouble interpreting one another's motives.

Before Thomas jumps to the conclusion that Gianni and his lawyer friend are law-breakers and cheats who have no moral code, he should pause for a moment and ask himself what lies behind their attitudes and behaviour. Similarly, Gianni should ask himself what makes Thomas react in what seems, to him, such a rigid and unimaginative way.

Where Thomas comes from, people tend to have faith in the State. Switzerland is famous for actively involving all of its citizens in the democratic and lawmaking process. Honest, upstanding citizens who have faith in the way their society is governed, and who believe their judicial system is transparent and fair, tend to regard obeying the laws of their land as a moral duty. The limits are very clearly defined: for example, paying taxes is right; evading them is wrong.

Gianni, on the other hand, has little faith in the State. Indeed, he has developed a fairly cynical attitude towards it. You only have to look at the lamentable performance of successive Italian governments to understand why? And the legislation they have produced is so complex, and the bureaucracy so labyrinthine, that Gianni would find it difficult to follow laws and procedures to the letter even if he tried. So he's a pragmatist. He has to be. If he weren't, the excessive regulation he lives with would paralyze him. What his lawyer friend suggested is certainly illegal. But to Gianni's mind, it is not immoral.

The fact that he sees nothing particularly wrong with breaking certain laws does not mean that he has no moral code. Far from it. In his personal relationships he demonstrates a very high level of loyalty and integrity. He genuinely wanted to help both his Swiss friend to save some money and his lawyer friend to supplement his income. The partners of the law firm earn a huge salaries. So where's the harm in redirecting a little of their income to a more deserving cause? It's quite possible, in any case, that the partners are aware of what their more junior colleagues are doing, and have pragmatically chosen to ignore it.

No one can expect Thomas to do something that he regards as morally wrong. But, equally, he will find it hard to do business successfully in a relative truth culture like Italy if he immediately jumps to the conclusion that Gianni and his lawyer friend have no moral values. And when Gianni does business with people from a fixed truth culture, he may well have to modify his highly pragmatic approach. If not, there's a danger it will undermine his business partners' confidence in his integrity.

Whatever kind of moral dilemma you're confronted with, the golden rule is to try to evaluate the situation as calmly and objectively as possible:

When a large German company set up a plant in China, they sent Klaus- an experienced manager in one of their home plants - over there to run it. One Sunday, a couple of years later, Klaus was doing some work on a report for HQ when he realized he had left a disk he needed in his office at the plant. He decided to go and pick it up. As he was about to leave, he heard noises coming from the factory. No one worked on a Sunday, so he thought he had better investigate. He could hardly believe his eyes: one of the production teams was running a line. What they were doing was obviously 'unofficial', but Klaus was careful not to over- react He simply shouted a warm greeting to Mr. Li (the foreman), said he needed to see him on Monday morning, and then discreetly left for home.

Next day, Mr. Li told him the truth: 'We were just trying to earn a little extra income,' he said. 'really, am very sorry. But we were only using the line; we bought in all our own materials from outside.' Klaus knew that Mr. Li was very well connected with local politicians. So, again, he was careful not to overreact. He simply explained that the machines had a specific 'MTBF' (Mean Time Between Failure) and that they were depreciated on that basis. Mr. Li thought for a moment and then made a suggestion that would get round the problem: he and his team could pay the company a hire charge for the use of the line.

Though this was highly irregular, Klaus decided to accept his proposal. The result was a very motivated workforce and a very cooperative Mr. Li. Unfortunately, the 'income' had to be recorded in the accounts, and it wasn't long before German HQ asked Klaus for clarification. Klaus tried to explain the reason for his decision and the benefits it had produced; but the CFO refused to listen and insisted that Klaus put a stop to the unofficial production immediately.

Two weeks later, the local safety standards officer paid a surprise visit to Klaus's plant. He produced questionable evidence which they were in breach of certain safety regulations and closed the plant down. It remained closed for six weeks. When it reopened, the workforce never regained their previous levels of effort and motivation.

Who do you sympathize with here? The entrepreneurial, but seemingly underhand, Mr. Li? The highly principled, but obviously dogmatic, CFO? Or the pragmatic, but possibly too liberal, Klaus? Once again, your answer will depend, to some extent, on how comfortable you personally feel about bending the rules to suit the circumstances.

The Chinese production team certainly knew that what they were doing was highly irregular. But, did they think it was immoral or illegal? Did they think anyone was going to suffer, or lose out, as a result of their actions? If you consider the norms and attitudes that are prevalent in Chinese society, you would probably conclude that they did not. But what about the safety standards officer? Was it Mr. Li who called him in? And if he did, what were his motives? No one could know for sure, but Mr. Li was very well connected with local politicians.

The fact is, despite recent changes in the fast-developing areas around cities like Shanghai and Guangzhou, China is still largely a vertical, paternalistic, Confucian society. Mr. Li's business world is intensely personal and closely linked to the extended circle of family and friends who are at the centre of his universe. The members of this extended circle have a strong sense of duty and responsibility towards one another and will always be willing to exchange favours. And Mr. Li will try to achieve as much as possible through these guanxi (connections). In all his dealings with them, he will practise the art of mian zi (giving face). That means doing everything to make the other person feel good, and trying to avoid conflict wherever possible.

Personal connections are also used to obtain goods and services that would not be available in the open market. Zhou houmen (literally, going through the back door) has become common practice. This unofficial economy far exceeds most black markets in its size and complexity. Recent history has taught Mr. Li to live for today; to take a practical, short-term approach. So it's not surprising that he and the production team were quick to seize this golden opportunity to make a bit of extra money on the side. After all, what harm would it do? They weren't stealing the company's materials. And once they knew about the MTBF problem, they were perfectly willing to pay for the use of the line.

So was Klaus right to legitimize this unofficial operation? That depends on your point of view. From the CFO's perspective, appropriating company property for private use was unquestionably wrong. By giving in to Mr. Li, Klaus may have made his own life easier in the short term. But he had given entirely the wrong signal to the Chinese workforce: here was a manager they could manipulate. In the long term, showing that he was prepared to bend the rules could have disastrous consequences. To us, as Brits, on the other hand, it seems that everyone would gain by Klaus's creative compromise. But then the British tend to have a fairly deregulated mentality; as long as people play fair, who cares for the rules?

Whether Klaus's decision was right or wrong is a matter of opinion. But there's no denying that the way he reacted on that Sunday afternoon, and his behaviour towards Mr. Li the following day, were absolutely right. During his two years in China, Klaus had learnt a lot about the local culture. He knew all about connections, giving face and going through the back door. So he wasn't in the least surprised that Mr. Li had not told him about their unofficial operation. The Chinese team had often withheld information from him in the past.

Indeed, to save face and maintain harmony, they usually said very little about problems or irregularities. Instead, they tried to present him with as positive a picture as possible of what was going on. Klaus knew that to manage his Chinese team effectively he needed to invest plenty of time and effort in getting to know them, and earning their trust. And, perhaps most importantly, he had learnt that if he wanted to gain their cooperation, he needed to modify the frank, direct and explicit communication style that came naturally to him and his German colleagues.

So, on that Sunday afternoon, Klaus was very careful to avoid a direct confrontation with Mr. Li. Of course, he was shocked to see what was going on. But he didn't show it. He remained calm, greeted Mr. Li courteously, and discreetly told him that he needed to see him the following day. The next morning, he maintained a constructive and positive attitude. He didn't pass judgement on Mr. Li's actions. Instead, he patiently told him about the MTBF problem. Given this firm but fair approach, if Klaus had decided to stop the unofficial production there and then, we believe he could have done so without damaging the relationship.

Back home in Germany, Klaus would most probably have taken the same view as the CFO. But he wasn't back home. He was in China managing a team whose attitudes and beliefs were different from his. So he did everything he could to try to bridge the culture gap. If you find yourself in a similar position to Klaus, we recommend that you follow his example:

- Don't overreact or pass hasty judgements;
- Keep an open mind;
- ask yourself why you think what's happening is wrong; and why the people you're dealing with draw the line in a different place;
- Re-examine the situation as objectively as possible;
- Look for ways of resolving it that will be acceptable to both parties' moral values and beliefs;
- Remain calm and constructive at all times.

Having gone through this process, Klaus decided that he could accept Mr. Li's proposal to pay a hire charge for the use of the line without compromising his own, or indeed the company's, moral beliefs. And if the CFO had not withdrawn the privilege, the Chinese workforce would most probably have continued to repay their German boss's flexibility and fairness with continued cooperation and productivity. Of course, if you had been in Klaus's position, you might well have made a different decision. Which is fine. No one can expect you to condone something that you believe to be wrong. Whatever the situation, you have to remain true to yourself.

GIFTS, FAVOURS AND BRIBES

Bending the rules is one thing. But how comfortable do you feel about exchanging gifts and favours with the people you're doing business with? Your answer will, to some extent, depend on where you fall on the given below scale:

Functional	**Personal**
We need to focus on business first and personal relationships later in order to do successful business.	We need to build a personal relationship first in order to do successful business.
50 40 30 20 10 0	10 20 30 40 50

In cultures where business is personal, gift-giving and exchanging favours tend to be commonplace. After all, what better way of developing goodwill and demonstrating your wish to keep the relationship going? The problem is, where do you draw the line between a gift and a bribe? How do you distinguish between reasonable business entertainment and thinly disguised corruption? How do you identify the point at which doing someone a favour becomes sharp practice? Following the many corruption scandals that have been reported in the press in recent years, the world's leading multinational companies are being forced to give these questions some careful thought.

In 2002, Transparency International - the global anti-corruption organization - published a Corruption Perceptions Index (CPI) and a Bribe Payers Index (BPI). The former looks at levels of perceived corruption 'at home' in 102 countries; the latter at the propensity of companies from 21 leading industrial nations to offer bribes 'away from home' in emerging markets. Both polls use the same scoring system which ranges from 10 (no corruption) to 0 (widespread corruption).

As you would expect, levels of corruption 'at home' were, on the whole, perceived to be at their lowest in rich and politically stable democracies, and at their highest in poorer, less developed countries. Finland, Denmark and New Zealand, for example, got the three highest (that's to say 'cleanest') scores; while Bangladesh, Nigeria, Paraguay, Madagascar and Angola got the three lowest (or 'dirtiest') scores. It's worth noting, however, that only 32 of the 102 countries surveyed scored more than 5. And while the USA and the leading member states of the EU fell into this category, the levels of perceived corruption in each of these countries varied considerably:

UK	8.7
USA	7.7
Germany	7.3
Spain	7.1
France	6.3
Italy	5.2

And even those nations whose levels of corruption are perceived to be low 'at home' have little room for complacency (self-satisfaction) when it comes to the way their companies behave overseas. In the majority of cases, the BPI score was lower (ie 'dirtier') than the CPI. In some instances, the difference between the two scores was very pronounced: HongKong's clean 8.2 at home, for example, contrasted starkly with a fairly dirty 4.3 overseas. Among the other countries that got noticeably cleaner scores at home than abroad were: Singapore, the USA, the UK, Japan, and Taiwan. Of the countries whose perceived levels of corruption were low at home, only Australia, Switzerland, Austria and Belgium (all of them fixed truth cultures, note) got similarly clean scores for their conduct abroad.

When the CPI and BPI were published, a Vice-Chairman of Transparency International said:

Developed countries have a special humanitarian responsibility, given the resources at their disposal, to investigate and prosecute the companies within their jurisdictions that are bribing. Their bribes and incentives to corrupt public officials and politicians are subverting the orderly development of poor nations, already trapped as they are, in a vicious circle of crippling poverty, hunger and disease.

The trouble is, when a multinational company is competing for business in a country where bribing public officials is commonplace, they're confronted with a real dilemma: slip someone some money and get the contract; or make a stand against corruption and lose the business to another firm who are prepared to be less scrupulous. It seems that there are still a lot of companies around who operate a double standard: while publicly deprecating corruption and expressly forbidding their employees from offering or accepting bribes, they appoint a local agent to act on their behalf overseas, and then turn a blind eye to (deliberately ignore) how he spends the large fees they pay him.

Corruption has always been with us, and no doubt always will be with us in some form or other. Even so, Transparency International's message does seem to be having some impact on the way the international business community behaves. Multinationals from some countries - particularly those in Northern Europe - are now so anxious to avoid any hint of corruption that they won't even allow their employees to pay for a business associate's dinner; or, indeed, to accept a meal. And even in Japan - a relative truth culture, where business is personal - a number of leading companies have now banned the traditional, twice-yearly exchange of gifts. Until recently, most Japanese business people presented beautifully wrapped gifts to a whole network of business associates during the official summer (o-chugen) and winter (o-seibo) gift-giving seasons.

International, national and individual beliefs do evolve, and behaviours do change. But it's a slow process. Some Japanese companies may have banned the traditional gift-giving, but that doesn't necessarily mean they have suddenly come to the conclusion that this age-old custom is wrong or corrupt. Perhaps they're simply adapting to the way their US and Northern European partners behave. Or maybe they just see it as a convenient way of cutting costs without losing face.

Why some companies in the USA and Northern Europe have banned business entertainment is perhaps a little easier to understand. Few people would see anything wrong with taking a client out to dinner in a reasonably priced restaurant once every six months or so. But there are many who would think that inviting an overseas official and his wife for an all-expenses-paid trip to New York, Zurich or London was in the same category as bribery. As there are many grey areas between these two extremes, it's hard to establish clearcut rules about what constitutes acceptable business entertainment and what does not. For people from a fixed truth culture, it's far easier simply to ban entertainment altogether. That way, the rule is absolutely clear and everyone can follow it to the letter.

Adapting to other people's expectations without going against company policy is rarely easy. But if you think objectively and flexibly, you should be able to find ways in which you can show warmth without compromising your own or your company's moral values. The British personnel manager of a large multinational's subsidiary in East Africa offers some useful advice:

Building a relationship with local officials is one thing; paying bribes is quite another. Our policy is absolutely clear: we never, ever pay money to anyone; and we never offer anything in return for a contract. But to build the relationship, we do offer help and, occasionally, small presents. For example, one of the ministers wanted to send his son to a public (fee-paying) school in the UK. I wrote a letter on his behalf to a headmaster I knew. Sending small birthday presents to an official's children is another good way of building a warm relationship: it means a lot to them that we know how old their children are.

Dr Jehad Al-Omari - Jordanian author of books on Arab business culture and one of Canning's associate training consultants - offers very similar advice:

As business is personal, exchanging favours is very common in the Arab world. There is no stigma or sense of shame attached to the giving and receiving of favours. So you should neither be embarrassed to ask for a favour, nor reluctant to grant one when asked. This is especially true for small favours: for example, arranging to visit your host's son who is studying in the West; sending medicine to his sick mother; arranging to meet a friend at the airport. These would be standard favours that would not cost much financially, nor interfere with general moral codes.

Whoever you're doing business with, you will find that sometimes even the smallest of favours can have an unexpectedly dramatic effect. When a French manager at Renault (let's call him Yves) saw that one of his Japanese colleagues from Nissan (we'll refer to him as Hideki) was in an embarrassing situation, he didn't hesitate to offer him some highly practical assistance.

It was in the first few years of the alliance between these two companies when their managers were still learning about one another's cultures and how best to bridge the gap between them. The impact of Yves' spontaneous act of kindness took the members of both companies by surprise:

On the first morning of a two-day meeting in Paris, Yves noticed that every time Hideki stood up, he kept self-consciously pulling his trousers up. Yves took him discreetly to one side at the coffee break. 'I see you're having problems with your trousers', he whispered. 'Yes', said Hideki. 'I forgot to pack my belt.' Without a moment's hesitation, Yves took his own belt off and handed it to Hideki: 'Here you are', he said. 'You can borrow mine.

I don't need it.' Hideki quietly thanked him and unobtrusively put the belt on straight away. When he returned to Tokyo, he sent the belt back to Yves with a warm letter of thanks. From that moment on, relations between the two men and their teams improved beyond recognition. News of Yves' generous act spread to other departments in Nissan. And those managers who tended to think these gaijin (foreigners) were cold and unfriendly started to look at their French colleagues through different eyes.

The moral to this tale is clear: however different their cultural values may be, your international business associates are human beings with the same basic needs and emotions as you. Small acts of kindness that demonstrate empathy and concern can often do as much, if not more, for the relation- ship than expensive gifts or nights out on the town.

Of course, there will be times when someone offers you a gift or entertainment. As we've already seen, some US and Northern European companies have banned their employees from accepting either. Many multinationals, however, take a slightly more pragmatic approach. An American IT company we know of helps its staff distinguish between gifts and bribes by offering the following advice:

Don't accept anything that can't be consumed in a day.

So the occasional business dinner is OK; a weekend in the Bahamas is not. You can accept a bottle of whisky with an easy conscience; but if someone gives you a case of whisky, you'll have to send it back.

NEPOTISM

Some cultures put nepotism in more or less the same category as corruption. Others regard giving jobs or contracts to members of their family, or clan, as a perfectly normal, logical and acceptable thing to do. On the status scale we looked at in last chapter, the former would probably lean towards the left; the latter to the right:

Acquired Status	**Given Status**
People should be judged on what they do, not who they are.	Other factors – such as family, class, nationality, race, education, age, sex, religion – should also be taken into account.

50 40 30 20 10 0 10 20 30 40 50

And when people from opposite ends of this scale meet, they're often genuinely puzzled by one another's attitudes:

A Swedish company had established very clear global purchasing guidelines: no more than 30 per cent of any particular item could be supplied by one vendor; quotes had to be obtained from at least three different suppliers; and contracts were to be awarded purely on the basis of price, delivery terms, reliability and quality. Anders, the Swedish regional manager for South-East Asia, was disturbed to note that, despite several reminders, the subsidiary in Vietnam did not appear to be following these guidelines. In fact, the range of suppliers they used seemed to be very limited, and most of them were Chinese. The subsidiary's Chinese manager seemed very unconcerned when Anders raised this problem with him. 'Well, of course most of our suppliers are Chinese,' he said. 'I only use vendors I'm related to.' Anders was shocked and remained silent for a moment. Then he calmly explained that this practice was against company guidelines. 'But why?' asked the Chinese manager. 'Because it's unethical and anti-competitive. We're not allowed to do it in Sweden, and we can't allow our subsidiaries to behave in this way.' It was the Chinese manager's turn to be shocked: 'But I can't see what the problem is,' he said. 'My family are much more loyal and reliable than people I don't know. I can call them any time of day or night. They can't escape me. And, of course, they give me much better discounts. Surely you don't want me to use suppliers I don't trust.'

Anders raised and lowered his eyebrows, and remained silent. After having a little thought he realized that there was a lot of sense in what the Chinese manager was saying. He felt sure that HQ in Stockholm would be happy as long as the Vietnam plant appeared to be sourcing supplies from a number of different vendors. So he and the Chinese manager agreed to create a number of 'shadow' companies for each supplier. That way, the names on the invoices would be different and it would look as if they were complying with the 30 per cent rule.

How do you feel about Anders' decision? Would you have done the same thing? Or would you have insisted that your Chinese colleague follow HQ guidelines? Anders would probably fall towards the acquired status end of the scale above; he may well also feel that rules and procedures should be followed to the letter. But when he was confronted with this moral dilemma, he followed the golden rules: he was careful not to overreact; he asked himself why he thought giving contracts to relatives was wrong; and why the Chinese manager thought it was not only right, but actually beneficial to the company; then he re-examined the situation as objectively as possible; and found a way of resolving it that was acceptable to himself, his company, and his Chinese colleague.

Anders was only prepared to accept this compromise because he could see that it was beneficial to the company. But there are occasions when family loyalties seem to be seriously disrupting efficiency and discipline:

Jon, an Englishman, was sent to Botswana to run his bank's main branch in Gaborone. All the other managers and staff were locals. During the first couple of months, Jon noticed that the members of the back-office team seemed to be taking a lot of unofficial leave. In most cases, they were asking for an official holiday on a Friday, and then calling the bank the following Monday to say they wouldn't be able to return to work until the Wednesday or Thursday. Jon asked Busang - the bright, well- educated young back-office manager - what was going on. Busang went through the timesheets with him and offered a number of explanations: 'This woman had to go to a family wedding; that man had to attend his nephew's circumcision ceremony; these two people had to go back to their village and help with the ploughing,' and so on. 'But why didn't they return to work on the Monday?' Jon asked. Well because, apparently, they had missed the bus, or the journey had taken longer than they had expected. When Jon explained that these unofficial absences were damaging the bank's efficiency, Busang looked puzzled. 'But when someone's away, we always share their work between us,' he said. Sensing that Busang was unwilling or unable to exercise his authority over the team, Jon decided to have a word with the bank's deputy manager.

As you have probably guessed, most of the employees in the back-office - and indeed the bank - were members of the same family or clan. When Jon said that this was unacceptable, the deputy manager reacted in a very similar way to the Chinese manager in Vietnam. Unlike Anders, however, Jon was convinced that allowing nepotism to flourish was not in the company's interests. Clearly, firing people at this stage wasn't an option But Jon was able to use the deputy manager's argument to put a stop to the unofficial leave-taking: 'You said that relatives are easier to control than outsiders,' he pointed out. 'In which case, I expect you and all the departmental managers to exercise that control. This absenteeism is unacceptable and I'd like you to make sure that it stops right away. If it doesn't, people will lose their jobs.' Though the situation improved dramatically, Jon still felt very uncomfortable with the fact that most of his staff were related to each other. From that moment on, he took part in all recruitment interviews and made sure that candidates from outside the clan were given equal consideration.

Towards the end of his first year in Botswana, Jon was surprised to discover that the family relationships inside the bank could sometimes work in his favour.

Busang's own timekeeping had started to deteriorate and he was always complaining of being tired. On some occasions he arrived up to an hour late and often left early. Jon asked the deputy manager what he thought the reason was: 'Oh, he has a few problems at home; his children have been ill,' he said, somewhat unconvincingly. 'I'll have a word with him.'

But Busang's performance didn't improve. In fact, it seemed to get even worse. One day he went out of the office very early and left an important job undone. Jon was furious. So furious, in fact, that - without naming names - he told his chauffeur what had happened during the drive home that evening. The chauffeur - a man in his late fifties - listened in silence. As he pulled up outside Jon's home, he turned to him and said: 'If you permit, Sir, I would like to tell you about my nephew. He works for our bank here in Gaborone. In fact, it was he who recommended me for this position as your driver. When our family realized he was a bright boy with a lot of potential, we all paid for his education. And now that he has a good job, of course, it's his duty to support anyone in the family who needs help. The problem is, he doesn't earn enough at the bank to meet all his obligations. So he's had to find a second job - just like a lot of young men in his position. For the last six months, he's been driving a taxi in the evenings.'

Jon thanked the driver for his help, and fixed a meeting with Busang. He handled it as sensitively as he could, but the general message was: 'I know what's been happening. I'll give you an x per cent salary increase, on condition that you give up the evening job.' The young manager obviously knew that his uncle had interceded on his behalf, and accepted the offer right away.

It would not necessarily occur to a manager from an acquired status culture that his chauffeur would be able to help him with a personnel problem. But, to the majority of the world's people, age brings wisdom; elders are always consulted and often obeyed - regardless of the job they do or the income they have at their disposal. Without the older man's intervention, Jon would probably never have found out why the back-office manager's performance had deteriorated so sharply. Nor would he have been able to work out how best to resolve the problem.

This European bank's employment contracts specifically banned staff from taking a second job. So why didn't Jon simply fire Busang? Well, because - as his chauffeur had explained - nearly all the well-educated young people in Botswana were in a similar position to the back-office manager. So any successor would find it equally difficult to meet their family obligations on the salary that went with the job. By showing empathy with Busang's position, Jon was able to propose a solution that was firm but fair: 'If you want to stay at the bank, you have to give up the second job; I realize you're having problems so I'll give you a salary increase.' Now that he understood how the family relationships worked, Jon was confident that the uncle would make sure Busang honoured the agreement.

Unlike Anders, Jon remained firmly convinced that giving jobs or contracts to family members was unequivocally wrong; he didn't accept Busang's claim that the bank's efficiency was unaffected by the unofficial leave-taking; and he couldn't allow him to carry on doing a second job. Even so, he was careful not to overreact. Instead of reprimanding Busang for his failure to control the team - which is what he would probably have done back home in the UK - Jon discussed the problem with someone who understood the local culture. And when his deputy manager argued that family members were easier to control than outsiders, he calmly and very reasonably insisted that the managers should exercise that control. Instead of issuing an official policy document that would have been incompatible with local cultural values, he quietly and pragmatically decided to take charge of the recruitment process himself. And instead of firing

Busang for doing a second job, he showed empathy with the young man's position and offered him a firm but fair solution to his problems.

DISCRETION VERSUS DISHONESTY

No examination of differing moral values would be complete without some reference to where you draw the line between discretion and dishonesty. Successful relationships in every culture are based on trust and mutual respect. And, most people would agree, it's virtually impossible to build trust if the other person thinks you're behaving dishonestly or telling outright lies. The trouble is, what one culture perceives to be an outright lie, another may regard as discretion or even honourable behaviour:

When an Italian company wanted to export specialist food and beverage products to Japan, it sought the advice of a Dutch consultant who had lived and worked in the country for many years. He put them in touch with a local importer/distributor with whom he had done business on many previous occasions. With the Dutch consultant's help, the Japanese importer and Italian exporter reached agreement on sales volumes, batch sizes, delivery dates, payment terms and so on, and a deal was set up.

For 18 months, everything seemed to go according to plan. The Italians delivered the goods as agreed, and the Japanese settled their invoices in full and on time. As far as the Dutch consultant could see, however, none of the retail outlets who had been named by the Japanese distributor as major potential clients seemed to be carrying the Italian goods. The Japanese distributor offered the following explanation: 'Most of our current clients repackage the goods and sell them under their own name. But you should start seeing the Italian brand in the shops within a few months.'

When, several months later, there was still no sign of the Italian brand, the Dutchman was fairly sure something was seriously wrong. So he went to see his old Japanese friend and spoke frankly to him about his concerns. The Japanese distributor looked embarrassed, but was unable to offer a satisfactory explanation. At the end of the meeting, however, he invited the Dutchman to accompany him to the warehouse. As soon as they got there, the Dutchman realized what the problem was. The warehouse was full of Italian goods - many of them past their sell-by date. The distributor had not been selling anywhere near the volumes that had been agreed. But he hadn't felt able to admit this to his Dutch business partner.

If the Japanese distributor hadn't had such a strong relationship with the Dutchman, he would probably have cancelled the contract as soon as he realized there was little demand for the product. As it was, however, he felt a very strong on (personal obligation) to meet the targets that had been agreed. And he couldn't see any way of telling the Dutchman what was really going on without damaging their relationship and losing face. Indeed, his sense of obligation to the Dutchman was so strong that he was even prepared to endanger himself financially to honour it.

The Dutchman comes from a culture where people have been brought up to tell the truth, whatever the circumstances. Attitudes to the truth run very deep. So even though he had considerable experience of working in Japan, it still took him a while to understand what was going on. Someone with less experience of Japanese culture might have jumped to the conclusion that the distributor was being deliberately dishonest.

Of course, the Japanese distributor wasn't actually telling lies. But he was withholding the truth. Everyone does this to one degree or another. Discretion about company and personal matters is a quality that is prized the world over. And there are occasions when even the most brutally frank people will keep opinions or information that may hurt or offend to themselves.

But what if there's bad news that you have to communicate? Do you tell people as directly and as soon as possible? Or do you prepare them gently and gradually to receive the bad news?

When I lived in the UK, I phoned my family in Jordan every week. And, of course, I always asked for news of my grandfather. When he died, my relatives kept it from me for several weeks. 'How is he?' I asked. 'Oh, he's not feeling too well.' Then, 'He's not well at all'; then, 'He's gone to hospital'; then, 'He's in a critical condition.' Throughout this period, I was being mentally prepared to take the bad news. Westerners might feel cheated or deceived; but I did not. I knew it had been done out of care for me, to cushion the blow.

If you lean towards the monochronic end, you may not feel comfortable until the bad news has been given and you can carry on working your way methodically through your agenda. For Jehad, however, time is more circular. He feels no need to get one task out of the way before he starts on another:

In the Arab world it is timing rather than time that is important. In the West, when you invite people for drinks at 7.30 pm and dinner at

8.00 pm you expect them to turn up at that time. Among Arabs you serve dinner when the time is right, when everyone is comfortable and ready to eat.

You follow the mood rather than the schedule. It's the same thing when you have to break bad news. You don't do it straight away. You wait until the time is right - when the person is ready to take it.

SUMMARY

Wherever you work in the world, you will occasionally come across people who are doing things which, by almost any standards, are deeply wrong. And when that happens, all you can do is follow your own conscience. Unless you are very unlucky, however, it's likely that most of the people you meet will be trying to do what their own culture regards as acceptable. It just seems wrong to you because you're looking at it from your own cultural standpoint.

When you're working internationally, navigating your way smoothly through the moral maze (labyrinth) will often require more time, more thought and more flexibility than it does at home. So remember the golden rules:

- Don't overreact;
- Keep an open mind;
- Don't pass hasty judgements;
- Ask yourself why do you think what's happening is wrong; and why the people you're dealing with draw the line in a different place;
- Re-examine the situation as objectively as possible;
- Look for ways of resolving it that will be acceptable to both parties' moral values and beliefs;
- Remain calm and constructive at all times.

As the people in the situations we've looked at discovered, there's no room for casual assumptions or quick judgements. You may regard something as normal. But is it necessarily right? Is what the other person is doing really wrong? Or is it just unusual or irregular? Before you leap to any hasty conclusions about an international partner's moral probity, or lack of it, think carefully about your respective cultural assumptions. Once you know and understand your own limits and theirs, you should be able to work out how best to bridge the gap.

There will be some occasions when, like the Swiss businessman in Italy, you decide that you can't condone what the other person is doing. There will be others when, like the Swede in Vietnam, you decide that you can accept what's happening without compromising your moral principles. We would never suggest that you ignore your own sense of right and wrong. But if you look in the history books, you'll find plenty of examples of people - Galileo, to name but one - who were harshly punished for acts that were merely unusual, rather than wrong. Beware of falling into the same trap. Don't let an irrational fear of the unusual lead you to hasty decisions. And whatever decision you do reach, make every effort - as Klaus did with Mr. Li - to treat people as they expect to be treated.

Note:1. Best practical example is Infosys. In 2001 it was rated Best Employer in India by Business Today. Infosys won the Global MAKE (Most Admired Knowledge Enterprises) award, for the years 2003, 2004 and 2005. Infosys was rated best employer to work for in 2000, 2001, and 2002 by Hewitt Associates. For detailed information, reader may visit this site: http://www.infosysblogs.com

25

Knowing the Form

Most psychologists agree that human beings form an impression of one another with lightning speed. This impression is based on innumerable signals that neither person may be consciously aware of sending. When you meet someone for the first time, you'll evaluate their general conduct and interpret their eye, face and body language within minutes, if not seconds. And as soon as the other person starts talking, you'll very quickly reach a decision about what they're like.

Good manners are all about showing warmth, consideration, deference and respect to others. But the good manners you learnt at your mother's knee go way beyond saying please and thank you or using the correct form of address. Without realizing it, you also absorbed the right way to use your eyes and body, the right things to say, the right way of saying them, and the right time to say them. You know and instinctively follow the form (socially acceptable behaviour). And when you meet people who don't, you may well judge them negatively. The trouble is, what you regard as good form may be considered very bad form somewhere else - and vice versa.

Business: people all over the world shake hands with visitors when they arrive and when they leave. But the French also shake hands with everyone in the office every morning when they go into work. And, as a British friend of ours who was living in Paris soon discovered:

People: That's often the way one nation's negative stereotypes of another are built up. It was only when Thomas had lived and worked among the English for a while that he realized they had the same impulse to be courteous and warm as any other nation. They just had a different way of showing it.

It's astonishing that such a minor difference in social form could create so much misunderstanding. But it happens all the time. There will always be some kind of gap between your social conventions and those of your international business partners.

Finding out what the main differences are and making a conscious effort to honour local custom is relatively easy. Battling against your own subconscious can be much harder. In many respects, the way you relate to people is instinctive. And the way you interpret the signals they're sending is involuntary. Buried somewhere deep inside you is the belief that your own social form is universal. And before your conscious mind has time to remind you that these people come from a different culture, your subconscious has already interpreted their behaviour in the light of your own social norms - often unfavourably.

It's hard to build a warm and constructive business relationship with someone if your instincts have told you they're arrogant, rude, cold, dishonest or whatever. This chapter takes you through some of the areas in which social form differs from one culture to another. Our own experience has taught us that the more you know about the differences and the better you understand them, the easier it will be to overcome any negative judgements your subconscious mind may form.

GREETING PEOPLE

We started with the apparently superficial question of when you shake hands with people. However, it's not just when you shake hands, but also how that sends different signals to different people. We asked three colleagues - A (male), B (male) and C (female) - to shake hands with a German, a Swiss, a Frenchman, a Frenchwoman, an Italian and a Brit. Colleague A gripped each person's hand very strongly indeed, B's grip was firm but not excessively so, C exerted no pressure at all with her hand. We then asked each person for their impressions:

A (male) - firm grip

German and Swiss:

He had a firm handshake. And he looked me straight in the eye. He seems very honest and straightforward.

Frenchman, Frenchwoman, Italian:

Ouch! He gripped my hand so firmly, he almost crushed my bones. People who do that are usually aggressive and pushy. My first impression is not favourable.

Oh dear! This guy's going to be a real bore.

B (male) - firm but not excessive pressure

Italian:

His handshake was OK. But he didn't strike me as being a very warm person. He stood such a long way away from me.

Everyone else:

Good firm handshake. More or less what I would expect. Looked me in the eye. I wouldn't have any trouble trusting him.

C (female) - no pressure at all

German, Brit:

(recoiling in horror): Argh! That's horrible! I'd try to keep an open mind but that's given me a very bad first impression. I don't trust her. She's not my kind of person. And she stood right on top of me. I hate people who invade my personal space.

Swiss:

A lot of women have gentler handshakes than men. But, personally, I like a woman who grips my hand firmly. It shows they're strong and straightforward. I wouldn't give this woman a job. She's got no spirit.

Frenchman, Frenchwoman, Italian:

It was softer than I would expect - even for a woman. If a man shook hands with me like that, I would think he was dishonest.

Of course these are very personal reactions and if you tried the same experiment with some other people from the same cultures, you might well get a different response. What's more interesting is the cultural conditioning that lies behind some of these comments. The Italian, for example, thought that B might not be a very warm person because he stood such a long way away from me. And the German and Brit thought that C was invading their personal space and it made them feel very uneasy.

One of the first things you absorb at your mother's knee is how comfortable people feel with physical contact and closeness. And, as our colleague Dr Jehad al Omari discovered, the form varies considerably from culture to culture:

When I first came to the UK as a student, I was struck by the lack of human interaction. I did some part-time work in a shop in Guildford.

One day the female manager had a visit from another woman. Afterwards, she said the woman was her aunt. I found it hard to believe. No hugs, no kisses, nothing.

Where I come from, there's so much touching. As a child, you are handed from one lap to another. As a boy, you often carry one of your cousins or relatives around you. You see Arab children whose cheeks are covered in red marks; they come from kissing. From the moment you are born, you're taught to express yourself physically as much as verbally. And it doesn't stop when you grow up. When you meet someone you have not seen for a while, you kiss - even one man to another.

During my first year at college in the UK, my Arab friends and I enjoyed shocking the British. We would kiss each other on both cheeks - just to see their reaction. It took some time for the joke to wear off. After I had lived in the UK for several years, I visited Jordan. I was walking along the street with one of my male cousins when he held my hand. My reflex action was to withdraw my hand immediately. I had not realized how British I had become! It took me a few minutes to remember that I was now at home and that it was perfectly normal for two men to hold hands. I took hold of my cousin's hand again. This was my first lesson in learning how to be at ease with both cultures.

The Italian in our handshaking experiment would lean towards the physically close end of the scale too. He told us, for example, that when he greeted his friends with a handshake, he would also squeeze their arm with his left hand. And if they were very close friends or family, he would find it quite natural to kiss them - men and women alike. The Brit and the German, on the other hand, would be likely to place themselves in the middle or slightly towards the physically distant end of the scale. If a man kissed either of them, or walked along the street holding their hand, they would probably feel extremely uncomfortable.

A while ago, Chris - the Welsh, rugby-playing co-writer of this book - worked for a week in London with a Turkish manager. As he said goodbye at the end of the course, the Turk gave Chris a perfectly normal (by British standards) handshake. A few weeks later, they met one another by chance in Istanbul.

The Turk beamed with delight, rushed up to Chris, gave him a hug, and kissed him on the cheek. Despite the fact that Chris is an experienced cross-cultural trainer, his instinctive reaction was: Help! Why's he kissing me? He never did that in London. This is really embarrassing.

After a few seconds, of course, he was able to overcome this subconscious reaction and analyse the situation objectively. In London, his Turkish friend had adapted his behaviour to suit British expectations. Now he was at home in Turkey, there was no reason why he shouldn't greet friends in the way that came naturally to him.

If it's up to the visitor to know and honour local customs, then presumably the next time Chris meets his Turkish friend in Istanbul, he should initiate the hugging and kissing himself. Well no, not if it makes him feel awkward and uncomfortable. He would only come across as clumsy or insincere. But he should be careful not to show surprise or embarrassment when his Turkish friend hugs him. And, of course, not to allow his own social conditioning to lead him to false or negative judgements.

Everyone who took part in our handshaking experiment said that they found it hard to trust people who didn't look them into the eye. But they were all European. To the Japanese and other Asian cultures, people who look you in the eye too directly and too long can appear aggressive and disrespectful. So if a German and a Japanese meet, should Klaus try to keep averting his gaze? And should Takashi force himself to stare non-stop into Klaus's eyes? Well, they should both make an effort to modify their behaviour slightly, of course. But you can't undo a lifetime's conditioning; you can't be expected to act in a way that makes you feel uncomfortable or unnatural. What you can do, however, is stop yourself from jumping to the wrong conclusions. Klaus isn't being aggressive or deliberately trying to behave disrespectfully; Takashi isn't being devious or dishonest. They're both trying to be courteous. They've just got different ways of showing it.

So where would you place yourself on the physically distant scale? If you're from an individualist culture (for example, the USA, the UK, Northern Europe), you will probably fall somewhere in the middle. But if you're from a group-oriented culture, you may well fall sharply towards one end of the scale or the other. Arabs, Africans, Indians, South Americans, Southern Italians and Greeks tend to be very tactile. With them, handshakes can go on forever, and they're likely to stand very close to you In East and South-East Asia, on the other hand, people tend to be far more physically distant. In Japan, for example, physical contact between business people in the office is almost non-existent. Interestingly enough, however, when Japanese colleagues are socializing together in the bar after work, they seem to become more tactile and it's not unusual to see them touching one another on the arm or patting someone on the back.

While bowing rather than handshaking is the cultural norm, most Japanese businesspeople these days expect to shake hands with their foreign business associates. But it's worth remembering that, if you grip their hand too firmly, they could assume you're being aggressive. So if your natural handshake is very firm, you'll need to make a conscious effort to apply slightly less pressure when you're greeting your Japanese business partners.

MAKING SMALL TALK

So you've got through the introductions successfully. Regardless of how your business partners shook your hand, how directly they looked you in the eye, and how close they stood to you, you've kept an open mind about what they're like. Good. Now let's get down to the small talk. How long should it go on, do you think? Two minutes, five minutes, 10 minutes, 45 minutes? Ah, well, once again your answer will be influenced by what's considered good form where you come from. As we've already seen, some cultures prefer to focus on business first and personal relationships later; others feel the need to build a personal relationship before they can do business.

At the beginning of a meeting with someone from the Arab world, for example, people expect to spend plenty of time in getting to know one another, or cementing the relationship, and the conversation can extend to all aspects of life (family, hobbies, travel, current affairs, the economy etc). And even when the business talk finally starts, people often continue to intersperse it with more small talk and pleasantries. In Japan, too, the aim at early meetings will be to develop personal trust. And while Takashi may not engage in social pleasantries for very long - especially if he's forced to do so in English or another foreign language - he'll probably expect to spend plenty of time exchanging information about your two companies before he's ready to discuss specific business proposals. In more functional cultures, on the other hand, people expect to start on the business agenda within minutes of sitting down. With Germans, Swiss, Scandinavians and Finns, for example, small talk is often no more than a couple of sentences.

So if the person you're meeting spends longer on small talk than you regard as normal, hide any irritation you may instinctively feel; and overcome any urge you may have to force the pace. Remember, it's unlikely that they're trying to annoy you or waste your time. They're simply following what their culture regards as good form. Similarly, if the other person launches straight into business without what you would regard as even the minimum of pleasantries, don't assume they're being deliberately cold or unwelcoming. They're probably just trying to be professional and businesslike - qualities that their culture puts a high value on.

PLAYING THE CONVERSATION GAME

Of course, it's not just how long you spend on small talk that differs from culture to culture. The way you actually play the conversation game also sends signals that may be misinterpreted by your international business partners.

I once visited an Englishman, called Paul, who had been working in Germany for many years. He started telling me about his company. As he spoke, I interrupted him several times with comments and questions - in an interested and friendly way that would be considered quite normal in the UK and the USA. Paul began to look more and more annoyed. Finally, I realized why. I said, 'You don't like me interrupting you, do you, Paul?' He said, 'No, I find it really irritating. Quite rude, in fact.' He had been in Germany for so long that he was no longer used to the interactive way his compatriots discuss things. He expected me to let him finish before I took my turn.

The Englishwoman was neither rudely or aggressively shouting Paul down, nor was she continually cutting across what he was saying. That would be considered bad form virtually everywhere. She was just showing a friendly and respectful interest. She was playing the conversation game according to the rules of her culture. Maybe if Paul had been German, she would have tried not to interrupt him. But he wasn't; he was a fellow Englishman, and so it took her a while to realize what the problem was.

Some cultures (the UK and the USA, for example) expect conversation to be fairly interactive. To them, interrupting with the odd relevant comment or question is good form. The Americans, for example, will often make comments in the affirmative that build on what the other person is saying, while the British tend to interact by asking questions.

And when people from these two cultures are confronted with a business partner who sits and listens to them in absolute silence, it can make them feel uneasy. They may wonder if they have said something wrong, or even jump to the conclusion that the other person is cold or lacking in personality.

Other cultures (the Japanese and the Finns, for example) are used to waiting their turn to speak. For them, conversation is often like a series of mini-monologues. They're not used to being interrupted, and when they meet someone who expects to conduct a conversation in a more interactive way, their instincts may tell them that he or she is ill-mannered, disrespectful or superficial. Such cultures are often very comfortable with silence. It shows that you're thinking about what has been said. With them, rushing to fill the silence can send completely the wrong signal, as a British salesman discovered on his first-ever trip to Finland:

The first guy I met was unbelievably taciturn (unwilling to converse). Everything I said was greeted with a long silence. To be honest, I thought there was something wrong with him - you know, some kind of personality disorder. Being a typical Brit, I believed at the time that everyone in the world could be charmed with a bit of smooth-talking. So, every time there was a silence, I filled it. This was a fatal mistake. I soon learned that the Finns actively mistrust people who are too effusive.

How do you instinctively play the conversation game? Your answer will, to some extent, depend on where you would place yourself on the scale below:

Reserved	**Effusive**
I think you should talk only when you have something relevant to say.	Lots of talk indicates warmth and interest. Silences should be avoided.

50 40 30 20 10 0 10 20 30 40 50

At the far left of the scale you would probably find the Finns, while people from the Arab world would be likely to place themselves at the far right. The British and Americans would probably lean towards the right, while the Germans and Swiss might well lean towards the left. Interestingly enough, though, while the Germans are not used to interrupting people mid-flow, they are not particularly comfortable with silence. In this respect, they are more similar to the British and Americans.

CHOOSING WHAT TO SAY AND HOW TO SAY IT

You're bound to draw conclusions about what people are like from what they choose to say, and how they choose to say it. The trouble is, the way even the most basic and universal sentiments are expressed can vary considerably from culture to culture. Take saying thank you, for example.

It's something every child learns to do from a very early age. And you'll find an equally short and simple equivalent - merci, gracias, dankeschön, arigato and so on - of these two 'important little words' in virtually every language. But that doesn't necessarily mean that the way your international colleagues instinctively express their gratitude will be the same as yours.

In cultures where there's a strong oral tradition, for example, the use of metaphors, poetic language and colourful turns of phrase are usually much admired. When Penny was working, a while ago, with a senior businessman from Saudi Arabia, he thanked her for a very simple piece of advice she offered him by saying: These are jewels you are giving me. Really jewels. I am so grateful. Using a metaphor to express his gratitude came perfectly naturally to him. That's because, from a young age, he had listened to his elders in the majlis. This is a large room in which the men of the tribe regularly gather together to discuss family affairs and to socialize. Though the name of the room varies from place to place (for example: madeef in Syria and Iraq, madafa in Jordan, diwanihey in Kuwait), these gatherings are commonplace throughout the Arab world. And it's there that young boys sit with the men and learn the art of conversation and storytelling. Good raconteurs are much admired so naturally the boys are keen to memorize the stories that are told and to imitate the metaphors and colourful language that is used.

In other parts of the world - much of Northern Europe, for example - people tend to express themselves more plainly and simply. During a recent one-week intensive language course, one of the group members - a German - had to take a morning off to attend a meeting. Naturally our colleague was anxious to help him catch up with the rest of the group. So she spent her lunch break typing up a summary of everything he had missed. When she handed the notes to him after lunch, he simply said: Thank you. To him, this was a perfectly normal and well-mannered response. But someone from a culture where people express themselves more effusively and colourfully might well have found it rather terse, and even have concluded - quite wrongly - that the German was ungrateful. And, of course, the kind of language the Saudi Arabian used might well make a plain-speaking Northern European feel uncomfortable or even suspicious of the other person's motives.

So even something as simple as the way you choose to say thank you can be open to misinterpretation. That's why documents that have been translated from another language sometimes sound strange or even slightly comical. You see, it isn't just a question of converting the actual words or phrases that are used in one language into their nearest equivalent in another. You have to really understand the cultural sentiments, attitudes and assumptions that lie behind the words and then find the most appropriate way of expressing them in the other language.

If, for example, a Frenchman says C'est pas normal, the inexperienced translator might be tempted to go for It's not normal. But that would be a pretty inaccurate and misleading translation. In French, the word normal has a cultural context. It brings to mind the whole French attitude towards logic, their Cartesian sense of the right way to think and the right way to do things. So if Jean-Claude tells you C'est pas normal, he expects you to be able to interpret what he means. Depending on the situation, it might be That's completely unacceptable; or, You're going about this in completely the wrong way; or He has absolutely no right to do that.

As we saw in a previous chapter, low context communicators (such as Americans, Germans, Scandinavians, Finns) tend to express themselves in explicit, concrete, unequivocal terms. There's little cultural baggage or 'context' attached to the words they use and you can usually take what they say at face value. High context communicators (such as Arabs, Japanese, French) tend to communicate more implicitly. They expect you to be able to interpret what they mean from your knowledge of what lies behind the words, what they're actually talking about at the time, their tone of voice and, of course, their eye and body language.

English has become the lingua franca of international business. So, is it a high context or a low context language, do you think? Well, the fact is, you can't always equate language with culture. When George Bernard Shaw described the British and the Americans as 'two nations divided by a common language' he wasn't just referring to their accent, or the odd difference in vocabulary. Most Americans - apart from people who come from the narrow East Coast belt - are relatively low context. Like the Germans, they will tend to say what they mean in a fairly explicit, open and direct way.

The British, on the other hand, are relatively high context - but in a rather different way from, say, the French. Our cultural conditioning has taught us that making direct and open criticisms, issuing unequivocal orders, or making a fuss (unnecessary demands or complaints) is very bad form. So whatever the merits or demerits of a situation, we will automatically understate them; and if we have a difficult message to deliver, we will instinctively try to soften it. We think we're being sensitive or showing a very reasonable wish to compromise. Most of the rest of world thinks we're being indecisive, pessimistic, insincere, two-faced, sarcastic... and so on. Many of our compatriots are completely unaware of the impact our communication style has on other nationalities. Your writers have known about it for a long time. And we've had a lot of practice adapting our approach to other nationalities' expectations. Even so, everything we say or write betrays our cultural conditioning - as our American readers, in particular, will have noticed from the very first page of this book.

The difference in British and American communication style doesn't just mean that the two nations misjudge one another. They often misunderstand each other too. If you're American and your British boss says: You might like to consider changing the launch date, what do you think he means?

A: This is an option you should consider, but the final decision will be yours.

OR

B: I'd like you to change the launch date, please.

Well, as you've probably guessed, he means B. Would you have realized that before you read this chapter? We know of some Americans whose boss said something similar, and they thought he meant A. So they considered changing the launch date, and decided against it. Their British boss was not impressed.

How you communicate is central to who you are and how you perceive yourself. And few people are willing - or indeed able - to behave in a way that conflicts with their own self-image. But you don't need to transform yourself into a completely different person every time you do business with someone whose values are different from yours. All you need to do is be curious, be observant, and keep an open mind. The better you under- stand yourself and others, the less likely you are to misinterpret your partners' motives. And the easier it will be for you to avoid sending the wrong signals to them.

Put yourself in the following situation:

You're running an international project with very tight deadlines. Your colleague, Susan, knows that she needs to send you a detailed progress report at the end of every month. It's now July and Susan's June report has only just arrived - nearly a week late. To make matters worse, some of the figures are inaccurate. You decide to call her.

How would you instinctively handle the conversation with Susan? Would you feel more comfortable taking approach A, or approach B?

Approach A

You: I'm calling about your June report. It was a week late and some of the figures were inaccurate.

Susan: Yes, I know. I'm sorry about that. A couple of my people were off sick.

You: Yes but, Susan, you must respect the deadlines. If you don't, we'll fall behind schedule. And, in future, please make sure that you check all the figures very carefully.

Approach B

You: I'm calling about your June report.

Susan: I was just about to call you. I'm sorry it was late, but a couple of my people were sick.

You: Oh dear ... The thing is, I've just been through the figures and

I'm afraid of some of them don't seem to add up.

Susan: Don't they? Oh, I'm sorry. I had to put them together very quickly.

You: Right. But what about this month? Will you be able to spend a bit more time on them?

Susan: Yes, of course.

You: Great. Because, as you know, there's an important deadline coming up, and we'll be in real trouble if we miss it.

Clearly, approach A is low context. The speaker says what he means clearly, directly and explicitly. Susan knows, without any doubt, what she has to do. Approach B, on the other hand, is high context - in a peculiarly British way. The speaker tries to avoid direct criticism or recrimination. And instead of using an imperative, he asks a question. His message is the same as speaker A's, but he tries to soften it.

Of course, we're not trying to suggest that every German, Scandinavian or American you meet would always be as frank, direct or explicit as speaker A; nor that every Brit would be as diplomatic, indirect or implicit as speaker B. What people say and the way they choose to say it depends, above all, on the relationship, what's gone before, and the actual situation. When two Brits are having a tough discussion, they're capable of using as many imperatives and concrete messages as lower context cultures do. And when the situation demands it, people from lower context cultures are equally capable of expressing themselves more indirectly or implicitly.

But, there's no denying that the way people instinctively communicate does vary from culture to culture. And unless you are aware of these differences, you may well misjudge your international colleagues' motives. If Susan were British, for example, and speaker A always spoke to her in this way, she could easily form the impression that he was autocratic, insensitive and uncompromising. And if she were German, American or even French, she might end up thinking that speaker B was diffident, indecisive and, possibly, insincere.

It's very hard for non-native speakers of any language - however fluent they are - to know exactly what impact they're making, or indeed to understand exactly what their native-speaking partners are saying. The high-low context communication gap compounds these problems. So if you're dealing with someone whose communication style and native tongue are different from your own, you need to think carefully about the way you're expressing yourself and to monitor the other person's reactions very closely. And if they seem confused, irritated or offended, don't just carry on; stop and ask them what's wrong. When Rosie, a colleague of ours, was giving some advice to a German client, she couldn't understand why he looked so annoyed. You don't look very happy, Dieter, she said. What's the problem? He replied: Well, you're the trainer; I expect you to give me the answers, not ask me to supply them. When she thought about what she had said, she realized that all her suggestions had been phrased, in typical British fashion, as questions: Why don't you...; Wouldn't it be better if you...; How about...; What if you.... But, of course, to the low context Dieter, these turns of phrase sounded too indirect and indecisive. He expected the trainer to phrase her advice more positively and explicitly: I think you should...; I recommend that you...; In my experience, the best way to solve this problem is.... Because she had been prepared to ask Dieter what was wrong, Rosie was soon able to clear up the misunderstanding. Dieter learnt something important about British communication style, and Rosie made sure she phrased her subsequent suggestions more positively and explicitly.

TRYING TO BE FUNNY

Often the British cannot be serious because they are afraid of making fools of themselves... They know and accept the rules of the game, but otherwise nothing is sacred. Nor do they draw the line at self-irony. That is why they are predestined to make compromises, the precondition for a life without absolute truths.

Irony involves saying the opposite of what you mean. So it's a relatively high context way of communicating. The British love it and most people - from ambassadors to shop assistants, tycoons to taxi drivers - use it almost without thinking. Unfortunately, this style of communication doesn't always travel well:

Two British women in their early thirties were on holiday in Florida. One evening, they went to a bar where there was music and dancing. An American man, also in his thirties, politely went up to one of the women and asked her if she would like to dance. She wasn't interested in dancing, but she didn't want just to say 'No thanks' in case she offended him. So she smiled pleasantly and said: 'I won't just now, thanks. The old war wound's playing up again' (my war injury is causing problems). It was a line she had used, on a number of occasions, in London. British guys would usually laugh, make an equally ironic comment, and then walk away with their egos intact. But the American guy looked at her sympathetically and said: 'Hey, that's too bad. Which war were you in?' When the woman explained that she had been joking, he walked away looking confused.

Of course, there are plenty of Americans who would have seen the joke and responded with an ironic, or humorous, comment of their own. You only have to watch an episode of the popular American cartoon series, The Simpsons, to see that irony is alive and well in the USA. It's just that, for many Americans, irony doesn't seem to be the 'default' form of communication as it is for most Brits. As a result, Americans may sometimes take their British counterparts' ironic comments literally and, if they do, this can lead to genuine misunderstanding on both sides. So if you're British, you would be well advised to try to avoid using irony when you're doing business internationally. And if you're American, or any other nationality for whom irony is not the norm, try not to jump to the conclusion that the British are making fun of you, or being deliberately opaque. As often as not, they're making fun of themselves, or trying to defuse a tense or embarrassing situation.

Every culture has a sense of humour; everyone enjoys laughing and joking with their friends. But not everyone laughs at the same things:

A group of high potentials in a multinational company had flown to HQ from all over Europe and the USA to attend the first module of an in-house training programme. Some of the sessions were to be run by the company's own trainers; others by some of our colleagues from Canning. The first two-hour session was facilitated by one of the in-house trainers - a Norwegian. To 'break the ice', the Norwegian facilitator asked each participant to draw a self-portrait using any combination of squares, circles and triangles. The unnamed sketches were then pinned on the wall, and the Norwegian explained what the three different symbols signified. He finished with triangles which, he solemnly told them, related to erotic characteristics. As he had hoped, the group seemed amused by this announcement and the ice was indeed broken as they tried to guess who had drawn which sketch.

The participants were then invited, one by one, to stand up and give a short self-introduction. After each presentation, the rest of the group had to try to match the speaker with one of the sketches. The last speaker was an American woman called Beth. When she told the group which sketch was hers, Steve - a British man - quietly joked to his French neighbour: 'But that can't be her. The triangles aren't big enough.' When he said 'triangles' he briefly placed his hands in front of his chest. There was a ripple (small wave) of laughter from the people sitting near him. The group then went to the coffee lounge for their morning break.

Shortly after the break, the Norwegian approached the Canning trainers - who were working in an adjoining room - and said: 'I need your help. The Americans are threatening to withdraw from the programme.' Our colleagues accompanied him into the seminar room and encouraged the group members to discuss what had happened. One of the Americans spoke first: 'What Steve said about Beth and the way the rest of you guys laughed constitutes sexual harassment. Back home, all of our employment contracts include a sexual harassment clause. Don't yours?' Well, no, they didn't. And it was clear that some of the Europeans found it very hard to understand their American colleagues' reaction: 'How could anyone take offence at such an innocent joke?'

Whether you sympathize with the Americans or the Europeans, the moral to this tale is clear: what you think is a harmless bit of fun may well cause serious offence elsewhere. By all means show that you have a sense of humour, but stick to safe, inoffensive topics. And be aware that if you make sexist jokes in the USA, you could well end up being taken to court. Remember, too, that in a lot of places (such as Germany, Scandinavia, France, Japan), jokiness in meetings and presentations may be seen as frivolous and unprofessional. So when you're doing business with people from these cultures, keep your jokes for the bar, restaurant or sauna.

AVOIDING HIDDEN DANGERS

If you passed through Heathrow airport in early 2003, you may have noticed a series of large advertising posters in which an international bank highlighted its cross-cultural expertise. The posters featured a range of gestures, colours, numbers, and symbols that mean different things in different places: for example, making a circle with your thumb and fore-finger which says OK in the USA, but something very vulgar in Mediterranean countries and the Middle East; or red, which signifies danger in much of the Western world, but symbolizes good luck to the Chinese; and so on.

Clearly, it's useful to know about differences such as those. Otherwise, you could - without realizing it - do something which causes embarrassment, distress or offence to the people you're working with. If, for example, you put four candles on a Japanese colleague's birthday cake, he may misinterpret your kind gesture: in Japan, four is a very unlucky number; it symbolizes death. If you want to get some flowers for your French or Italian hosts, don't buy chrysanthemums; these are the flowers that people traditionally put on their family graves on All Saints Day. When you're in a meeting with someone from the Middle East, keep your feet planted firmly on the ground; showing an Arab the soles of your feet is the gravest of insults. And if you come from the Arab world, be careful about the kind of questions you ask your European colleagues:

When I first came to London from the Middle East - at the age of 14 - I was met at the airport by a company representative whom my father had asked to look after me. As we were driving from London to Norwich, I put my foot in it: 'Who did you vote for at the last election?' I asked. 'Young man,' he replied, 'you don't ask that kind of question over here.' I found it odd and offputting that I could not ask personal questions; that is how I had learnt to deal with people. Now I had to find another route.

And if you're American or European, avoid talking about your Arab colleagues' female relatives:

In the Middle East you can ask questions; any questions. The only questions you do not ask are about mothers or sisters. A Saudi friend once invited an American banker to dinner at his house and introduced him to his wife. The following day, in an attempt to be polite, the banker said: 'Your wife is lovely.' He was shocked when the Arab replied: 'My wife is not the subject for conversation.'

There are a number of hidden dangers such as these. And it's worth taking the trouble to find out what they are before you start doing business in a culture that is new to you. Gestures, symbols, numbers, colours, rituals for exchanging business cards, correct seating arrangements, drinking and dining etiquette, taboo topics of conversation and so on do, of course, vary from country to country. But, unlike many of the less obvious differences that we've focused on in this chapter, they are fairly well and widely documented. You can find out what the main DOs and DON'Ts are from any reputable country guide. And we strongly recommend that you do so. After all, it would be a pity to put a promising business relationship at risk by doing something that is relatively easy to avoid.

SUMMARY

The impulse to be courteous is universal. And most of the people you meet will be as keen to show warmth, consideration, and respect as you are. But, as we've seen, you can't assume that they will do so in exactly the same way as you. No matter how carefully you do your homework, you're bound to find yourself in some situations where you simply don't know what the form is. Which is why it's so important, at all times, to keep your eyes and ears open:

- Be observant;
- Be curious;
- Be sensitive to how others are behaving, and to the impact your behaviour seems to be having on them;
- Make a conscious effort to adapt to the style and rhythm that comes naturally to the people you're dealing with;
- If they appear confused, irritated or offended, ask questions and try to clear up the misunderstanding;
- By all means show that you have a sense of humour, but stick to safe, inoffensive topics;
- Above all, don't jump to hasty conclusions about what the other person is like.

Note: There is no better example than Toyota Motor Corporation. Toyota's management doctrine has developed from the company's origins and has been reflected in the terms "Lean Manufacturing" and Just in Time Production. The Toyota Way has four components: 1) Long-term thinking as a basis for management decisions, 2) a process for problem-

solving, 3) adding value to the establishment by developing its individuals, and 4) recognizing that continuously solving root problems drives organizational learning. The Toyota Way incorporates the Toyota Production System. For further knowledge, reader can visit Toyota's site: http://www.toyota.co.jp

26

Making Presentations

Imagine, for a moment, that you are an area sales manager with a company that produces fast-moving consumer goods. Last quarter - January to March - the results for your region were very bad. In fact, sales were 10 per cent below target. Understandably, the sales director wants to know why there was such a serious shortfall, and how you propose to reverse the situation next quarter. He has asked you to make a presentation to him and the finance director between 10.00 and 10.30 next Monday morning.

There were a number of reasons for your area's poor performance and none of them was your fault. You have all the facts and figures to show what went wrong and why. The overriding problem, however, was that you simply don't have enough sales representatives to cover the region. You pointed this out last October when you submitted your budget, but HQ rejected your proposal to recruit extra staff.

As you sit down to prepare your presentation, which of the approaches below do you instinctively feel it would be better to take?

A. Spend most of the presentation looking back over the last quarter making sure that your bosses understand exactly what went wrong and why?

B. Say very little about the last three months; concentrate, instead, on explaining how, with one or two extra sales representatives, you'll be able to meet, and most probably exceed, next quarter's target.

And how do you propose to give your bosses all the facts and figures you've prepared?

A. Show a series of slides as you are making your presentation.

B. Give them a written handout to study at their leisure afterwards.

And what about timing? How do you plan to use the 30 minutes you've got?

A. Spend most of the time presenting with five minutes or so at the end for questions.

B. Make a brief speech and leave at least 20 minutes for questions and discussion.

Clearly your decisions would depend, to a large extent, on how well you know the bosses, what kind of people they are, and what they're interested in. What's gone before and how much is at stake (to be gained or lost) would be key factors too. But if you found yourself in a similar position to this area manager, which of these approaches would come more naturally to you? And if you were one of the bosses, what would you expect from this presentation? Which of the approaches would you be more inclined to listen to?

It's quite possible that you are wondering why we're asking these questions. It's perfectly obvious which of the approaches is right, you may be thinking. Why are these people insulting my intelligence?

Well, actually, we aren't trying to insult your intelligence. The fact is, what people expect from a presentation varies from culture to culture. For example, some people think the best presentations are thorough and detailed with plenty of supporting facts and documentation; others will only listen to you if you're brief and selective. Some audiences are impressed by a logical structure; others by a creative one. Some presenters instinctively aim to inform; others to persuade or entertain. So while it may have been immediately obvious to you that approach A or B was the right one, you can't assume that your international colleagues will share your view.

But surely, you may say, there must be some rights and wrongs that are universal; some presentation styles and techniques that are guaranteed to succeed with any audience? Well, we wouldn't go so far as to say there are universal rights and wrongs. But there is one golden rule that successful presenters the world over follow: no matter what message they're trying to get across, they put the audience first. That may sound simple and obvious. But, as our international clients often tell us, it isn't always easy to do.

When you're having a conversation with someone, you can see or hear their reactions. And, provided you're willing to try to put yourself in their position, you can adapt what you say and the way you say it as the conversation progresses. But when you sit down to prepare a presentation, the members of your audience aren't around. You have to put the whole thing together, from start to finish, without any input or feedback from them. And you may well be tempted to concentrate on the message you want to deliver and what you want to achieve. As we keep repeating, however, focusing on yourself and your own agenda is the major block to successful communication, whatever context you're operating in. If you want your audience to really sit up and listen, you have to make sure that everything you say and every visual you show is interesting and relevant to them. And you can only do that if you put yourself in their shoes (position) at every stage.

Planning and delivering an effective presentation is hard work - even if you know your audience well and they're from the same national and corporate culture as you. When they're from a different country and you don't know them personally, it can be harder still. In our experience, the greatest challenges for an international presenter are: choosing a style that will suit the audience's expectations; putting the message you want to deliver into a concrete context that your audience can relate to; and speaking in a way that will be clear and accessible.

CHOOSING THE RIGHT STYLE

As we mentioned in earlier chapter, many of the management techniques that businesses adopt originate in the USA. So, too, do many of the techniques that are taught on international presentation skills courses. The Americans, perhaps more than any other culture, seem instinctively to try to build a personal rapport with their audience and to put their message across persuasively and positively. In this respect, we believe, they have a lot to teach the rest of the world. But, as our international clients often tell us, they also have a lot to learn:

When a Swiss company decided to award 'loyalty' points to their customers, they asked their in-house IT department to develop the software they needed to operate the scheme. The project was scheduled to take two years. After 18 months, however, it ran into serious difficulties. Two and a half years later, they were still trying to solve them. The company moved Connie, one of their brightest and most competent Swiss managers, on to the team. They gave her six months to get the system up and running. By June - the new deadline - she had indeed established the basic framework and solved the major difficulties. The relatively minor problems that remained could, she decided, be sorted out gradually over the next two years - at a cost of 5 million Swiss francs per year. The Swiss manager who was responsible for the loyalty scheme accepted Connie's proposal. A couple of months later, however, he left the company and was replaced by an American called Robert.

One of the first things Robert did was to ask Connie for a progress report on the project. She prepared a well-structured, informative and clear presentation. She had, in fact, performed a miracle during her six months on the team.

But, being Swiss, it didn't occur to her to 'sell' herself or highlight the remarkable job she had done. Instead, she explained - in the calm, methodical, low-key style that came naturally to her - why the project had run into difficulty and what progress had been made. She then moved on to what the remaining problems were, how long it would take to solve them, and how much it would cost.

Robert was not impressed. All he heard was 'a number of problems remain' and 'it'll take two years and an additional budget of 5 million a year to solve them'. As far as he was concerned, Connie had failed to reach the targets she had been given; the problems had to be solved by the end of the current year; and he was going to put in a new team to make sure that they were.

Connie didn't try to argue with him. She simply applied for a job in a different department and left the new team to take responsibility for the project. By the end of the year, they seemed to have created more problems than they had solved. The project continued for a further two years and went way over the budget Connie had projected. The Swiss were all convinced that if Robert had left Connie to handle the project her way, it would have been completed much faster and cheaper.

So why didn't Robert accept Connie's proposal? Well, we can't read his mind. But Connie, who had worked with Americans before, was convinced that it was because he had been unable to bridge the gap between American and Swiss culture. 'In my experience,' she told us, 'Robert's reaction was typically American.

They always take the short- term view. They never want to hear about problems; just quick solutions. And they expect you to tell them everything is wonderful, even if it isn't. Well, I'm sorry, but that's not the way we do things in Switzerland.'

In our view, Connie was probably right about the culture gap. She and Robert would be likely to fall at opposite ends of the following scales:

Short-term										**Long-term**
I prefer to focus on the here and now.										I need to see beyond the horizon and plan accordingly.
50	**40**	**30**	**20**	**10**	**0**	**10**	**20**	**30**	**40**	**50**
Upbeat										**Low-key**
I always try to emphasize the positive aspects of a situation. And I am not afraid to talk openly about my own achievements and successes.										I always try to give a factual and balanced view of a situation. And if I've done a good job, I let the facts speak for themselves.
50	**40**	**30**	**20**	**10**	**0**	**10**	**20**	**30**	**40**	**50**

As everyone knows, of course, the USA is a relatively young country. It was only in 1620 that the Pilgrim Fathers settled in Plymouth, Massachusetts - the first permanent colony in New England. There have been many waves of other immigrants since then, most of them trying to escape the religious persecution, political unrest or extreme poverty of the old world; and all of them attracted by the freedom and opportunities that were on offer. Between the 1840s and the early 1920s, for example, some 30 million people immigrated to the USA. These immigrants were determined to build a new and better life for themselves. They were convinced that, with hard work and a little luck, there would be no limit to what they could achieve. For most presenters, though, choosing the right style to suit their audience is vital:

George, a senior fund manager with a British asset management firm (let's call them BAM), came to Canning to polish up a presentation he was going to make to his firm's largest American client. His aim was to persuade the Americans to renew BAM's mandate. The trouble was, the performance figures for the previous and current year looked very bad, and the Americans were threatening to take their business elsewhere. George would have just half an hour to change their minds. He was planning to spend most of that time looking back over the previous 18 months, and justifying the way in which BAM had managed the fund. His trainer persuaded him to take a much more upbeat approach. Instead of looking at what had gone wrong in the past, George tried to focus on the good results BAM could achieve in future: 'Stay with BAM and we'll beat the target you have set us' was his new central message. This new approach made his presentation much shorter. George practised it again and again, paying particular attention to his tone of voice. By the end of the two-day coaching session, he knew the introduction and conclusion off by heart. And he really sounded positive and optimistic.

The following week, George phoned his trainer in triumph: 'They've renewed the mandate,' he said. 'Thank God you made me change my central message! When I arrived, their consultant told me I only had 5 minutes, not 30. So I just went in and presented the introduction and conclusion. According to their consultant, the trustees were very impressed that I had been able to adapt so flexibly to the time constraint. And they had confidence in me because I sounded so positive and didn't give them any of the "usual British bullshit".'

On the strength of this five-minute presentation, over a hundred million dollars of pension fund money were allocated.

All of us carry around very fixed images of other cultures. These stereo- types are often negative, and nearly always the result of measuring what foreigners do or say against our own cultural norms. When George's client referred to the usual British bullshit, we knew exactly what he meant. On our cross-cultural workshops, we always ask the participants how they perceive other nationalities. And we have discovered that the image the Americans and British have of one another is remarkably consistent. For example, on one course we ran for the European head office of a major American company, the expatriate American managers said that, in their view, the British were:

- Always talking about problems, not solutions;
- Always focusing on what has happened, and not on what will happen;
- Gloomy (pessimistic) and depressing, even when they are giving good news;
- Rude and disrespectful;
- Badly prepared.

The trouble is, taking the kind of upbeat, positive attitude that impresses the Americans doesn't come naturally to the British. As we saw in earlier chapter, our culture values understatement, irony and self-deprecation. Maybe that's why the British managers on the course told us that, in their view, the Americans were:

- Always over-optimistic;
- Not prepared to analyse a problem properly in order to reach workable solutions;

- Boastful and superficial;
- Not prepared to disagree with superiors, even when they are wrong;
- Badly prepared.

A few years ago, Canning was considering the possibility of offering an e-learning service. We invited a number of software consultancies to present their proposals for a tailored solution. One of the consultancies was American and they flew two of their vice-presidents over to the UK to do some research and make their proposals. The presenters were friendly, dynamic and enthusiastic. They started their presentation something like that: It's a real privilege for us to be here. And we're very excited about the prospect of handling this project for you. They then spent what seemed like 20 minutes telling us, in glowing terms, about their personal experience and many successes. As they spoke, they showed us slide after slide, and animated graphic after animated graphic, taken from the e-learning programmes they had developed for other clients - few of whom seemed to be in the same business as Canning. When they finally started talking about us, it was immediately clear that they had little understanding of our training style or our clients' needs. During the question and answer session at the end, we raised many objections to their proposals. Instead of trying to answering these objections, they simply said things like: We've got a lot of experience in this field. We'll be able to work through that kind of issue when the project's under way.

The audience were all international communication trainers who were more prepared than most to make an effort to bridge the culture gap. And if these presenters had been able to show us that they really understood our business, we would have forgiven them for the emphasis they had placed on their own achievements and successes. But because they weren't prepared to engage with the problems we raised, we left the presentation feeling mildly angry that they had wasted so much of our time. And even we allowed ourselves to think, for a few moments, that their performance had been typically American. In other words, that it had conformed to most of the negative images in the list above.

Clearly, when you're presenting internationally, you have to make a conscious effort to avoid reinforcing negative stereotypes such as these. If not, there's a danger you will alienate the audience almost as soon as you open your mouth. That's not to say you should try to change your natural style so radically that you feel uncomfortable. No one could have expected the American software consultants to stop sounding enthusiastic and positive. Indeed, we believe that putting your message across persuasively and positively is something that all presenters should aim to do. But there has to be something behind the positive noises you're making. You've got to show the audience that you understand their needs and expectations. And you've got to make sure that everything you say is relevant and interesting to them. The American consultants seemed to have made little effort to understand us. And the many successes and achievements that they presented were simply not relevant. That was why we found them superficial and boastful. If they had put us first, we would probably have been very favourably impressed by their upbeat and dynamic style.

Similarly, when Canning was helping George from BAM to prepare his presentation, we did not, for one moment, expect him to say anything that made him feel uncomfortable. We didn't, for example, ask him to tell his clients how excited he was about the prospect of managing the fund next year. We simply suggested that, to suit the expectations of his American audience, he should try to look forward rather than back. And once he did that, he was able to find a central message: Stay with BAM and we'll beat the target you have set us, that his clients could relate to. His whole presentation was structured around this upbeat, forward-looking message. So when he only had time to deliver the introduction and conclusion, it came across loud and clear to his clients. All the more so because he tried very hard to sound positive and optimistic.

It would be wrong to assume, from the examples we've looked at, that the British and Americans are at opposite ends of every scale. The two cultures actually have a lot of views and values in common. Both nations would, for example, probably fall to the left of the following scales:

Short	**Long**
I keep my presentation short and to the point, never go over an agreed time limit, and speak as concisely as possible.	I allocate as much time to the subjects as it deserves and try to speak as eloquently and impressively as possible.
50 40 30 20 10 0	10 20 30 40 50
Selective	**Comprehensive**
I select only the key points and avoid clouding my message with unnecessary detail.	I make sure my presentation is thorough and detailed with plenty of supporting facts and documentation.
50 40 30 20 10 0	10 20 30 40 50

Of course, there are plenty of American and British presenters who include a lot of detail and talk at considerable length. The American software consultants spent 20 minutes telling us about their successes and achievements; and George originally planned to talk to his clients for half an hour. But the American presentation didn't succeed; and George's original structure and style would have lost him the mandate. In general, American and British audiences respond best to presentations that are short and selective. As you might expect, not every culture shares their expectations:

An English manager was at a meeting in Milan. The Italian participants belonged to a network of professional service companies who wanted to pool their skills. Each of the delegates had been asked to prepare a brief presentation of their company. The Englishman was annoyed to find that his fellow delegates ignored the request to keep their presentations brief and in some cases spoke for as long as 20 minutes. When it was his turn to speak, he delivered a two-minute presentation. It had a clear message, was well structured and gave the key information relevant to his listeners. As he sat down, there was an awkward silence; and then polite applause. After the meeting, which finished two hours late, an Italian friend came up to the Englishman. 'Why,' he asked, 'didn't you explain in much greater detail the many things I know your company can offer the group?'

Where you would place yourself on the short-long and selective-comprehensive scales will be heavily influenced by the educational norms in your country. At school and university in Italy, the examinations are often oral. So, throughout their education, Italian students are taught all the rhetorical skills; and they learn to give long, impressive speeches that will show their examiners how much they have learnt and thought about the subject. Naturally enough, when they come to make a business presentation, they take the same approach. They aim to be eloquent and positive; and, of course, to speak for as long as it takes to show the audience that they have thought of all the points.

The British education system, on the other hand, encourages a crisper, more concise style. When your writers were at school, we had lessons and exams where we had to précis texts - in other words, reduce several pages of complicated prose into one short, simple paragraph. As we mentioned above, we were also conditioned, from a very early age, to understate our abilities and give our messages indirectly. When the Englishman made his short, low-key presentation, he was really sending the signal 'less is more'. This would have been fine for a British audience, but the message was completely lost on (misunderstood by) his Italian listeners. The structure he chose came across to them as over-simplistic and far too low-key. They expected him to illustrate the facts with relevant examples and opinions, to argue his case with eloquence, and to project a positive and upbeat attitude.

To most Brits, the word rhetoric describes a speech that sounds impressive, but isn't actually sincere or useful. For the Italians, however, it's the art of speaking eloquently, impressively and persuasively. Rhetorik is also an important part of the academic and business school syllabus in Germany. But the Germans seem to interpret the word in a different way again. In his comparative study of German and British culture, Thomas Kielinger suggests that his fellow Germans most value people who are konsequent (logical, consistent, uncompromising) and grundlich (thorough). So, for them, Rhetorik is the art of presenting a logical and detailed sequence of arguments - as reflected in the dialectical methods of Hegel and Marx. For German students to pass their oral exams, there's no need for them to put forward a lot of new or original ideas. They simply have to learn all the facts and present them in a logical and thorough way.

Maybe that's why the Germans tend to dislike presentations that sound like a sales pitch. While the Italians, Americans and Brits would fall to the left of the scale below, the Germans would most probably fall to the right:

Persuade	**Inform**
I state my own opinions and conclusions upfront and focus only on those areas that support my argument.	I give a detailed and balanced view of the whole situation, so that the audience can draw their own conclusions.
50 40 30 20 10	0 10 20 30 40 50

So, if you're presenting to a German audience, avoid the hard selling concept. Try, instead, to construct a logical and convincing argument using plenty of relevant facts. And if you're German, remember that - with the possible exception of the Scandinavians, Finns and Japanese - few other cultures are as fascinated by exhaustive lists of facts as you are. So make a conscious effort to select only the data that support your central message and are relevant and interesting to your audience. If you don't, there's a very real danger that they will fall asleep. That doesn't mean you should abandon your logical approach - particularly if you're presenting to the French. The French, like the Germans, would fall at the far right of this scale:

Creative Structure	**Logical Structure**
What I appreciate most is a creative structure that surprises and intrigues.	What I appreciate is well-structured, logical sequence of arguments.

50 40 30 20 10 0 10 20 30 40 50

The French enjoy debate, value eloquence and, above all, expect the presenter to give them a logically consistent argument that can't be demolished. In French schools, pupils are taught to present their arguments in a very Cartesian way: thèse, anti-thèse, synthèse (thesis, antithesis, synthesis). As we mentioned earlier, many of the techniques that are taught on international presentation skills courses originate in the USA. And the Americans tend to state their central message at the beginning of their presentation. But this technique does not come naturally to the French. That's because a good central message is effectively a synthesis or conclusion. And the French are taught from an early age to lead up to the conclusion step by step - not state it upfront at the beginning.

It's quite possible that, at this point, your head is starting to spin. Don't worry! There may be over 200 countries in the world, but we aren't going to try to talk about all of them. The cultures we have looked at, and the scales we have shown you, cover the main style differences you will come across.

Before you can adapt to your audience's expectations, you need to do two things: first, analyse your own style and preferences as objectively as possible; and second, resist the temptation to believe that you are right and the rest of the world is wrong. If you know yourself, keep an open mind and make every effort to know your audience, you can always find a way to bridge even the widest culture gap.

FINDING A CONCRETE CONTEXT

In a typical year, many of the international business people we work with have to attend at least 25 presentations. But when we ask them how many of these presentations they would describe as really impressive or memorable, their answer is nearly always the same: No more than 20 per cent.

So what do the presenters who belong to this elite minority do that sets them apart from everyone else? Well, part of the answer is in the quotation at the head of this chapter: they realize that people only see something when they have the right metaphor to perceive it.

Imagine for a moment that you work for a large pharmaceutical company which is about to launch an anti-fungal cream. As product manager, it's your job to present the new cream and ways of selling it to each of the four regional sales teams in your country. So what do you think you should do: deliver exactly the same presentation to each of the four teams; or try to adapt it each time?

In our experience, most people would see nothing wrong with delivering exactly the same presentation to each of the teams. And many would also assume that, in this situation, it would be perfectly acceptable to let the facts speak for themselves. After all, they argue, there's no need to agonize over what might appeal to these audiences. They all work for the same company and they're all salespeople. So they're bound to be interested in the product and how to sell it.

Well, yes, that may be true. But it doesn't mean they will necessarily be fascinated by what you have to say. What if they already know a lot of the information you're planning to present? What if they've already decided that some of your new sales policies are wrong or unsuitable for their region? What if the members of one team are at war with their colleagues in one of the other teams?

It doesn't matter how relevant you think the subject matter is, you've still got to try to put it in a context that the audience can relate to. And, as every audience is different, you're going to have to change the context to suit each one. We don't believe you can create a universal presentation that will be equally relevant and memorable to a series of different listeners. What interests and appeals to one group may well bore or irritate another.

The situation we asked you to imagine - like all the situations in this book - was a real one. After some research and careful thought, the product manager concerned came up with a neat way of making his message relevant to each of the teams. He had discovered that nearly all the sales representatives were keen football fans. So he worked out a way of describing the new sales strategy in footballing terms: the sales team was to be divided into strikers who would go out and find new customers, defenders who would concentrate on cultivating existing customers, sweepers who would be sent out to solve problems, and so on. He was sure that this metaphor would be equally attractive to each of the four sales teams. But he knew it would have even greater impact if he could show them a picture.

That was when he realized how he could tailor his presentation to each region. He got his graphics department to prepare four different visuals. Each one showed football players wearing the colours of the top local team. When he showed the visual, the sales reps immediately identified with the players and started teasing one another. On a couple of occasions, their jokes gave the product manager a clearer under- standing of their needs. And he was able to adapt his presentation accordingly.

But what can I do, our clients often ask us, if I don't know the people I'm presenting to? Well, if you don't know the members of your audience personally, ask yourself what you know about them as a group: are they, for example, all engineers; do they all come from India; are they all in their twenties? You have to keep asking questions about them until you find some common denominator.

But what if the audience do different jobs, come from different countries, and are all different ages? you may ask. Surely the only common denominator then is the information I'm going to present. Well, no. You're forgetting the most important thing they have in common. They're all human beings. And no matter where they come from or what they do, all human beings have certain needs and aims in common. It's just a question of finding which of their needs and aims you could most effectively appeal to in this particular presentation. Often, the answers won't come to you straight away. But if you want your audience to really take notice of what you're saying, you need to persevere.

Finding a context and developing a concrete image your audience can relate to takes time, patience, effort, and a bit of imagination. But it isn't rocket science. In fact, as the example below shows, it's often the simplest ideas that work best:

Our colleague Danny was running a presentations course for a group of six Finns. They worked for a large industrial conglomerate whose core business was paper production. On the first day, Danny invited each of them to make a short presentation about their company. The first five presentations were almost identical: 'Our company employs thousands of people in many different countries. We have factories in this town, that town and the other town. We produce paper, paper-making machinery, drilling platforms, power plants...' and so on, and so on, and so on. Danny was desperate for a cup of coffee. Even so, he decided to get the last presentation out of the way before the mid-morning break. The sixth guy was called John and his presentation went something like this:

John: Danny.

Danny: (surprised) Yes?

John: Which newspaper do you read?

Danny: (even more surprised) The Guardian.

John: Ah! That's a paper for students and left-wingers, right?

Danny: (impressed) Well, I suppose it is, yeah. I started reading it when I was a student. Though I'm more of a liberal democrat these days.

John: OK. But what problems do you have when you read The

Guardian?

Danny: Well, I don't always agree with their politics. And they make a lot of spelling mistakes.

John: And what about your hands? What do they look like when you have finished reading the paper?

Danny: My hands? Well, pretty dirty usually. It's a real nuisance.

John: Exactly. And you're one of our customers, Danny. We supply over 30 per cent of the newsprint that's used in the UK. And we want you to have clean hands. That's why our R&D people are trying to find a way of keeping the ink on the paper and off your hands. You see...

Danny was hooked. He forgot all about the coffee break and would have been happy to let John speak for far longer than the three minutes he had been allotted.

John ended up presenting more or less the same information as his five colleagues. But unlike them, he put Danny first. He focused on the human element and found a concrete example that Danny could immediately relate to. As a result, Danny really listened to him and, to this day, still remembers what he said.

Clearly, Danny and John have quite a lot in common. They're both Europeans; they're both from developed, stable democracies; they're both widely travelled. So it was relatively easy for John to put himself in Danny's shoes. Finding the right context for an audience whose cultural values and expectations are very different from yours can be more challenging. That's because many of your perceptions are so instinctive that it doesn't even occur to you that there's another way of looking at the world. This was certainly the case for Al - a young American Peace Corps volunteer - whom Danny worked with in Africa in the 1970s:

Al was in his early twenties when he arrived at the junior high school in a large village in southern Africa to teach mathematics. The village consisted of traditional mud huts where the 40,000 inhabitants lived, the school (eight large rectangular buildings), a church and a hospital (both built by Scottish missionaries). At first, Al was very impressed with the pupils' enthusiasm and aptitude for his subject. But when he moved on to geometry - starting with squares, rectangles and triangles as he did in the States - they seemed to lose interest. They simply couldn't see the point of the exercises their teacher was asking them to do. After a particularly frustrating lesson, Al went for a walk to clear his head. He climbed a nearby hill, stood at the top, and looked down at the village. 'But of course!', he thought. 'Most of the buildings in the village are circular. No wonder they're not interested in right angles. Why didn't I see that before?'

Next day, he started the maths class by saying: 'I want you to imagine you're an eagle. You're looking down on the village. What do you see?' The children immediately drew a lot of circular huts and walls. 'OK,' said the teacher. 'So how much space do you have in each hut? And how far is it from the edge of the hut to the edge of the wall?' From that moment on, the children were hooked. They eagerly learned about 'pi', and were soon working out circumferences and areas. And they were just as interested when the teacher moved from circles to tangents and from tangents to angles.

From a Western perspective, it makes no sense to start with circles and end with squares. In fact, that's doing things the wrong way round. But for these young Africans, it was the right way round. And the American teacher only realized that when he started to see the world through his pupils' eyes. Making a conscious effort to step outside your own cultural preconceptions is the key to finding the right context for your international audiences.

Sooner or later, you will make or attend a presentation where one of the visuals is a map. When you learnt geography at school, you probably assumed that the maps your teachers gave you were universal. After all, everyone lives in the same world and countries are a fixed shape and size. And it probably never occurred to you that different cultures see the world, literally, through different eyes:

A Swedish professor was presenting the results of some clinical trials at an international pharmaceutical symposium in Florence. A high proportion of the delegates were from the Middle East and Asia. To show where the people who had taken part in the trial came from, the professor had a slide with a map of the world on it. Instead of illustrating his point, however, the slide seemed to be confusing the audience. Some of them frowned, others exchanged glances, and one or two of them raised their eyebrows. From that point on, the professor sensed that he had lost the audience's attention. 'I can't understand what the problem was,' he confided to a friend several days later. 'I mean, this is the slide I used. Can you see anything wrong with it?' His friend looked at the slide for a moment, smiled and asked: 'Where did you get this map from?' The professor replied: 'I don't know.

The people in our graphics department produced all the slides. Why?' His friend said: 'Well, they shouldn't have put Sweden right at the centre of the map, should they?' The professor looked puzzled: 'But that's where most of the clinical trials took place.' His friend shook his head and pointed to the tiny landmass that represented the Indian sub-continent: 'Yes, but most of your audience came from this part of the world. I expect they were pretty shocked to see that you thought Sweden was three times the size of India.'

The world map that many Americans and Europeans are used to seeing is based on Mercator's projection. And according to Mercator's projection, North America is bigger than Africa, Scandinavia is bigger than India, and Europe is bigger than South America. But, in fact, this is a gross distortion of the world. A map using an equal area projection (eg Arno Peters') reveals that North America is far smaller than Africa; India is three times the size of Scandinavia; and South America is twice the size of Europe. When we show a Peters' world map on our presentation courses, some of the participants react quite negatively. They declare that it's wrong; that the continents are shaped wrongly. Maybe they expect the industrialized countries to look bigger than the developing ones because they're richer. Or maybe they've simply never realized that the world maps they've always used give an inaccurate impression of each country's size and are, therefore, not universally accepted.

That was certainly the case with the Swedish professor. The last thing he wanted to do was offend or alienate his audience. If only he had asked someone from India or the Middle East for their advice while he was preparing his presentation. It's such a simple and obvious thing to do. And yet, in our experience, it's something that far too many presenters forget - particularly when the presentation they're preparing involves a lot of creative work:

A large European company were trying to sell their high-tech systems to clients around the world. They tailored each presentation to the individual client's interests, but there was one key metaphor and visual that they always used: 'Your problems,' they told their clients, 'are like lions - wild, unpredictable, and hard to control. But with our systems, you can be a lion tamer. You can subdue the lions and keep them under control.' This worked very well until they went to a country in Africa. As soon as they showed the visual, the audience looked horrified. The lion was a symbol of their country, and the image that came across to them was of a colonial power subduing their State. The Europeans lost the contract to a competitor.

The trouble was, these Europeans had invested a lot of time, money and effort in developing the lion-tamer image. In any case, it had already been tried out on a number of audiences and worked very well. So they didn't see any reason why it shouldn't succeed with their prospective African clients too. For the international presenter, this is a dangerous position to be in. It's only human nature to believe that an idea you've worked hard to create is sure to succeed. But before you get too attached to it, you need to check it out with a local expert, and act on the advice they give you. And you should never assume that, just because an image has already succeeded with one audience, it will necessarily have the right impression on another. Remember, every audience is different. What engages and amuses one group of people may mystify or offend another.

SPEAKING WITH IMPACT

There's one thing, however, that every audience in the world has in common. If a presenter uses language that is unclear, or speaks in an over- complicated or monotonous way, they will fall asleep.

Try to read the sentence below out loud:

With the installation of our new manufacturing software platform, and the implementation of the seven-step quality initiative which, as some of you are probably aware, represent a substantial investment of some 15 million, our ultimate objective, once these two projects have been implemented at the end of next year, is the achievement of optimal production performance, a reduction in lead times, and an overall improvement to customer service...

It sounds horrible, doesn't it? If you speak like this, you'll lose your audience's attention before you even get to the end of your first sentence. So what's going wrong here? Well, more or less everything, to be honest.

For a start, there are far too many nouns: installation, implementation, investment, objective, achievement, performance, reduction, improvement. And look at them. They're all very long - three syllables or more; and most of them are very abstract. Can you actually visualize implementation, achievement, or performance? You certainly couldn't draw a picture to explain what these abstractions mean. And listen to the rhythm: installATion, implemenTATion, inVESTment, and so on. In every case, the stress falls on the next to last syllable. That kind of rhythm is guaranteed to send an audience to sleep - as your writers know from long experience of listening to the first presentations our clients make when they come on one of our courses.

So why do people use these long abstract nouns? Well, for the native speaker of English, they're the kind of words you find in very formal, written documents - economic reports, academic theses and contracts, for example. So they probably think that using them in their presentation will make them sound more intellectual or impressive. And, of course, a lot of non-native speakers use these words all the time - particularly the Germans and the Italians - because that's the way they speak in their own language.

But English is a language that loves verbs. If you want your audience to be able to visualize what you're saying, you need to talk about people doing things. For example:

We're going to install some new production software.

We're going to set up a better quality control system.

We're investing more than 15 million in these projects.

What we're aiming to do is boost output, cut lead times, and improve customer satisfaction.

All these verbs are short - no more than two syllables. And the minute you start using them, you can help your audience understand what you're saying by stressing the parts of the sentence that you think are important. For example:

We're going to install some NEW production SOFTware and SET UP a BETter quality conTROL system.

You see, in natural spoken English, every sentence is a combination of long beats and short beats, rather like the drum rhythm in a pop song. As soon as you stress the important parts of the sentence, you adopt this natural rhythm. And you start sounding like a real person talking to other real people - rather than someone who is reading from a script, or delivering a pedantic lecture.

So the sentence we asked you to read out loud has far too many long, abstract nouns. But that's not the only thing that's wrong with it.

The sentence itself is much too long. Successful international presenters keep their sentences short and simple.

If you try to put too many ideas into one sentence, you'll be forced to use subordinate clauses: which, as some of you are probably aware, represent a substantial investment of some 15 million; and once these two projects have been implemented at the end of next year. And subordinate clauses make it very difficult for your listeners to remember how the sentence began. If you want to speak with impact, aim for one idea per sentence. And, where possible, keep your sentences active:

Instead of: once these two projects have been implemented (passive verb construction)

Say: once we've implemented these two projects (active verb construction)

Instead of: The new machines were checked by us.

Say: We checked the new machines.

Of course, there will be occasions when you need to use a passive construction. You may well prefer, for example, to say a lot of mistakes were made rather than the sales director made a lot of mistakes. But when you're not worried about saying who did what, active sentences generally have far greater impact.

So if you follow all the advice above, and also try to add some 'you-appeal' - in other words, make sure that what you're saying is relevant to the audience - this speech might sound something like this:

What can we do to boost our output? How can we cut lead times? How can we improve customer service? These are questions you've been asking for some time. And today, I've got some answers for you. We've decided to spend 15 million updating our systems. First, we're going to install the latest production software. And, second, we're going to set up a much tighter quality control system. Both projects should be up and running by the end of next year...

OK. Are you ready for a short exercise? If so, look at the sentence below, and work out how you would replace the nouns with verbs:

It is necessary to have a detailed examination of the specification before the installation of the new line.

If you are a non-native speaker of English, you will probably instinctively say something like this:

We need to examine the specification very carefully before we install the new line.

If you are a native English speaker, your proposal may be more like this:

We need to go through the spec with a fine-tooth comb before we put the new line in.

English has an enormous vocabulary - twice as big, for example, as French. Words are derived from two main language streams: Germanic (German and Scandinavian) and Romance (Latin-based). Native speakers tend automatically to choose short Germanic verbs (for example: get, go through, put in, tell) in preference to their Latin-based equivalents (obtain, examine, install, inform). That's because, to their ear, Latin-based verbs sound too formal for speaking, and are more appropriate for writing - rather like the long, abstract nouns we looked at above.

But non-native speakers have most probably learnt written rather than spoken English. This means that they are likely to feel far more comfortable with words that are derived from Latin. Even people, like the Japanese, whose own language has no connection with Latin, tend to feel this way. And, somewhat paradoxically, many Germans prefer Latin-based words too. That's because they sound more formal and, therefore, more similar to High German. We still have Germans on our language courses who believe that get isn't correct English. And, of course, to speakers of Romance languages - French, Spanish, Italian, Portuguese, Romanian - Latin-based words are much easier to understand.

The fact that English has become the common language of international business should be very good news for the monolingual American, Australian, New Zealander or Brit. All too often, however, the native English speaker is at a disadvantage. Some years ago, an East Asian airline chose to buy flight simulators from a French firm rather than a British one: as their pilots would have to be trained in English to use the simulators, the airline preferred to buy them from the people who spoke the clearer English - in other words, the French. And one of Italy's top companies refuses to have American or British consultants running their courses; they prefer Swiss or Dutch people who can speak English in a way that will be understood by all their staff.

If you're a native English speaker and you're presenting to an audience for whom English is a second or foreign language, you need to choose the kind of verbs they're likely to understand. That means, for example, saying examine rather than go through; and install instead of put in. And rather than use idiomatic expressions like with a fine-tooth comb and abbreviations like spec, you should say very carefully and specification instead.

And try to control your tone and tempo. Many presenters, particularly native speakers, make the mistake of speaking too fast. But, of course, if you speak too slowly, you could sound artificial and patronizing. The secret is to keep your natural tone, enunciate clearly, and pause at the end of a phrase or sentence - not after each word. When you're rehearsing your presentation, record part of your speech and listen to yourself critically. Do you sound natural? Are the pauses long enough? Whoever you're presenting to, you'll need to pause more frequently and for longer than you do in normal conversation.

Even if you're a native speaker presenting to a native-speaking audience, you can't assume that they will immediately understand what your main points are and how they link together. Listening to a presentation isn't like reading a book. Your audience can't see when you are 'starting a new paragraph'. If they miss a step in your argument, they can't go back and 'read' it again. It's your job, as presenter, to guide your audience through your speech. At every step, you need to tell them where they are, where they've been, and where they're going. So try to create plenty of beginnings, where you summarize your argument so far, and tell them what the next step is.

SUMMARY

Wherever your audience is from, your presentation will only be successful if they really listen to what you're saying and remember the message you're trying to get across. Following the guidelines below will help you achieve this objective.

Try to express in one clear, punchy sentence what the presentation is about and what the audience will gain from listening to you. In his introduction, for example, George told his American clients: I'm going to show you how, if you stay with BAM, we will beat the target you have set us. This has much more 'you-appeal' than his original central message: A lot of things went wrong last quarter but, as you will see, this was out of our control.

Even if you're presenting to an audience who value a lot of facts and background information, it's still vital to be selective. The most dangerous subject for you as presenter is the one that fascinates you; the one that you're the world expert on. If you're in this position, check your motives.

Why are you including this point? Is it because your audience really needs to know it? Or is it just because you find it interesting - and, perhaps, want to show people how much you know?

Choose only the points that support your central message and are relevant to your audience. Ask yourself which end of the selective-comprehensive and short-long scales your audience falls. If they are, for example, German, Scandinavian or Japanese, support what you say with plenty of relevant facts and figures. If, on the other hand, they're from the USA or the UK, go for a broad overview which includes only details that are absolutely essential.

If you're presenting to the Americans, focus on future solutions rather than past problems and don't be afraid to give your own opinions and recommendations upfront. If your audience is from Germany, on the other hand, avoid the hard sell. Try, instead, to give a detailed, balanced and logical view of the advantages and disadvantages. And if your audience is French, make sure that your argument is logical and consistent.

Even if the members of your audience seem to have nothing in common with each other, keep asking yourself questions until you find a common denominator. Remember, people only see something when they have the right metaphor to perceive it. Finding that metaphor will often turn a satisfactory presentation into a brilliant one.

Note: Reader can go to site www.members.microsoft.com for detailed in-depth knowledge on making presentations.

27

Making Deals

Have you noticed that, when a deal falls through (fails), most negotiators automatically blame some practical issue: the client couldn't afford to pay for the kind of quality we offer; or we don't have the capacity to supply the volumes they're looking for. Very few people are prepared to admit that they lost the contract because they didn't handle the client or the negotiation in the right way.

In the international arena, however, it's your negotiating style above all else that can make or break a deal:

Two companies had been short-listed for a major infrastructural contract in Mexico. One was North American, the other Swedish. Both companies were invited to Mexico to present their proposals to the relevant ministry and to start negotiating the terms of a deal.

The Americans put a lot of effort into producing a high-tech, hard-hitting presentation. Their message was clear: 'We can give you the most technically advanced equipment at a price our competitors can't match.' The team - which consisted of senior technical experts, lawyers, and interpreters - flew down from their New York head office to Mexico City where they had reserved rooms in one of the top hotels for a week. In order to put on the best possible performance for the minister and his officials, the Americans had arranged to give their presentation in a conference room at the hotel; and they had brought all the necessary equipment with them from the States. All the arrangements had been written down in great detail and sent to the Mexican officials two weeks earlier.

At the agreed time the American team were ready to present, but they had no one to present to. The people from the ministry arrived at various times over the next hour. They didn't apologize for being late, but just began to chat amiably with the Americans about a wide range of non- business matters. The leader of the American team kept glancing anxiously at his watch. Finally, he suggested that the presentation should start. Though the Mexicans seemed surprised, they politely agreed, and took their seats. Twenty minutes later the minister - accompanied by some senior officials - walked in. He looked extremely angry and asked the Americans to start the presentation again from the beginning. Ten minutes later, he started talking to an aide who had just arrived with a message for him. When the American presenter stopped speaking, the minister signalled that he should continue. By this time, most of the audience were talking amongst themselves. When invited to ask questions at the end, the only thing the minister wanted to know was why the Americans had told them so little about their company's history.

Later, during lunch, the Americans were very surprised to be asked questions about their individual backgrounds and qualifications, rather than the technical details of their products. The Minister had a brief word with the American team leader and left without eating or drinking anything.

Over the next few days, the Americans contacted their Mexican counterparts several times in an attempt to fix a meeting and start the negotiations. They reminded them that they had to fly back to the States at the end of the week. But the Mexicans' response was always the same: 'We need time to examine your proposal amongst ourselves first.' At the end of the week the Americans left Mexico angry, frustrated and empty-handed.

It was the Swedes who won this lucrative contract, and we'll have a look at how they handled the initial stages of the negotiation later. But first, let's try to work out why, despite their best intentions, things went so badly wrong for these negotiators from the USA. There's no doubt that they really wanted this contract. And they clearly invested a lot of time, money and effort in trying to make the best possible impression: they picked a first rate team; they looked round for a prestigious venue; they scheduled a carefully timed itinerary; they planned a comprehensive agenda; they put together an extremely competitive offer; and they thought very carefully about how they were going to communicate. A prospective client from the USA would certainly have found it all very hard to resist. The trouble was, the prospective clients weren't from the USA. They were Mexican. And the North Americans failed to take account of that. As a result, they chose the wrong negotiating team; they tried to deal with the Mexicans at the wrong pace and in the wrong place; and they misread the signals that were being sent. This chapter aims to help you avoid making the same costly mistakes.

PICKING THE RIGHT PEOPLE

YOUR TEAM

At first sight, you might think that the Americans had selected their team very carefully indeed: there were technical experts who could give a good impression of the company's expertise and answer any difficult questions; lawyers who could negotiate a watertight (comprehensive and free from errors) contract; and interpreters who would make sure that everything was communicated clearly and accurately.

So why was that the wrong team for Mexico? Well, not every culture shares the American view that people should be judged solely on what they do. Mexico is a given status culture where other factors such as age and position are also taken into account. The technical experts might have been very knowledgeable, but their level of seniority was way below that of the Mexican minister and his senior officials. So, from the Mexicans' perspective, there was no way they could negotiate on equal terms. To show the kind of respect the Mexicans were expecting, the American team should have been led by a board member, at the very least. As the minister himself was involved, a president, chairman or CEO would probably have been more appropriate - particularly for the initial exchanges.

Including lawyers on the team was another serious mistake. For the Mexicans, business is personal. If you want to make deals with them, you have to build a personal relationship first. Filling the room with lawyers at the very first meeting does little to develop mutual warmth and trust. Why on earth would people who trust each other need lawyers to record and check everything that was being said? Of course, you'll need to bring your lawyers in when you start drawing up the contract. But until then, you should leave them at home.

A few years ago, at the height of the American craze for political correctness in their universities, students were encouraged to sign contractual checklists of what they were and were not willing to do with a potential sexual partner on a first date. That way both partners could be sure they weren't exploiting one another. To much of the rest of the world (and, to be fair, to many Americans), this took all the mystery and romance out of the dating game. It reduced it to a purely functional transaction. Maybe that's what the Mexicans thought the lawyers were doing to the negotiation.

And why did the Americans decide to bring external interpreters with them? Theirs was a huge company with offices all over South

America. Surely they could have found a Spanish speaker who was in a senior enough position to take an active part in these negotiations. Interpreters are very useful, of course. And there will be some occasions when you have to bring them in. But if you can find someone from within your own organization who speaks the local language, they'll be able to help you get much closer to your partners than an interpreter can. Only one of your own people can show the empathy that is needed to develop a warm and trusting relationship between your two organizations.

The team that the Americans put together reflected their own cultural values. As this was a major infrastructural contract, they assumed that the Mexicans would be interested, above all, in technical expertise, legal guarantees and safeguards, and clear, straightforward communications. But, as we have seen, what the Mexicans were really looking for were partners they could trust; people who showed them warmth and treated them with respect. The team the Americans picked sent all the wrong signals. As a result, they didn't even make it to the negotiating table.

THEIR TEAM

Picking the right people for your team is vital. It's equally important to make sure that you are meeting the right people.

A very prestigious German company had a long-term relationship with a client firm in North Africa. The firm employed a large team of technical experts with impressive qualifications. And, during the year, the Germans had frequent and successful contact with them. But when the terms of the contract were renegotiated at the end of every year, these technical experts weren't present. Their president, whose technical expertise was fairly limited, would fly over to Germany on his own and conduct the negotiations himself. That was because his instincts told him that top companies expect to deal with very senior managers. But, of course, for the functional, acquired status Germans, he was the wrong person. They would have been much happier to deal with one of the technical experts. Their annual meetings with the president were a nightmare. They had to explain every single detail to him and it took hours to put the deal together. After one particularly long and frustrating session, the Germans politely suggested that, next time, the president should bring one of his technical experts with him. To their relief, he agreed.

The following year, the Germans arranged for one of their own board members to take care of the president while they negotiated with the technical guy. The president was delighted to be taken to lunch and shown round the company art galleries by someone of his own status. And the Germans were equally delighted to be able to put the deal together so quickly and easily.

Of course, in this case, the two companies already had a long-standing relationship. So meeting the wrong person didn't break the deal. Even so, relations might have deteriorated over time if the Germans hadn't found a way to meet the right person while still showing respect for the president's status. If you meet the wrong person in the initial stages of your relationship, however, the door to that company may be closed to you forever.

When Wim, the managing director of a Dutch tool manufacturer, was looking for a distributor in Asia, he was delighted when Watanabe-san, the chief executive of a major Tokyo firm, agreed to meet him. Wim knew that Japanese corporate structures tended to be much more vertical than in the Netherlands. And so he assumed, logically enough, that the guy at the top of the tree would be the one who made and executed the real decisions.

The chief executive's son-in-law, Paul - an Irishman who had worked for the Tokyo firm for many years-acted as interpreter. The meeting was warm and friendly and, as he flew back to Amsterdam, Wim felt very pleased with himself. He was convinced he had found the right business partner. As the weeks passed, however, he heard nothing back from Watanabe-san. Wim tried calling him, but he was never available. He sent him several letters, but they remained unanswered. What had gone wrong? Paul - the Irishman who had acted as interpreter - told us the other side of the story:

It was really embarrassing. As soon as I walked in, I realized that Watanabe-san wasn't remotely interested in making a deal. You see, he hadn't invited any middle managers to the meeting. And, over here, they're the ones who really put deals together and make them work. But poor old Wim was obviously delighted to be talking to the top guy. As far as he was concerned, that meant the deal was as good as done. For us, it was just a rather meaningless ceremonial discussion between our top man and theirs.

In many parts of the world, a one-to-one meeting with the chief executive would be a very positive signal indeed. But, as we saw Japan's business culture is highly group-oriented. Strategic decisions are only taken after a thorough consultation process (nemawashi). Your meeting may be with the top man, but if he's the only one who's listening to your pitch, it's highly unlikely to result in a deal.

When you're trying to make a deal with a company whose cultural values are very different from your own, it's not always easy to work out whether the person you're meeting is the right one or not. Our advice, as ever, is to resist the temptation to jump to any hasty conclusions about your prospective partner's motives. Instead, try to read the signals they are sending from their cultural perspective, not yours. If, for example, you're from a group-oriented culture (like Japan, the Arab world or China) and you're doing business with an individualist one (such as the USA, Germany or Britain), don't immediately assume that the deal has no future if there's only one person present at the meeting. As long as you're talking to the right person, there's no reason why the deal shouldn't go ahead.

Similarly, if you're from a given status culture (Latin America, say, or India) and you're meeting someone from an acquired status culture (such as the USA, Australia or the Netherlands), don't be offended if your partner is younger than you, or has a more junior position. She has almost certainly been sent to this negotiation because she has the technical expertise, skills and knowledge to put this particular deal together.

In short, whether you're putting your own team together or evaluating your partners' team, it's vital to make a conscious effort to step outside your own cultural perspectives. As the Americans found to their cost, picking the wrong people can break a deal before you even get to the negotiating table.

THINKING ABOUT PACE AND PLACE

The Americans paid meticulous attention to the schedule and agenda for their presentation and initial meetings with the Mexicans. They also spent a lot of money on the venue. From their perspective, conducting the negotiations at one of the most prestigious hotels in the city had two major advantages: they could offer the Mexicans the kind of top class hospitality that would obviously be expected; and they would keep control of the negotiating environment. Indeed, their main instinct seems to have been to remain in control; to leave nothing to chance. And to make absolutely sure that nothing would go wrong, they wrote all the arrangements down in great detail and sent them to the Mexican officials well in advance of the meeting.

When they were thinking about pace and place, the Americans assumed that it was vital to demonstrate how serious, well organized and professional they were. As we have seen, this was the wrong assumption to make.

PACE

As we saw in previous chapter, the North Americans are highly monochronic. In their culture, people are judged by how well they can control their time. And people who can't do so are not to be trusted. The Mexicans, on the other hand, are highly polychronic. To them, how you nurture relationships is much more important than how you manage your time. Far from being impressed by the Americans' detailed and carefully timed schedule, the Mexicans probably thought they were being pushy or even arrogant.

The two prospective partners would fall at opposite ends of this scale too:

Speed	**Patience**
Too much analysis lead to paralysis.	Taking my time helps me make the right decision.

50 40 30 20 10 0 10 20 30 40 50

The Mexicans wanted to discuss the proposals among themselves in a leisurely fashion; and they couldn't understand why the Americans were in such a rush. The Americans, on the other hand, were impatient for a decision; they couldn't understand why it was taking the Mexicans so long to consider such a straightforward and attractive offer.

But, of course, the Mexicans weren't simply thinking about the proposals the Americans had made. In fact, they were far more interested in forming an impression of the members of the American team: Are these the kind of people we want to work with? Can we trust them? Could we build a good relationship with them? The answer they came to, in each case, was No. And that was largely because, at every stage, the Americans tried to force the pace: they looked anxious and surprised when the Mexicans were late; they started the presentation before the most important person arrived; and they kept reminding the Mexicans of their imminent departure in an attempt to force them to the negotiating table.

When your prospective partners are from a polychronic, patient culture, you won't get anywhere if you tie yourself to self-imposed deadlines or show you are desperate to catch the plane home. You need to allow plenty of time to get to know one another and build the relationship. You have to follow the mood, not the schedule.

When the Mexicans arrived late for the presentation, it was an ideal opportunity for informal and relaxed small talk. The Americans failed to take advantage of this because they were so obsessed with the schedule. For them (as well as the Germans, Swiss and Dutch) time is money. And there's no point in spending too much of either on unproductive small talk. But, for many cultures small talk is an essential part of building or cementing the relationship. So, when you're negotiating internationally, our advice is to follow your partners' lead. And if you come from a culture that is uncomfortable with small talk, make sure you have plenty of open questions ready to use. The more questions you ask, the better you will understand your partners. And that's bound to help you make a better deal.

Communicating clearly across cultures is never easy. So if they had managed to reach the negotiating table, the Americans would certainly have needed an agenda of some kind. But it was a serious mistake to prepare such a rigid agenda without consulting their Mexican partners. An agenda should always be agreed, never imposed. And you need to make sure that you handle it in a way that suits the natural pace and rhythm of the local partner. The linear, timed agenda favoured in monochronic cultures such as the USA and Germany is not universal. In polychronic cultures, like the Arab world, people feel very uncomfortable discussing and finalizing one issue at a time. They tend to take a more circular approach and may well revisit the same point again and again in the course of the meeting. We believe that nothing is agreed until everything is agreed; in other words, that successful negotiators link all the issues. In this respect, the way polychronic cultures instinctively handle the agenda can give them a considerable advantage over their more monochronic partners.

American pace is fast by almost any standards. Maybe that's because, perhaps more than any other culture, they embrace change, look constantly to the future, and have little respect for tradition. In fact, they would probably fall to the far left of this scale:

Future	**Past**
Tradition gets in the way of progress.	Change needs to respect tradition.

50 40 30 20 10 0 10 20 30 40 50

The Americans (and other future-oriented cultures like the 'new Russia') tend to see tradition as one of the main barriers to progress.

When top Wall Street analyst, Byron Wien, described Europe as 'an open air museum', he wasn't paying a compliment.

The gap between future- and past-oriented cultures is considerable. While the latter (for example, Europe and Latin America) are likely to focus on problems, the former will be more interested in solutions; while the Americans will be keen to introduce new systems, the Mexicans will be more interested in working out what went wrong with the old ones. These differing perspectives will have a marked impact on the pace of the negotiation and both parties need to be willing to adapt. If you place too much emphasis on the past, the Americans will think you're gloomy, conservative and lacking in dynamism; if you focus exclusively on the future, the Mexicans and Europeans will perceive you as superficial.

It's not just your pace and rhythm that may need to be adapted. You also have to think carefully about where your partners expect to conduct the negotiations.

PLACE

If your colleagues tell you they have just taken part in an international negotiation, what image immediately springs to mind? If you're from a highly functional business culture, you will probably picture the two teams of negotiators facing each other across a conference table in some smart hotel, your company's board room, or the corner of a colleague's office. It's unlikely that you will picture the negotiators sweating in a sauna, sipping malt whiskies in a nightclub, or reclining on sunbeds in the garden of someone's weekend home. But for people from highly personal business cultures, these informal venues are often where the real business takes place.

The Americans naturally assumed that a five star hotel with luxurious conference rooms was the obvious venue for an important international negotiation. But they would have had a much better chance of making a deal if they had been prepared to meet their Mexican partners in a series of more informal, personal settings. Instead of making an attempt to meet them on their own ground, however, they made the Mexicans come to them. The hotel conference room, with all its high-tech equipment flown in from the USA, was an extension of the Americans' territory. They were the rich neighbours and they were going to show their poor relatives how things should be done. At least, that's how the whole arrangement must have appeared to the Mexicans.

The Americans believed that they were acting as attentive and generous hosts and that they were treating their prospective clients as honoured guests. This would have been fine if they had been in the USA. But while they were in Mexico, they should have let the Mexicans play host.

Mexico is a given status culture. That means there are certain protocols which have to be observed when you're dealing with senior people, and behaviour 'onstage' at the negotiating table tends to be fairly formal. In such cultures, it's often more constructive to take the negotiation 'offstage' so that your partners can relax and get to know you. Only then will they feel free to speak frankly and openly.

'Offstage' negotiating can help you get round other problems too - as a French negotiator recently found. He had attended a Working with the Japanese course at Canning. A few weeks after the course, he sent us some feedback:

Last month, I took part in a negotiation with our Japanese partners. In the course of the meeting, I asked one of their negotiators a number of questions that related to his area of expertise. But each time, he evaded the question. I was beginning to get very frustrated when I remembered what you had said about taking the negotiations 'offstage'. So I called a break and took this guy into a corner. Once he was away from his colleagues, he happily answered all my questions in full. When we got back to the table, the negotiation started moving again. Going 'offstage' had made an enormous difference.

The Japanese guy wasn't being deliberately obstructive. He just didn't feel comfortable about expressing his opinions in front of so many people. That's because, in his highly group-oriented culture, individuals are not expected to push themselves forward during group meetings. Personal views are usually only exchanged during the informal, one-to-one discussions that take place during nemawashi. If the Frenchman had continued asking the same questions again and again - or worse, shown his frustration at the lack of answers - he would have blocked the negotiation and probably damaged the relationship. But because he showed that he under- stood his Japanese counterpart's difficulties by suggesting a break and having a quiet word with him in the corner, he reinforced the relationship and got the negotiation moving again.

If the Mexican minister had invited the Americans to spend the weekend at his hacienda, they might well have been reluctant to accept. As we saw in last chapter, fixed truth cultures often regard extravagant entertainment as a form of bribery. Or they may even suspect that their partners are trying to play some kind of dirty trick.

One of the main problems in international negotiations is that one person's dirty trick can be another person's standard negotiating behaviour. The key is to keep an open mind. If you travel the world assuming that all foreigners are trying to play dirty tricks on you, you'll never forge strong international relationships.

For the past few years, we've been asking the participants on our international negotiations courses to fill in a questionnaire about their personal negotiating style. The questions are designed to find out, for example, how important personal relationships are to them, and how important they think they are to their partners. As you might expect, the vast majority - 85 per cent - claim that personal relationships are very important to them; but only 50 per cent believe that they are important to their partners. Our participants come from a very wide cross-section of the world's multinationals and many of those firms deal with each other. So clearly these negotiators are misreading the signals their partners are sending. And differing attitudes to pace and place may well be one of the causes.

Take the American-Mexican deal we've been talking about. The Americans would undoubtedly have claimed that building a personal relationship with their partners was of paramount importance to them. But the Mexicans clearly didn't think that this was the case. And, like 72 per cent of our participants, the Americans would probably also have said that they always look for common ground rather than try to impose a solution on their partners. But, again, the Mexicans would probably have been astonished to hear it.

Your international partners can't read your mind. They can only try to interpret the signals you're sending to them. And the way they interpret those signals will be strongly influenced by their own cultural norms. The Americans didn't get as far as the negotiating table because the Mexicans were offended by their choice of team and the way they tried to force the pace. Even if you reach the negotiating table, you will still have to work very hard to play the game to win.

PLAYING THE GAME TO WIN

In our experience, international communication is often of a very low standard. Diplomacy is generally the first casualty; clarity the second. We regularly ask the business people who come on our international negotiations courses to play a game called 'The Prisoners' Dilemma'. Two people are asked to imagine that they're in jail. The trainer - in the role of prison guard - asks each of them, again and again, whether they're prepared to squeal (inform) on the other prisoner or not. They're not allowed to communicate with each other. But they know that:

- If both of them stay silent, they'll both go free (i.e. get two points each);
- If they both squeal, they'll both go to jail for a very long time (i.e. get one point each);
- If one prisoner talks and the other doesn't, the squealer will be released and given a fat reward (i.e. three points); his silent partner will be taken out and shot (i.e. get a zero score).

After each round, the players are told what their fellow prisoner has decided to do. As you would expect, in a mono-cultural group where the two players already know one another, they find it relatively easy to predict how the other is likely to behave in the next round. And they usually fall, fairly quickly, into a pattern of remaining silent. Ultimately, of course, this is what most pairs of prisoners end up doing. But, in a multi- cultural group - particularly where the players don't know each other - it usually takes them much longer to reach that point.

Say, for example, the two players are Renate and Gianni. For the first two rounds they both remain silent. Here's an opportunity thinks Gianni. Renate is obviously a 'sucker' (someone who is easily deceived). She's sure to remain silent in the third round, so I'll squeal and claim the reward. Sure enough, Renate does remain silent in the third round. And when Gianni squeals, she's extremely annoyed. So what does she do in the fourth round? Well, she may bear a grudge (feeling of anger or dislike towards someone who has harmed you) and squeal. Or she may remain silent in an attempt to teach her cheating partner the right way to behave. If Gianni continues to squeal, however, the game soon deteriorates into a fight to the death. And both players get very low scores.

The analogy between this game and a negotiation is clear. For both players to 'win' they need to trust one another and interpret accurately the signals their partner is sending. When you're negotiating with people from your own or a similar culture, you can usually recognize an aggressive move, a gesture of faith or a capitulation relatively easily. But when your partners are from a different culture, the signals can be much more difficult to read. And if you want to play the game to win, you will need to make a conscious effort to understand what lies behind their behaviour and, of course, to think very carefully about the way you express yourself.

UNDERSTANDING THEIR BELIEFS

Clearly, what your partners believe will have a marked impact on how they behave; and, of course, on how they interpret your behaviour.

A couple of years ago, Chris was running a negotiations course for a group of project leaders - among them Pascale and Bruno - at an engineering firm in France. Pascale's clients were in Austria; Bruno's were in Algeria. Apart from location, the two projects were very similar. They were of an identical size and both were in the public sector. After the initial negotiation, in each case, a written contract had been drawn up. The Austrian document ran to 132 pages; the Algerian one was a mere 7 pages. Out of interest, Chris asked the two project managers how often they actually looked at the contract. Pascale replied that she took the 132-page document with her every time she met her Austrian clients; and that it formed the basis of most of their discussions.

Bruno simply said: 'I took the contract to a meeting in Algeria once. But I'll never make the same mistake again.' Apparently, as soon as he pulled the contract out of his briefcase to clarify a couple of points, his Algerian counterpart exploded: 'Why do you need to look at the contract?', he asked. 'If there's a problem, just tell me. And we can find a solution together. I can't believe you're doing this. I thought we trusted each other.' Bruno had to work very hard to get the relationship back on track.

How can something that is accepted as common business practice in Austria cause so much offence in Algeria? Well, part of the answer lies in the two cultures' preferences on the following scale:

Written	**Spoken**
For serious issues I prefer the written word.	For serious issues I prefer oral communication.

50 40 30 20 10 0 10 20 30 40 50

Along with most Northern Europeans and North Americans, Pascale's Austrian partners would place themselves towards the left of this scale. For them, memoranda of understanding, written summaries and e-mailed offers may carry much more weight than what people say in a meeting; and contracts almost certainly will. That's probably why the Americans took their lawyers to the first meeting with the Mexicans. Bruno's Algerian partner, on the other hand, comes from a culture that has a strong oral tradition. He accepts that contracts are a necessary part of any international deal; but they don't define or shape the relationship as they do in a more written culture.

If you lean towards the left of this scale and you're trying to make a deal with someone who falls to the right, remember that your partners will probably take what you say more seriously than what you write. So keep the contract out of sight, don't make verbal promises you're not prepared to keep, and beware of taking too many notes. If you spend the whole meeting writing down what they say, they'll think you don't trust them. That's not to say you shouldn't take any notes at all. International negotiation is hard enough, particularly if one or both partners are speaking a language which is not their native tongue. And it's vital to make sure that you've understood one another correctly. But your first priority should be to look at your partners, listen carefully to what they say, and talk to them. If you summarize what has been discussed frequently, you should have no problem remembering the points that have been raised. Summarizing will also enable you to check that you've understood one another correctly. Once something concrete has been agreed, summarize it together verbally, and only then write down a few brief notes.

The Austrians and Algerians will also fall at opposite ends of this scale:

Choice						**Destiny**				
I am in charge of how I live my life.						Forces beyond my control determine what happens in my life.				
50	**40**	**30**	**20**	**10**	**0**	**10**	**20**	**30**	**40**	**50**

People from much of North Africa, the Middle East and parts of Asia would place themselves to the right. For them, the black and white certainty of a contract is in conflict with their religious and spiritual beliefs. Forces beyond their control could intervene at any time and disrupt their plans. So how can a document possibly define what will happen in the future? That's probably why the Algerian contract was only seven pages long. If you believe in destiny, there's no point in having a contract that covers every single eventuality. When Muslims are negotiating, they will often qualify what they say with the phrase Inshallah (if God wills it). They're not demonstrating an unwillingness to commit to the deal. They're just recognizing that circumstances can change; and reminding you that, if they do, partners who trust each other can always renegotiate the terms of the deal.

When Bruno pulled the contract out of his briefcase, then, his Algerian partner was very offended: partly because it was a signal that Bruno didn't trust him; and partly because it went against his deeply held beliefs about the meaning of life. Fortunately Bruno didn't repeat his mistake. From then on, he left the contract at home and made a conscious effort to show patience and respect for his Algerian partner's beliefs.

All of this is not to say that people from destiny cultures make no attempt to protect their own interests. Far from it. There's an old saying in the Middle East which neatly sums up their approach: Trust in Allah, but always tie your camel.

How much importance you attach to the contract isn't the only thing that can send the wrong signals to your partners:

Two firms in the brewing industry, one Dutch and the other Japanese, were in the final stage of negotiating a contract. Neither side was prepared to concede on some minor details. It was Sunday afternoon in one of the Japanese company's breweries. The Dutch team asked for a break and, when offered drinks, requested some beers - they were in a brewery, after all. The Japanese left the room. Instead of the usual 10 minutes, the break lasted nearly an hour. On their return, the leader of the Japanese delegation bowed deeply and said they were now prepared to accept all the remaining demands the Dutch had made. The delighted Dutch and considerably less enthusiastic Japanese shook hands on the deal. Only later did the Dutch discover that their request for alcohol had been interpreted by the Japanese as a subtle: 'Accept our demands or the deal is off.' Traditionally in Japan, alcohol only comes out to celebrate an agreement.

At first sight, this might look like a great result for the Dutch. They accidentally achieved an unexpectedly big 'win'. But there's little point in achieving a result that your partners will struggle to deliver. Which was exactly what happened in this case. The Japanese negotiators had shaken hands on the deal and so, naturally, they signed the contract. But because they had accepted the revised terms without first getting the agreement of each of their colleagues, there were bitter disputes about the concessions they had been forced to make. The Dutch hadn't been trying to cheat on their Japanese partners. But it must have looked that way to many of the Japanese managers who were responsible for executing the deal. As a result - like Renate in 'The Prisoners' Dilemma' - they turned into grudgers. And it took the Dutch a long time to regain the trust that was needed for both partners to truly 'win' the game.

If the Dutch could have gone back and changed their drinks order, you can be sure that they would. But you generally only get one chance. And if you send the wrong signal, you could break the deal or cause serious damage to the relationship. So before you do business in an unfamiliar culture, find out about local customs. If you ask people who know the culture well to tell you what the hidden dangers are, you will probably - like us - be astonished at some of the stories they tell you:

A Japanese banker, Akihiko, was in Amsterdam putting a deal together with a Dutchman, Ton, from a big European bank. Ton offered to take Akihiko for a beer. Akihiko scratched his nose in mild embarrassment, explained that he didn't really drink, and asked if they could go to a coffee shop instead. Ton assumed, from the hesitant way Akihiko made the suggestion, that he wanted to visit one of Amsterdam's famous marijuana coffee shops. Ton was happy to oblige. And, as they sat down, he rolled a joint and offered it to Akihiko. The poor man was horrified. But he didn't want to cause any embarrassment, so he accepted Ton's offer.

From that day, Akihiko couldn't do enough for Ton. He was the most flexible of partners and the entire two-year relationship went exceptionally well. It was only after the deal had come to an end that Ton discovered why Akihiko had been so accommodating. Apparently, he had been terrified that his bosses in Tokyo might be told that he was an habitual dope smoker. So he had been very careful not to do anything that might upset Ton.

If Ton had realized the impact the coffee shop incident had had on Akihiko, he too would have been horrified. If only Akihiko had told him that there was a misunderstanding. The trouble was, he couldn't. He was too embarrassed. That's because Japan is a culture that is concerned with maintaining face. It had been difficult enough for Akihiko to refuse Ton's offer of a beer. He probably wanted to die of shame when he realized that his Dutch counterpart thought he wanted to smoke marijuana instead. How on earth could he explain the misunderstanding without causing considerable embarrassment to them both?

Of course, you're unlikely ever to find yourself in such an extreme situation as Ton and Akihiko. But there will be plenty of occasions when your cultural conditioning leads you to jump to the wrong conclusion. Which is why it's vital to keep checking that you've understood your partners correctly. Many people will find it hard to understand why Ton even contemplated offering Akihiko the opportunity to smoke marijuana. Maybe it was something his other international colleagues had been keen to try while they were in a country where the practice had been decriminalized. Even so, he shouldn't just have assumed that was what his Japanese colleague wanted to do.

When Akihiko asked to go to a coffee shop, Ton should have tried to find some diplomatic way to check that he had interpreted the signals correctly. A general statement like: There's a nice coffee shop round the corner, but I'm not sure you would like it; some of their customers go there to smoke marijuana, would quickly have cleared up the misunderstanding, and also provided them with an interesting topic to discuss wherever they did end up having their coffee.

USING THE RIGHT LANGUAGE

It's a pity the Americans in our first case study never got to the negotiating table. If they had, their Mexican partners would most probably have liked them a lot. Earlier in the chapter, we mentioned the global negotiations survey we've been conducting.

Another of the questions we ask is: Who would you most like to be in partnership with? Interestingly enough, the majority of our participants say that their préferred partners are the Americans or the Germans because: You know where you are with them. They're direct and they say what they mean.

As we saw in last chapter, the Americans and Germans are low context communicators. So they tend to say what they mean frankly and directly. And while they may sometimes be perceived as brusque or aggressive, their transparency makes a welcome change from the confusion and misunderstanding that often plagues (troubles) international negotiations.

The least popular negotiating partners, according to our survey, are people from high context cultures (like the British, Italians, Japanese and Arabs). Their lack of clarity seems to confuse and exasperate people. And their partners often assume that they are trying to play dirty tricks on them.

Another interesting statistic is that the Americans seem to be almost twice as popular as the Germans. Maybe that's because they tend to take a more enthusiastic, upbeat and future-oriented approach; and, as we've already seen, they focus on solutions rather than problems. It may also be because they fall to the left of this scale:

Risk embracing										Risk averse
I like taking risks.										I avoid taking risks.
50	40	30	20	10	0	10	20	30	40	50

Being prepared to take risks means that the Americans rarely react negatively to an innovative proposal. They're more likely to regard it as an opportunity and to be willing to explore the options it presents with an open mind. The Germans, on the other hand, tend to be relatively risk-averse. As we have already seen, they also tend to be more past-focused and to express themselves in a fairly low-key way. As a result, they're likely to spend more time agonizing over problems; and to be less prepared to explore options that could carry too much risk.

Of course, no international business person likes to be thought of as conservative. But judged by American standards, many are. So while the Americans and Germans are both low context communicators, the former may sometimes feel frustrated by the latter's unwillingness to take risks.

As the Germans tend to take a functional approach to business, however, they're very unlikely to resort to deliberate abuse or aggression. Unfortunately, people from some of the more relationship-oriented cultures are sometimes tempted to make comments that are far too personal:

A British businessman was negotiating a large contract in Algeria. After some small talk, he presented his initial offer. His Algerian counterpart reacted very negatively and aggressively. Not only did he reject the proposals outright, but he made some extremely insulting and offensive comments about the Brit's mother and father. Though he was very shocked, the Brit remained calm and waited for the tirade to end. When it finally did, he leaned forward and said: 'Right. So are we ready to negotiate now?' The Algerian smiled: 'I like you,' he said. 'I like your style. I think we can do business together.' But, of course, the Brit didn't like the Algerian's style at all. And he did everything he could to avoid doing business with him again.

The Algerian was probably just testing the Brit. And he was doing so in a way that presumably would have been acceptable to partners from his own culture. But using this kind of aggressive and insulting language in the international arena is a serious mistake. Indeed, any attempt to destabilize your partners by putting them under unendurable pressure will rarely produce the best deal. The Brit perceived the Algerian guy's personal attack as a dirty trick and he resolved never to do business with him again.

You are bound to feel the need to challenge some of the claims your partners are making, or to reject some of the proposals they're putting on the table. But when you do so, you need to think carefully about the way you're expressing yourself. The most successful international negotiators attack issues, not people. They use language that is clear, direct and explicit while, at the same time, trying to convey a positive and upbeat attitude. That's what the Americans tend to do and, according to our survey, they seem to be the partners that most of our international clients prefer to negotiate with. If you want to follow their example, we recommend you try the three simple techniques below.

SOPHOP

This is the single most useful piece of advice we can offer to a negotiator who is trying to make deals in the international market. The most fragile aspect in international partnerships is the relationship between the people involved. (By maintaining a Be soft on people, Hard on Points) SOPHOP approach, you should be able to nurture the relationship, while still ensuring that you give no ground on the commercial issues. If your partners have decided that negotiating is about fighting, that's fine. Fight over the points, but do everything in your power to avoid making it personal. Eventually (like the players in 'The Prisoners' Dilemma'), they will follow your example. If you're the one who wants to fight, again, that's OK. But don't let it get personal. Few people in the world will warm to you if you irritate or offend them.

As we've already seen, some cultures treat business as purely functional; for others, it's intensely personal. The latter (for example, people from the Arab world) will often get so emotionally involved that business and personal issues become almost inseparable. So when someone from a functional culture makes what they think is a dispassionate criticism of a business issue, there's a real danger that their relationship-oriented partner will take it personally. To avoid this danger, you need to exercise control over the way you express yourself.

When you want to disagree with someone, or make a comment that may be perceived as negative, avoid the word you. That way, it will be clear that you aren't attacking them personally:

Instead of: What are you going to do about it?

Say: How are we going to solve it?

Instead of: I don't agree with you.

Say: I'm not sure I agree with that.

Instead of: That's not what you said before.

Say: Is that what we agreed?

KEEP EVERYTHING CONDITIONAL

The popularity of American negotiators is based on their ability to explore rather than reject. In other words, they're careful not to close doors or eliminate options too early. Again, it's all down to the language that you use. If, for example, you keep saying no, can't, don't or won't, a partner who is keen to put together a creative deal will soon become demoralized. The trick is to keep things conditional:

Seller: If you place an order for a full year's supply, (then) we could cut the price.

Buyer: If we ordered a year's supply, (then) would you extend the payment period?

Using If... (then)... sentences will help you to repackage your partners' proposals, reshape your own shopping list, and keep the deal open - even with a partner who is keen to eliminate possibilities. But you need to be careful how you use words like will/would, can/could, may/might; and to be aware that, for example, place or order will send very different signals from placed or ordered. Imagine, for example, that early on in the negotiation, the buyer says:

We need delivery in batches of seven hundred units monthly, starting in May.

Which of the two replies below would come most naturally to you?

Seller A: That gives us a very short lead time. But we can do it if you pay for the first batch in advance.

Seller B: That would give us a very short lead time. But we could do it if you paid for the first batch in advance.

In using the present tense - gives, can and pay - seller A is sending a clear signal that she is able to meet the delivery targets. Seller B, on the other hand, is using the past tense - would, could and paid - because he wants to explore the options in a more tentative and non-committal way. If you're a native speaker of English, switching between the more tentative, indirect (and sometimes hypothetical) past form and the more decisive, direct (and sometimes pushy) present form will come naturally to you. But you need to remember that non-native speakers often find it hard to distinguish between the two forms. Indeed, when the participants on our language courses discover that English frequently uses the past tense to talk about the future, they're often very surprised. This is particularly true of the Germans.

So if you're a native speaker of English, you need to make allowances for your non-native-speaking partners. Don't assume that they're deliberately using the more direct present form to send decisive, inflexible or even aggressive signals. If, for example, while you're happily exploring options together, you tentatively ask: Would you consider extending the payment period? and they say: We can't extend the payment period unless you order a full year's supply, don't assume that they're trying to eliminate this possibility. What they probably mean is: We might be able to consider extending the payment period if you ordered a full year's supply. They just don't know how to say it that way.

And if you're a non-native speaker who has not yet mastered this tentative past form, carry on using the present tense but try adding the words in principle to your sentence: Well, in principle, we can extend the payment period if, for example, you order a full year's supply. That should help you make it clear that you're exploring rather than eliminating options.

Of course, you'll only be able to explore the options properly if you've allowed enough room for the movement in your 'bargaining range' - in other words, the gap between your 'entry' and 'exit' points. How wide your partners expect your bargaining range to be will depend on where they come from. It's as foolish to pay the initial asking price for a carpet in Cairo as it is to try to negotiate over the price of a tube of toothpaste in a supermarket in Oslo. If you want the people you're negotiating with to take your bargaining range seriously, make sure that it's culturally credible to them. As a general rule, people from fixed truth cultures tend to keep their bargaining range narrow and may well mistrust you if you move too far from your entry point; people from relative truth cultures, on the other hand, tend to expect a bigger gap between your entry point and target. That's because they regard negotiating as a process to be enjoyed; and trying to close a wide gap gives them a good opportunity to assess their partner's character.

TALK ABOUT HOW YOU FEEL

If you keep everything conditional, you should be able to subtly train almost any partner in the world to take a positive, exploratory approach to negotiating. You can help this process further by talking about your feelings, and inviting your partners to do the same. If you use too many closed questions - ones that invite a Yes or No answer - you'll simply encourage them to reject your proposals. So try to find out how they feel:

Instead of: Can you accept this price?

Say: How do you feel about this price?

Instead of: Can you live with a lower margin on this?

Say: How would you feel about accepting a lower margin on this?

By avoiding Yes or No answers, you give yourself a much better chance of finding room for negotiation.

It doesn't matter whether your partners are given status Mexicans, functional Germans, high context Japanese, reserved Finns, polychronic Arabs, future-focused Russians, logical French, or risk-embracing Americans. You'll only make a successful and lasting deal if you send them the right signals, and interpret the signals they're sending accurately. Being soft on people, hard on points, keeping everything conditional, and talking about how you feel will help you to do that.

SUMMARY

As we mentioned at the beginning of this chapter, it was the Swedes who won the contract with the Mexicans:

The Swedish negotiating team flew to Mexico City a fortnight after the Americans. They, too, had worked very hard to prepare an impressive presentation. But when their friends at the ministry hinted at what had happened with the Americans they decided, at the last moment, to scale their presentation down to a short, formal talk and not to use any high-tech equipment. Their team, which was small, included a board member who spoke Spanish, the head of their Mexican representative office, and their company president. The first meeting with the minister was delayed by two hours. It only lasted 30 minutes and consisted of little more than small talk between the minister, the president and his Spanish-speaking colleagues. The Swedes were then invited to go on a tour of various potential factory sites over the next three days, followed by a day at the minister's hacienda. They readily agreed, even though their colleagues had already visited the potential sites at the tender stage. The Swedes had been in Mexico for six days before they were invited to the ministry to make their formal presentation. The minister responded with a speech detailing forcibly where he expected concessions to be made. The president then flew back to Sweden, leaving his team to negotiate the actual deal. Since they had built in quite wide margins on all their costings, the Swedes were happy to trade concessions with the ministry in order to go part of the way towards meeting the minister's demands. Within a month, the Swedish company's president and the minister signed the contract in front of the world's press.

If the monochronic, acquired status, functional Swedes had been the first to meet the Mexicans, they might instinctively have conducted their initial pitch and subsequent conversations in a very similar way to the Americans. Fortunately, they were able to learn from the mistakes their competitors had made. And, even though it meant moving quite a long way from their own cultural preferences, they made a conscious effort to adapt to their more polychronic, given status, relationship-oriented Mexican partners:

- They picked the right people. Unlike the Americans, they made sure they had people with local knowledge, a senior Spanish speaker, and the president. This made the Mexicans feel comfortable, and showed them the respect they felt they deserved.
- They let the Mexicans set the pace. They hadn't booked return flights to Sweden. Instead, they were prepared to wait patiently until the Mexicans were ready to see them. And once the negotiations started, they were careful not to impose a tight agenda on the discussions. As a result, the Mexicans were able to relax in the Swedes' company, and to focus on developing a relationship with them.
- They let the Mexicans choose the place. They happily visited the potential factory sites again, and graciously accepted the minister's invitation to spend the day at his hacienda. Away from the formality of the negotiating table, they demonstrated that they could form a partnership, rather than merely sign a contract, with their new Mexican friends.
- They played the game to win. Because they had read the signals correctly they kept their initial presentation short, low tech and personal. They had built wide margins into their costings so that, when the minister insisted on more favourable terms, they were able to explore ways of trading concessions and reaching a mutually beneficial deal.

In short, they remembered that, in the international arena, it's all about how you handle the client, above all else, that can make or break a deal.

Note: A sterling example is the company "General Motors". Today, General Motors Corporation is the world's largest automaker; it has been the annual global industry sales leader for 77 years. Founded in 1908, GM today employs about 270,000people around the world. For detailed information, reader can visit their site www.gm.com

28

Knowing Yourself

There will always be a culture gap of one kind or another between you and your international business partners. Most of the misunderstandings we've described arose because the people involved assumed that their own beliefs, attitudes and behaviour were normal. In many cases, it didn't even occur to them that the people they were dealing with looked at the world from a completely different perspective. As a result, negative stereotypes were reinforced, motives were misinterpreted, goodwill was damaged and, on some occasions, communications broke down altogether.

We believe that knowing yourself is the first and most important step towards bridging the culture gap. The second is to acknowledge that the way you and your compatriots look at the world is not universal. The third is to find out as much as you can about what other cultures value and what lies behind their beliefs. That's why, in the previous chapters, we've asked you to place yourself and people from differing cultures on a series of preference scales.

In this chapter, we invite you to look at all those scales again. To help you focus your mind on the key issues, we've grouped them under five main headings: relationships, communication, time, truth, and the meaning of life. What people expect of presenters is informed by their attitudes towards these key issues. But, for ease of reference, we've grouped the presentation style scales together at the end. After each set of scales, you'll find some simple tips - most of which have already appeared in the previous chapters - on how you could adapt your style when you're doing business with people whose preferences are very different from your own.

There are, of course, no magic formulae. No two cultures, or indeed individuals, are exactly the same. The number of variables is infinite. So there's no way that something as two-dimensional as the preference scales can provide you with a comprehensive and totally accurate model of your own or any other culture. But that is not their aim. They're simply there to draw your attention to some of the differences that, in our experience, exist from one culture to another. And to help you start the long process of building your own cultural models through research, observation, and objective analysis.

Similarly, human behaviour is complex and subtle. No one can do it justice in a simple list of DOs and DON'Ts. The tips we offer are necessarily very general. And, taken individually, some of them may seem very obvious to you. Again, they're just there as a starting point; to remind you that the way you do things in your part of the world is not necessarily universal.

When you look at the scales below, remember to examine each pair of statements in relation to your working life. Ask yourself what you personally value and try to achieve whenever possible. Then mark, only once, where your instinctive preference falls.

RELATIONSHIPS

Individualist-group-oriented

People from individualist cultures like the Americans, British, Dutch, Northern Italians and French tend to take personal responsibility for their own career development. They focus on the tasks set out in their job description and think it's normal for a boss to reward individual effort with public praise or rapid promotion. If something goes wrong - for example, a deadline is missed, or a mistake is made - they tend to give the reasons why rather than simply apologize. When you're doing business with someone from an individualist culture, you need to:

- Introduce yourself with confidence.
- Be prepared to state your own views forcibly and eloquently.
- Be prepared to challenge what people say.

Most Asian, Arab and African cultures are highly group-oriented. People tend to subordinate their personal goals to those of the group they belong to. And they often try to avoid open conflict with other group members. In Japan, for example, harmony must be preserved at all costs: If somebody conflicts with others and is excluded from the community, he cannot survive. No prima donnas are welcomed. When your business partner comes from a highly group-oriented culture, you should:

- Introduce yourself in relation to your company or team.

The card-exchange ritual so prevalent in many Asian cultures will help you do this. The information on the card puts you, the individual, in the context of the company or group.

- Talk early on about their company.
- Speak calmly and slowly, matching the pace of the discussion.
- Be ready to negotiate with and as part of a large team.

If you do business alone, you'll send negative messages. Not only does it lower your status, it insults your hosts - as it implies they are only worth one person. It also means they can't evaluate the effectiveness of your company's teamwork, a vital skill in any group-oriented culture.

- Be prepared to do the real business over a meal or in the bar.

Group meetings in many cultures are simply to exchange information or to confirm decisions. If you want your Korean, Japanese or Chinese partners to make concessions or explain a problem, this is often best done one-to-one away from the group. That way, there's no danger of public loss of face.

Flat Hierarchy-vertical Hierarchy

People from Scandinavia and Australia would probably fall to the far left of this scale (remember the 'Jante Law' and 'Tall Poppy Syndrome'). In Germany, Switzerland, Netherlands, the UK and the USA, company hierarchies are also relatively flat. Bosses tend to consult widely, and subordinates generally feel free to express their own views and challenge their boss's decisions. People from flat cultures expect you to:

- Take full responsibility for your area of expertise.

  Subordinates openly disagree and argue with their seniors. Such debate is regarded as healthy and likely to lead to good decisions.

- Tackle colleagues directly if there's a problem.

  If you run to the boss every time a colleague is being difficult, you'll make yourself very unpopular.

In France, Spain, Italy, Latin America, South-East Asia, India, China, Africa, and the Arab world, power in companies is held by a few people at the top. And managers are expected to tell people what to do. When the people you're doing business with come from one of these vertical cultures, you need to:

- Have clear lines of communication to senior management.

  Apart from Japan, where consensus (nemawashi) is the norm, decisions tend to be made by a small group, or one person, at the very top. You must have their/his (sadly, seldom her) ear.

- Keep valuable information to yourself.

  Only share it with those who can help you. Those in the know are much admired.

- Show a great deal of respect to the decision-makers.

  Avoid flattery, though. They will respect you if you demonstrate quick-wittedness and creativity. Don't get angry if your best ideas somehow become the brilliant solutions of the company president.

- Be autocratic in your dealings with subordinates.

  If you're a manager from a flat culture, you will find this very hard; but you must do it. If you seek the opinions of juniors, they will often simply tell you what they think you want to hear. Tell them firmly what you want done. Then watch and listen very carefully to see whether your demand is feasible or not. In many vertical cultures, senior people will have secretaries or assistants whose most important, but unstated, task is to tell the boss where he's going wrong. You should cultivate these people.

Acquired Status-given Status

The idea that businesses should be run along meritocratic lines is becoming more common. And many people would, at first sight, place themselves to the left of this scale. There are, nonetheless, many cultures that lean towards the right. Among them are Spain, Southern Italy, South America, India, China, Japan, the Arab world and Africa. In given status cultures, how fast you work your way up the hierarchy doesn't just depend on how well do you perform. Factors like age, gender, social status and educational background are also taken into consideration. And managers often behave in a paternalistic way. When you're dealing with people from the given status end of the scale, you should:

- Show respect for those older than you.

  This is true whatever their official position. Respect is often shown through body language. In many parts of Africa, for example, when you shake hands with someone older, you take the lower part of his right arm with your left hand.

- Consider the age and length of service of your staff when assigning jobs.

  A young person who has not worked long for your company may have all the technical skills, but they will still not be taken seriously in the most Asian, African and Arab cultures. Take this into account when you're choosing the members of your negotiating team or the new manager for an overseas operation.

- Be paternalistic with your subordinates.

  This is difficult for people from an acquired status culture. But you will be expected to look after your juniors: champion them for promotion or the best jobs, protect them in intra-company disputes, and advise them on personal matters. Much of a manager's time in Asian cultures is spent attending the weddings and funerals of his juniors' families, acting as a marriage arranger, dispensing financial advice, giving direct on-the-job training. As an outsider, you can't do all these things. But try to have plenty of one-to-one meetings with your subordinates where the discussion is largely about their personal lives. It may be small talk to you, but it will gain you their loyalty.

  And if you are a woman:

- Dress appropriately.

  Cover yourself up in Muslim countries (this includes many parts of South-East Asia). Dress soberly, but smartly, in Japan and Korea.

- Act demurely.

  This is the hard one. The dictionary defines demure as sober, grave, and modest. Many Asian cultures admire strong women and even elect them as their political leaders. But they dislike intensely the argumentative and assertive behaviour of some of the Western women they are forced to do business with.

Functional-personal

Everyone responds positively to genuine human warmth and empathy. Indeed, we believe it's at the heart of all successful business communication. If you're from a culture that falls to the left of this scale (for example, Germany, Switzerland, Scandinavia), however, you may not feel the need to build a close personal relationship with everyone you do business with. And you may feel surprised, or even impatient, if your business associates spend too much time on small talk or socializing. But, there are many cultures (for example, the Arab world, Asia, Southern Europe, Africa, South America) where people won't do business with you until they know and trust you. With them, you need to:

- Allow plenty of time.

  Don't expect to fly in, sign the contract and fly home on the same day. Be prepared to spend several meetings exchanging information about your two companies and the individuals involved before you start discussing specific business proposals.

- Engage in small talk.

  At the beginning of any meeting with someone from the Arab world, for example, it's not unusual to spend up to 45 minutes in getting to know one another or cementing the relationship, and the conversation can extend to all aspects of life.

- Be prepared to socialize with your colleagues and clients.

  In countries as diverse as Spain and Japan, much of the important information is exchanged in a social context over a drink or a meal.

- Be prepared to exchange favours and small gifts.

  Small favours, such as helping someone's son to find a school in your country, can do a lot to warm up the relationship.

Physically Distant-physically Close

People from individualist cultures (like the USA, UK, Northern Europe) tend to fall somewhere in the middle of this scale. There are some group- oriented cultures (e.g. East and South-East Asian) that fall to the far left of this scale and others (e.g. Arab, African, Indian, Latin American, Southern Italian, Greek, Turkish) that fall to the far right.

If you're doing business with someone from the middle of the scale:

- Give a firm, short handshake and look people in the eye.

  If your handshake is too soft and your eye contact infrequent, they may conclude you're weak and untrustworthy.

  When you're with people from the far left of the scale:

- Give them plenty of personal space.

  If you touch them, stand too close, or look them too directly in the eye, you will make them feel very uncomfortable.

When your business associates are from the far right of the scale:

- Don't show surprise or embarrassment if they get too close.

  In tactile cultures, handshakes can go on forever and you'll have almost no personal space. And it's often perfectly normal for men to kiss or hold hands with each other. Rejecting these signs of warmth will make you appear cold and discourteous.

COMMUNICATION

Low Context-high Context

Low context communicators tend to express themselves in explicit, concrete and unequivocal terms. There's little cultural baggage or 'context' attached to the words they use and you can usually assume that what they say is what they mean. The Americans, Scandinavians, Finns and Germans tend to fall at the far left of this scale. When you're doing business with them:

- Take what they say literally.

  If they say something is difficult, they mean it's difficult - but not necessarily impossible.

- Don't be offended if they openly contradict you or disagree with you.

  To them, stating the case clearly and unequivocally shows respect and honesty. They're not trying to be gratuitously insensitive or aggressive.

  High context communicators, on the other hand, tend to communicate implicitly. They expect you to be able to interpret what they mean from your knowledge of the cultural values that lie behind the words, what they're actually talking about at the time, their tone of voice and, of course, their eye and body language. People from China, Japan, the Arab world and France tend to be high context communicators. And the way the British use understatement, irony and allusion means that they too often lean towards the right of this scale. When you're doing business with high context communicators:

- Don't always take what they say literally.

  If a Japanese colleague says something is difficult, he's probably telling you it's impossible. Look at his eye and body language and ask yourself how far it supports or detracts from the actual words he's using. Think too about the context and what you know about the situation. Wait. Listen. Ask gently.

- Don't get suspicious or irritated if you find it hard to grasp their key message.

  Burying the key message in circular talk and allusion comes naturally to them. They're not doing it deliberately to confuse or mislead you. Be patient, listen hard, read between the lines, and ask questions to check you've understood them correctly.

Reserved-effusive

Your preferences on this scale will have a strong influence on how you instinctively play the conversation game. The Americans and British, for example, expect conversation to be relatively interactive. To them, interrupting with the odd relevant comment or question shows interest. The Japanese, Chinese, Scandinavians, Finns and Germans, on the other hand, are used to waiting their turn to speak. For them, conversation is often like a series of mini-monologues.

- Listen carefully to what they are saying without interrupting.
- Don't speak too effusively.

  You may think the whole world can be won over with a bit of charm and smooth talk. But very reserved cultures, such as the Finns, actively mistrust people who are too effusive.

  And, unless they are German or Swiss:

- Pause for a few seconds before giving your reply.

  The Scandinavians, Finns, Chinese and Japanese are usually very comfortable with silence and will often pause after someone has spoken to show that they're thinking about what has been said.

  If, on the other hand, your business partners are from a more effusive culture (for example, the Arab world, USA, Italy, the UK):

- Don't be offended if they interrupt you.

  They're not being ill-mannered or disrespectful.

- Actively show interest in what they are saying.

  People who listen in total silence make them feel uncomfortable. So try to make the occasional comment: I see or That surprises me or I didn't realize that.

Written-spoken

Most Northern Europeans and North Americans would lean towards the left of this scale. For them, memoranda of understanding, written summaries and e-mailed offers may carry more weight than what people say in a meeting; and contracts almost certainly will. When you're doing business with them:

- Don't be offended if they take a lot of notes during the meeting.

  People from written cultures generally feel more comfortable relying on the written word rather than memory. If they take notes, it's not a signal that they don't trust you. They're just trying to be professional and get things be right.

- Don't be surprised if they get their lawyers involved early on in the relationship.

  Again, it's not a signal that they don't trust you. They're just trying to make sure that everyone's interests are protected.

- Don't assume an agreement has been made until it has been confirmed in writing.

  For cultures (such as the Arab world) that have a strong oral tradition, on the other hand, the spoken word tends to be far more important. When you're trying to make deals with them:

- Don't take too many written notes during the meeting.

  If you do, they may think you don't trust them.

- Leave the lawyers at home.

  Oral cultures accept that contracts are a necessary part of an international deal; but they don't define or shape the relationship as they do in a more written culture. So don't bring the lawyers in until the whole deal has been agreed.

- Don't make oral promises you're not prepared to keep.

TIME

Monochronic-polychromic

In monochronic cultures (for example, Anglo-Saxon America and Canada, Australia, Scandinavia, Germany, Switzerland, Netherlands, the UK), time is linear, sequential, and can be cut up into blocks. People are judged by how well they can control their time. And those who can't do so are not to be trusted. The Germans and Swiss would probably fall at the far left of this scale. As they work out Die Tagesordnung (the Daily Order), they will often allot a specific and precise amount of time to each task - including their coffee breaks. When dealing with such cultures, that would be wise to:

- Fix appointments weeks ahead.

  By doing so, you're communicating that the subject is important and that you are in control of your time.

- Send meeting agendas in advance.

  Or, at least, be ready to agree them at the beginning of meetings.

- Arrive on time.

  The Dutch and British are not as insistent on this as the Swiss, Scandinavians and Germans.

- Start meetings at the agreed time.

  If you keep visitors waiting outside your office, they'll assume you are disorganized and, therefore, not to be respected or trusted; or worse, they'll think you're deliberately trying to make them feel inferior. Many negotiations have been weakened from the start because of this kind of misinterpretation. If there's an unavoidable delay, explain the reason and apologize.

- Keep to agendas, schedules and deadlines.

  If you don't stick to the point, you'll be regarded as devious or unprepared.

- Interrupt if you don't understand something.

  If you wait until the end before admitting this, they will think of you as a time-waster.

- Give bad news straight away.

  If you don't, they may well conclude that you're being dishonest or deceitful.

  Polychronic cultures (for example: Hispanic USA, Latin America, India, the Arab world, Italy) view time as more circular; it's their servant, not their master. To them, how you nurture relationships is more important than how you manage your time. When dealing with or in polychronic cultures, you should:

- Fix appointments in the short notice.

  Don't be surprised if, even then, they have to be changed at the last moment.

- Allow plenty of time between appointments.
- Be prepared to be kept waiting.

  Use the time to chat to the receptionist, secretary or other visitors. You'll be surprised at how much useful information you can gather.
- Try to fix an agenda at the start of a meeting.

  But don't stick to it rigidly. Allow the discussion to meander before gently trying to bring it back to the points you want to discuss. The way in which the other side meanders may well signal to you what points are important to them.
- Avoid rushing meetings.

  Present your case in stages; ask and answer questions; use the many interruptions and parallel discussions to observe, think and plan.
- Don't bind yourself to self-imposed deadlines.

  Follow the mood rather than the schedule. You will seriously undermine your negotiating position if you show you're desperate to meet quarterly targets or catch the plane home.
- If there's bad news, try to soften it.

  You don't have to delay passing on the bad news for days or weeks. But try to spend some time at the beginning of the conversation preparing them for what you're going to say.

Speed-patience

You might expect all monochronic cultures to be keen to get everything done as fast and efficiently as possible; and all polychronic cultures to prefer taking their time. Unfortunately, life isn't that simple. Though the monochronic Germans often expect their meetings to be well structured and fairly quick, they can be very slow in taking decisions. With the more polychronic Spanish, on the other hand, meetings can be long and rambling, but decisions are often taken very rapidly. And the Japanese, who are well known for taking a very long time to actually reach a decision, expect implementation to be lightning-quick once a decision has been made.

The critical issue for the international negotiator is how fast you expect to progress from initial contact to final deal. And closely linked to that question is how much time you're prepared to devote to developing a personal relationship with your partners. If, like the Americans, you lean towards the far left of this scale, and you're trying to make a deal with partners who lean towards the right:

- Don't try to force the pace.

  If you do, your partners may well perceive you as pushy or arrogant. No matter how straightforward and attractive you think your offer is, focus on the relationship first, commercial issues second. Give your partners time to get to know you and discuss your proposals among themselves in a leisurely fashion.

  And if, like the Mexicans, you lean to the far right of this scale, don't jump to any hasty conclusions about your prospective partners' motives. If the Mexicans in our case study had agreed to meet the Americans across the negotiating table, they would probably have liked them. And, who knows? The Americans might even have offered a better deal than the Swedes.

Short-term-long-term

In today's business world, shareholders of every culture put companies under pressure to show results in the short term. And even in Confucian cultures, like China, which are renowned for taking the long-term view, people are often quick to seize an opportunity for short-term personal gain.

Even so, there are some cultures which instinctively lean further to the right of this scale than others. While the Americans' impatience with time often leads them to insist on results in the short term, cultures as diverse as the Swiss and Japanese tend to take a longer-term view. If you fall to the left of this scale and you're trying to manage a team who lean to the right, you should be careful not to jump to hasty conclusions. Reportees - like Connie the Swiss IT project manager - who take a longer-term view than you might like, are not necessarily lacking in dynamism or vision. Indeed, as Connie's American boss Robert found to his cost, their longer-term plan might turn out to be much more effective than your short-term one.

Future-past

The Americans (and other future-oriented cultures like the 'new Russia') tend to see tradition as one of the main barriers to progress. For people in much of the rest of the world, traditional values and the lessons of the past have a contribution to make to future development. China,

Japan and India, for example, would fall to the far right of this scale, while many European countries would probably fall somewhere in the middle. While the futurists will be keen to introduce new systems, the traditionalists will be more interested in working out what went wrong with the old ones. If you place too much emphasis on the past, the former will think you're pessimistic, conservative and lacking in dynamism; if you focus exclusively on the future, the latter will perceive you as superficial.

So, when you're presenting to future-oriented cultures:

- Focus on the future, even if you're reporting on past results.

And when you're presenting to people who value tradition:

- Include plenty of relevant background (i.e. past) detail even if you're making proposals for the future.

TRUTH

Fixed Truth-relative Truth

If you believe there are clear rights and wrongs regardless of the circumstances, you will probably expect people to follow rules and procedures to the letter. North Americans, Australians and northern Europeans lean this way. People from these cultures tend to attach great importance to written contracts, organization charts, detailed quality control manuals and so on. And they admire honesty and directness, even if it hurts people's feelings. When you're doing business with them, you should:

- Pay full attention to the written clauses of any contract you are negotiating with them.

  In their eyes, you have committed to them - even if the situation changes. The language may look negative to you because it focuses on what to do if things go wrong; but the fixed truth culture sees it as no more than an insurance policy.

- Keep your bargaining range narrow.

  People who move too far from their initial offer/proposal could be regarded as liars and cheats.

- Be prepared for open criticism or direct rejection of your proposals.

  This may seem extremely rude to you; but people from fixed truth cultures often prefer to know where they stand. They don't pick up the correct messages if you're too vague and indirect. And they'll mistrust you if you keep them in the dark.

- Use arguments based on logic and the facts.

  Avoid ones based on emotional appeals to family and friendship.

- Be very careful when giving presents or doing favours.

  What you think of as simply a gift to strengthen the relationship, they may regard as a bribe.

In relative truth cultures (to be found in much of East, South-East and South Asia, Africa and around the Mediterranean), the circumstances dictate the way you behave. Your loyalty is more to your group (e.g. family, clan, friends and company) than to a set of abstract rules. When dealing with people from relative truth cultures, you need to:

- Focus on building the relationship before getting down to contractual details.

  Keep your lawyers under control. Better still, leave them at home. The letter of intent may be considered more important than the contract.

- Keep your bargaining range wide.

  Relative truth cultures regard negotiating as a process to be enjoyed and a good opportunity to assess the other person's character. Too narrow a gap between opening offer and target makes it difficult for such judgements to be made.

- Be ready to renegotiate a contract if the situation changes.
- Maintain continuity in relationships.

  The link is with the person, not the company. Any change of personnel needs careful handling. Give plenty of notice and make sure the old hand introduces his successor personally to your company's clients.

- Use emotional arguments which show the benefits to the person's group.
- Avoid being too direct in your opinions.

  What may seem always right to you, may be completely wrong at that moment to them.

- Accept small gifts and favours.

  They are signs of respect and friendship, not an attempt to corrupt you. Reciprocate by giving a present too; or if, for example, they have a relative or friend who plans to visit your country, offer to help them.

Analytical-intuitive

The French, Germans and Swiss would fall to the left of this scale. Their education has taught them to take a factual, balanced and above all logical view of any situation. If you want to get them on your side, make sure your argument is comprehensive and consistent.

By all means be positive, but make sure you can support your enthusiasm with solid facts and rational argument. If you don't, they may well jump to the conclusion that you're superficial, or even lazy; and that what you're saying is meaningless hot air.

The Americans are impatient with time, willing to accept mistakes and happy to improvise. As a result, they would probably fall nearer the middle of this scale. The highly pragmatic British would lean towards the right.

When you're dealing with more intuitive cultures, resist the temptation to give them too many facts. By all means construct a logical argument, but keep it short and to the point. If you don't, there's a danger they will think you are dull and unimaginative.

Theoretical-empirical

At first sight, you may think this scale is very similar to the previous one. But, actually, there are a number of logical cultures that prefer concrete experience to abstract theory. The Germans and Finns, for example, certainly favour logical argument, but they would fall to the right of this scale.

While the French also favour logical argument, they're more likely to base it on abstract concepts and would fall to the left of this scale.

The Americans, too, would probably lean to the left. Which might be why they're more prepared than, for example, the Finns to commit themselves to aims and values that are expressed in relatively abstract terms.

For most Brits, concrete experience is more important than theory. So they're at the same time intuitive and empirical.

So before you can work out how best to argue your case, you need to think about where your international colleagues fall on both the analytical-intuitive and theoretical-empirical scales.

THE MEANING OF LIFE

To many Westerners - even those who are regular churchgoers - religion is a private affair. It has little influence on their business lives. The meaning of life and death is for discussion in the university coffee bars and on late- night television. It comes as a shock to them when they find that many cultures have no such demarcation. In the Arab world, for example, religious and philosophical beliefs directly affect the way business is done.

When communicating in strongly and publicly religious cultures you must be careful to:

- Know and honour the local rules of behaviour.

  Many of them are based on religious practices. In Muslim and Hindu cultures, for example, eat and hand over documents with your right hand and don't show the soles of your feet. Don't offer alcohol or pork to Muslims. Be sensitive to the kosher food laws of orthodox Jews. In India and much of South-East Asia, accept that the contract will only be signed or the equipment installed on a day that is regarded as auspicious. Agree to have the site of your new factory blessed by Shinto priests in Japan and aligned correctly by the feng shui man in Southern China. Appreciate that the wrong doings in a previous life can explain your Indian employee's shortcomings in this one.

- Avoid blaspheming.

  Secular Europeans who casually swear (eg God or Jesus Christ) can cause great offence, not only to the many Americans, Africans and Asians (eg Koreans) who are strong Christians, but also to people of other religions. Some Muslim and Indian businessmen have told us that they would prefer to do business with a practising Christian than an overt atheist. How can you trust someone who has no beliefs?

- Assess attitudes to risk.

  In some cultures subordinates are encouraged to take risks and are rewarded for showing personal initiative. In others quite the opposite is the case and conformity is the norm. If you're managing a team from a risk-averse culture, you may need to be very patient and supportive if you want your staff to act in a more autonomous way.

PRESENTATION STYLE

Upbeat-low-key

In the presentations we described to you, it was the Americans who were at the far left of this scale, and the Swiss and British who were at the far right. No one can expect the Americans to stop sounding enthusiastic and positive. Indeed, we believe that putting your message across persuasively and positively is something that all presenters should aim to do. So, by all means, be upbeat and enthusiastic. But if you're presenting to a low-key audience:

- Make sure you can support what you say with relevant details and facts.
- Respond to their concerns realistically and factually.
- Don't put too much emphasis on your own successes and achievements.

If, like Connie the Swiss woman or George the British fund manager, you come from a low-key culture and you are presenting to the Americans:

- Try to find an upbeat central message that looks forward rather than backward.
- Make a conscious effort to be sound positive and optimistic.

Short-long/selective-comprehensive

American and British audiences tend to respond best to presentations that are short and selective. When you're presenting to them:

- Be concise.
- Never go over an agreed time limit.

Italian, German, Scandinavian, Finnish and Japanese audiences fall to the right of these two scales. When you're presenting to them:

- Avoid being oversimplistic.
- Support your arguments with plenty of relevant facts and data.

Even if you're presenting to an audience who value a lot of facts and background information, however, it is still vital to be selective. Remember that the most dangerous subject for you as presenter is the one that fascinates you; the one that you're the world expert on.

Persuade-inform

The Americans, Italians and British would all fall to the left of this scale. They expect presenters to interpret the facts for them. When you're presenting to them:

- Give them your opinions upfront and tell them directly what your recommendations are and why.
- Try to present your case as persuasively as possible.

The Germans, Scandinavians, Finns and Japanese, on the other hand, expect you to let them draw their own conclusions. When you're presenting to them:

- Avoid the hard sell.

Creative Structure-logical Structure

The Germans, Scandinavians, Finns and French fall to the right of this scale; the Americans and British to the left. Try to adjust the way you present your argument accordingly. But remember that, no matter where your audience is from, they will only listen to what you say and remember the message you're trying to get across if you create a concrete context they can relate to. In this respect, we believe that all presenters need to demonstrate creativity. In our experience, the right metaphor will appeal to even the most logical of audiences. And finding that metaphor will often help you turn a satisfactory presentation into a brilliant one.

Note: For the purpose of gaining depth of understanding into the subject, we can take the example of Nokia Company. In 2007, Nokia was listed as number one company in Europe and number three in the world in a "Top Companies for Leaders" study carried on by Human Resources Company "Hewitt Associates" in partnership with "Fortune magazine". For detailed information, reader can visit Nokia Website http://www.nokia.com

Bibliography

A. O'Reilly III and J. Pfeffer, *Hidden Value*, Cambridge, MA: Harvard Business School Press, 2000.

A. Priestland and R. Hanig, "Developing First Level Leaders," *Harvard Business Review,* June 2005.

A. Williams, P. Dobson, and M. Walters, *Changing Culture: New Organizational Approaches*, London: Institute of Personnel Management, 1989.

A.S. Grove, *Only the Paranoid Survive*, New York: Doubleday, 1996.

B. McLean, "Satellite tilled the Radio Star," *Fortune,* January, 2001.

Banai and L.M. Sama, "Ethical Dilemma in MNCs' International Staffing Policies," *Journal of Business Ethics,* June 2000.

Belson, "In U.S., Cell Phone Users Are Often All Talk," *The New YorkTimes,* December, 2004.

Birkinshaw, A. Morrison, and J. Hulland, "Structural and Competitive Determinants of a Global Integration Strategy," *Strategic Management Journal,* 1995.

C. Grant, "Whistle Blowers: Saints of Secular Culture," *Journal of Business Ethics,* September 2002.

C. Shapiro and H.R. Varian, *Information Rules: A Strategic Guide to the Network Economy*, Boston: Harvard Business School Press, 1999.

C, W.L. Hill, *International Business,* 6th ed., New York: McGraw-Hill, 2007.

C.K. Prahalad and Y.L. Doz, *The Multinational Mission: Balancing Local Demands and Global Vision*, New York: Free Press, 1987.

C.M. Solomon, "Success Abroad Depends upon More Than Job Skills," *Personnel Journal,* April 1994.

C.M. Solomon, "Unhappy Trails," *Workforce,* August 2000.

C.W.L. Hill and T.M. Jones, "Stakeholder-Agency Theory," *Journal of Management Studies*, 1992.

C.W.L. Hill, "Establishing a Standard: Competitive Strategy and Technology Standards in Winner Take All Industries," *Academy of Management Executive*, 1997.

D. Barboza, "An Unknown Giant Flexes Its Muscles," *The New York Times,* December, 2004.

D. Buss, "How to Pick Your Number 2," *Financial Times*, London, December, 2004.

D. Fisher, "GE Turns Green," *Forbes,* 2005.

D. Goleman, R. Boyatzis, and A. McKee, *Primal Leaders*, Boston: Harvard Business School Press, 2002.

D. Jones, "Critics Tie Sweatshop Sneakers to 'Air Jordan,'" *USA Today,* June, 1996.

D. Messick and M.H. Bazerman, "Ethical Leadership and the Psychology of Decision Making," *Sloan Management Review*, Winter 1996.

D. Nilsen, B. Kowske, and A. Kshanika, "Managing Globally," *HR Magazine.* August 2005.

D. Pritchard, "Are Federal Tax Laws and State Subsidies for Boeing 7E7 Selling America Short?" *Aviation Week,* April, 2004.

D.C. McClelland and D.H. Burnham, "Power Is the Great Motivator," *Harvard Business Review*, January-February 1995.

D.C. North, *Institutions, Institutional Change, and Economic Performance,* Cambridge: Cambridge University Press, 1990.

E. Freeman, *Strategic Management: A Stakeholder Approach*, Boston: Pitman Press, 1984.

E.E. Ghiselli, "Interaction of Traits and Motivational Factors in the Determination of the Success of Managers," *Journal of Applied Psychology*, 1968.

E.H. Schein, "What Is Culture?" in *Reframing Organizational Culture,* ed. P.J. Frost et al., Newbury Park, CA: Sage, 1991.

E.T. Hall and M.R. Hall, *Understanding Cultural Differences,* Yar-mouth, ME: Intercultural Press, 1990.

F. I. Carakaya, "Market Exit and Barriers to Exit: Theory and Practice," *Psychology and Marketing*, 2000.

G. Oddou and M. Mendenhall, "Expatriate Performance Appraisal: Problems and Solutions," in *International Human Resource Manage-ment,* ed. G. Mendenhall and M. Oddou, Boston: PWS-Kent, 1991.

G. Rice, "Doing Business in Saudi Arabia," *Thunderbird International Business Review,* January-February 2004.

G. Yukl and R. Lepsinger, "Why Integrating the Leading and Managing Roles Is Essential for Organizational Effectiveness," *Organizational Dynamics*, 2005.

G.S. Becker, *Human Capital,* 2nd ed., Chicago: University of Chicago Press, 1993.

H. Mint/berg, "Patterns in Strategy Formulation," *Management Science,* 1915.

H. Mintzberg, "Managerial Work: Analysis from Observation," *Management Science*, 1971.

H. Mintzberg, "Managing Exceptionally," *Organization Science*, 2001.

H. Mintzberg, "The Yin and the Yang of Managing," *Organizational Dynamics*, 2001.

H. Mintzberg, *The Nature of Managerial Work*, New York: Harper & Row, 1973.

I.C. Macmillan and RE. Jones, *Strategy Formulation: Power and Poltics*, St. Paul, MN: West, 1986.

IB; S. Greenhouse, "Nike Shoe Plant in Vietnam Is Called Unsafe for Workers," *New York Times,* November, 1997.

J. Bower and J. Dial, *Jack Welch: General Electrics Revolutionary*, Harvard Business School, April 1994.

J. Ewing and D. Foust, "DHL's American Adventure," *Business Week,* November, 2004.

J. Kahn, "Ruse in Toyland: Chinese Workers' Hidden Woe," *The New York Times,* December, 2003.

J. Pfeffer and G.R. Salancik, *The External Control of Organizations*, New York: Harper & Row, 1978.

J. Pfeffer, *Competitive Advantage through People,* Boston: Harvard Business School Press, 1996.

J. Pfeffer, *Competitive Advantage through People*, Cambridge, MA: Harvard Business School Press, 1994.

J. Pfeffer, *Managing with Power*, Boston: Harvard Business School Press, 1992.

J. Post and L. Preston, *Redefining the Corporation: Stake-holder Management and Organization Wealth*, Palo Alto, CA: Stanford University Press, 2002.

J. Rawls., *Theory of Justice*, rev. ed., Boston: Belknap Press, 1999; original edition 1971.

J. Schumpeter in *Capitalism, Socialism, and Democracy,* London: Macmillan, 1950.

J.A. DiMasi, R.W. Hansen, and H.G. Grabowski, "The Price of Innovation: New Estimates of Drug Development Costs," *Journal of Health Economics*, March 2003.

J.B. Barney, "Company Resources and Sustained Competitive Advantage," *Journal of Management*, 1991.

J.C. Collins and J.I. Porras, *Built to Last: Successful Habits of Visionary Companies*, London: Century, 1995.

J.Ci. Fernald and V. Greenfield, "The Fall and Rise of the Global Economy," *Chicago Fed Letters.* April 2001.

J.D. Thompson, *Organizations in Action*, New York: McGraw-Hill, 1967.

J.L. Badaracco Jr., "The Discipline of Building Character," *Harvard Business Review*, March-April 1998.

J.M. Kouzes and B.Z. Posner, *The Leadership Challenge,* 3rd ed., San Francisco: Jossey-Bass, 2002.

J.O. March and H.A. Si-mon, *Organizations*, New York: Wiley, 1958.

J.P. Kotter and J.L. Heskett, *Corporate Culture and Performance*, New York: Free Press, 1992.

J.P. Kotter and J.L. Heskett, *Corporate Culture and Performance*, New York: Free Press, 1992.

J.P. Womack, D.T. Jones, and D. Roos, *The Machine That Changed the World;* J. Palmer, "Can Anyone Stop Toyota?" *Barron s,* September, 2004.

J.R. Rest, *Moral Development: Advances in Research and Theory*, New York: Praeger, 1986.

J.Z. Namenwirth and R.B. Weber, *Dynamics of Culture*, Boston: Alien & Unwin, 1987.

K.. Kranhold, "GE Takes Big Steps in Its Strategy to Exit Insurance," *The Wall Street Journal,* November, 2005.

L. Hill, *Becoming a Manager: How New Managers Master the Challenges of Leadership*, Boston: Harvard Business School Press, 2003.

L. Himelstein, S. Hamm, and P. Burrows, "Inside Frank Quattrone's Money Machine," *BusinessWeek,* October, 2003.

L. Kahney. "Inside Look at Birth of the iPod," *Wired News,* July, 2004.

L.A. Hill, "What It Really Means to Manage," *Harvard Business School Teaching,* February 2000.

L.A. Hill, *Becoming a Manager*, Boston: Harvard Business School Press, 1992.

M. Busse, "Firm Financial Condition and Airline Price Wars," *Rand Journal of Economics*, 2002.

M. Friedman and R. Fried-man, *Free to Choose*, London: Penguin Books, 1980.

M. Friedman, "The Social Responsibility of Business Is to Increase Profits," *New York Times Magazine,* September, 1970.

M. Maremont, "Tyco Figures Will Be Jailed for at Least? Years," *The Wall Street Journal,* September, 2005.

M.D. Mumford et al., "Leadership Skills for a Changing World: Solving Complex Social Problems," *Leadership Quarterlv*, 2000.

M.E. Porter, "Strategy and the Internet," *Harvard Business Review,* March 2001.

M.E. Porter, *Competitive Strategy*, New York: Free Press, 1980.

Metthee, "Playing a Large Part," *Seattle Post-Intelligencer,* April, 1994.

N.W. Hatch and J.H. Dyer, "Human Capital and Learning as a Source of Sustainable Competitive Advantage," *Strategic Management Journal*, 2004.

P. Drucker, *Peter Drucker on the Profession of Management*, Boston: Harvard Business School Press, 1998.

P. Drucker, *The Practice of Management*, New York: Harper & Row, 1954.

P. Singer, *One World: The Ethics of Globalization,* New Haven, CT: Yale University Press, 2002.

Paul Roberts, *The End of Oil*, Boston: Houghton Mifflin, 2004.

Pfeffer and Salancik, *The External Control of Organizations.*

R. Brooks, "DHL Plans to Spend $1.2 Billion in Challenge of FedEx and UPS," *The Wall Street Journal,* June, 2004.

R. Bryce, *Pipe Dreams: Greed, Ego, and the Death of Enron*, New York: Public Affairs, 2002.

R. Charan, C. Burke, and L. Bossidy, *Execution: The Discipline of Getting Things Done*, New York: Crown Business, 2002.

R. Giuliani, "Rudy Giuliani on Leadership," *Leadership Excellence,* June 2005.

R. Mead, *International Management: Cross Cultural Dimensions*, Oxford: Blackwell Business, 1994.

R.E. Freeman and D. Gilbert, *Corporate Strategy and the Search for Ethics*, Englewood Cliffs, NJ: Prentice-Hall, 1988.

R.L. Katz, "Skills of an Effective Administrator," *Harvard Business Review*, September-October 1974.

Reitman and Schuman, "Men's Club: Japanese and Korean Companies Rarely Look Outside for People to Run Their Overseas Operations;" *Wall Street Journal,* September, 1996.

S. Fisher, R. Sahay, and C.A. Vegh, "Stabilization and the Growth in Transition Economies: The Early Experience," *Journal of Economic Perspectives*, Spring 1996

S. Gray and E. Smith, "Coffee and Music Create a Potent Mix at Starbucks," *The Wall Street Journal,* 2005.

S. Leung, "Armchairs, TVs, and Espresso: Is It McDonald's?" *The Wall* A *Street Journal,* August, 2002..

S. Walton, *Made in America,* New York: Doubleday, 1992.

S.A. Waddock and S.B. Graves, "The Corporate Social Performance-Financial Performance Link," *Strategic Management Journal*, 1997.

S.J. Kobrin, "Geocentric Mindset and Multinational Strategy," *Journal of International Business Studies*, 1994..

S.L. Berman, A.C. Wicks, S. Kotha, and T.M. Jones, "Does Stakeholder Orientation Matter?" *Academy of Management Journal*, 1999.

S.W. Gellerman, "Why Good Managers Make Bad Ethical Choices," *in Ethics in Practice: Managing the Moral Corporation,* ed. K.R. Andrews, Harvard Business School Press, 1989.

See J. Bhagwati, *In Defense of Globalization*, New York: Oxford Uni-versity Press, 2004.

See T.L. Beauchamp and N.E. Bowie, *Ethical Theory and Business,* 7th ed., Upper Saddle River, NJ: Pearson Prentice-Hall, 2001.

Staff re-porter, "Where the Money Is: The Drug Industry," *The Economist,* April, 2003.

T. Donaldson. *The Ethics of International Business*, Oxford: Oxford University Press, 1989.

T. Jones, "Ethical Decision Making by Individuals in Organizations," *Academy of Management Review,* 1991.

T. Levitt, "The Globalization of Markets," *Harvard Business Review.* May-June 1983.

T. Simons, "Behavioral Integrity: The Perceived Alignment between Managers' Words and Deeds as a Research Focus," *Organization Science*, January-February 2002.

United Nations, *World Investment Report 2005*, New York & Geneva: United Nations, 2005.

W.M. Bulkeley, "IBM to Export Highly Paid Jobs to India," *The Wall Street Journal.* December, 2003.

World Trade Organization, *2004 Annual Report*, Geneva: WTO, 2005.

Index

O

P

Q

R

S